PETER ELLIOTT

rambling towards jerusalem

JOURNEYS OF A FREMANTLE BOY

Ark House Press
PO Box 1722, Port Orchard, WA 98366 USA
PO Box 1321, Mona Vale NSW 1660 Australia
PO Box 318 334, West Harbour, Auckland 0661 New Zealand
arkhousepress.com

© Peter Elliott 2018

Some names and identifying details have been changed to protect the privacy of individuals.

Cataloguing in Publication Data:
Title: Rambling Towards Jerusalem
ISBN: 9780648441045 (pbk) 9780648507765 (ebk)
Subjects: Travel; Christian Living;
Other Authors/Contributors: Elliott, Peter

Design by initiateagency.com

By the same author

Reasons for Disbelief: a survey of the historical and theological beliefs of the Reorganized Church of Jesus Christ of Latter-Day Saints (2010, original 1980)

Asang: Trevor White and the Dusuns of Sabah (1997)

Church.History@WhyBother? (2012)

Edward Irving: Romantic theology in crisis (2013)

In memory of
Derek Taylor (1956-2011)
who really started it all

and for Deborah,
who married me anyway.

contents

This book has taken 40 years to write. It focuses especially on the years 1978 to 1981 and draws directly from the detailed diaries I kept during that period. The availability of the diaries presented me with a choice: I could either redact the material substantially from my later perspective, or I could largely let the diaries speak for themselves. The former option would have been by far the safer, resulting in a more sanitised version of events. I have, however, chosen the second option. In the course of my life, I have become convinced that history is under no obligation to be palatable, so it seemed only fair to apply the same standard to my own story. Honesty and risk are, I believe, natural co-travellers.

chapter 1

A School of Ghosts

Let's begin in 1969 in a Fremantle high school built on working class aspirations and the bones of pioneers. The oval of John Curtin Senior High was on the old Skinner Street cemetery site. The cemetery closed in 1899, and in the 1930s, some of the blasé dead had been disinterred and unceremoniously relocated to the Carrington Street cemetery. I say "some" for good reason: a lot of body parts ended up in our backyard. We lived near the school on a sloping block in Burt Street which had been filled with soil from Skinner Street; let's just say that trainee forensic pathologists would have found gardening at our place *very* interesting.

It was not enough that we had to throw our teenage bodies into physical contortions above the dismembered and decayed; the school was immediately behind one of Australia's most haunted buildings – the old insane asylum. In short, they expected us to get an education in a virtual necropolis. The odds were against us.

I would like to say such metaphysical sensitivities were the reason I quickly lost interest in participating in sport and physical education on the oval, and succumbed to the lures of the local snooker hall, but you'd see through that in a moment. The reality was that for an overweight kid with braces, snooker offered far greater fulfillment than athletics. But snooker held its own terror, namely Plastic Man, the chief attendant. None of us ever summoned the courage to ask what happened to him, but neither could we summon the courage to look at him for more than a couple of seconds at a time. Had he suffered from injuries in the First World War? Perhaps dragged from the flames of a car wreck just in time? In any case, his face was a Hammer films nightmare amalgam of melted flesh and budget reconstruction. Plastic Man held court in the Stygian gloom of the Princess Billiard Saloon, above Trees' Panel Beaters, just in front of the asylum. But we knew one thing for sure – it was worth braving Plastic Man to avoid sport on Wednesday afternoons and indulge ourselves on the full-size snooker tables.

Of course, life at high school wasn't all dead people and snooker: as an only child, one of my first goals on arriving at John Curtin in 1969 was to make friends. Derek Taylor and Bob Howard were two of the first. Derek, part of a family of £10 Poms, had arrived in Perth a year or two previously. He was a keen Crystal Palace supporter, Slade fan and amateur ornithologist; I hadn't heard of the first two and my main interest in birds was eating them. Bob had three attractive sisters and lived next door to someone with a full-size snooker table in their garage; clearly, a valuable ally. But even valuable allies have their moments…

Friday morning was phys. ed., which always struck me as a particularly stupid idea. It is a fact universally acknowledged that pubescent teenage boys become particularly pungent after violent exercise. So the idea of working them into a sweat at the beginning of the day, and then putting them back into uniform for another 5 ½ hours can only be described as perverse. One Friday, I made my token effort by running about half-way around the oval and collapsing back at the steps. The phys. ed. instructor had gone away for a moment (probably to conceal his laughter at my attempts) and for one delicious moment, lying on my back on the grass, I closed my eyes.

At that moment, Bob decided to throw a medicine ball at my head. As I'm sure this is not an experience shared by many of you, let me assure you that the immediate results were intense pain, distorted vision, and a strong desire for medicine of a different kind. In the midst of this, as I staggered back to the change rooms, there was also the desire to inflict revenge. I located Bob's bag, took it to a tap, and filled it with water.

The period immediately after phys. ed. was with Jenkins, the Maths Nazi, a title he had earned because he looked vaguely Germanic, drove a Mercedes, and seemed even more interested in some of the girls in the class than we were, which scarcely seemed possible. He was balding and ancient – at least thirty-five. Bob was the last one into class that morning, making a dramatic entrance in a dripping wet school uniform, earning a Teutonic sneer from Jenkins. From within the psychedelic rollercoaster still spinning in my head, I summoned what I hoped was a look of smug serenity.

Even in the 1970s, long before its reincarnation as an up-market College of the Arts, John Curtin contained students with amazing creativity. Rob, a student with hair below his shoulders, was one of these. He possessed the skill to knock flies unconscious without killing them. While the fly was lying on the desk, he would remove its legs and tie it to the end of one of his hairs. When the fly regained consciousness, it would fly around on its tether, unable to land. Often, there were five or six of these, orbiting Rob's head in frustration. This was my introduction to surrealism.

Then there was Keaney, a teacher who had little option but to believe that there was much more than his philosophy could account for in the halls of John Curtin High. He would be writing on the board when there would be a knock on the sliding door of the classroom. "Come in", he would call, but no-one came. He would go to the door and open it, but no-one would be there. This would be repeated a couple of times. Finally, he would ignore the knock, but then, the door would slowly slide open, but again, no-one was there. He was never able to see the drawing pin in the bottom of the door, or the fishing line stretching from it to the student at the back of the class, nor was he able to understand that while he was writing on the board, the student sitting closest to the door was quite capable of knocking on it.

Then there was Shaw, an English teacher who seriously over-estimated the levels of cooperation he could expect from teenagers. He wanted to read a poem about a farmyard and for us to volunteer to make the sounds of all the farm animals. Now this would have been an excellent learning activity for four year olds, but he'd missed the mark by a decade, and naturally had no volunteers. So he stood at the back of the class, making all the sounds himself. I eliminated teaching English as a possible career and tragically, some time after this, Shaw leapt to his death from the Legacy lookout at Dumas House near King's Park.

I soon discovered that there are two types of students in the world: those who do well even if they do little work, and those who will fail if they do little work. Derek and Bob were in the former category; I was in the latter. We shared a conviction that high school was to be enjoyed at all costs, but whereas they could afford to muck around and still pass, unfortunately I couldn't. This tension between how I wanted to spend my time and how I needed to spend my time resonated throughout my high school years.

chapter 2

Family Matters

"The Reorganized Church of Jesus Christ of Latter-Day Saints (RLDS), not the Mormons." This was how my grandfather, Oscar Stack, answered when people asked about his religious affiliation. Oscar and his wife Nell were stalwarts in the RLDS church opposite the war memorial in High Street, Fremantle. The building is in private hands today, a grand but decaying limestone structure with jarrah floors and ceiling, originally Girton College, then used to store coffins during World War II. A well-known Fremantle City councillor, Oscar was a barber by trade, operating from a shop in South Terrace (he was said to be so quick at cutting hair that if you cycled to his salon, he'd cut your hair and have you back on the street before your pedals had stopped turning). Oscar loved officiating at weddings, and was especially popular with Fremantle's Italian community. The Stack sunroom collected oddments of all kinds, including dozens of bomboniere from Italian weddings – diverse containers holding sugared almonds in various degrees of decay. Oscar was close to six feet tall, Nell a good foot shorter; they had only one child, Dorothy. Dorothy grew up playing the piano, singing, and convinced that her ideal future husband would be a non-drinker, non-smoker and non-gambler; perhaps it would have helped to have had some more positive characteristics on her list. When her secretarial skills landed her a short-term job in Canberra, she found someone who met her criteria; she brought Frederick Elliott back to Perth and married him in January 1954.

The unhappy marriage between my parents lasted for seven years and I was the result, and, perhaps indirectly, the cause of their separation. During one of their frequent arguments, as a four year old, I asked my father, "Why don't you love my mummy?" Many years later, my mother told me this was the moment she decided the marriage was over. She had run down the hill to Bicton Baths after that encounter, planning to throw herself into the Swan River (she couldn't swim), but her maternal instincts stopped her. She walked back up Braunton Place, determined to end the marriage. When in 1962 they began the five year separation leading to their divorce, I had just started at Richmond Primary School. My father dropped me at school the first day and kept going, across the Nullarbor, back to his native New South Wales.

My primary years were dominated by RLDS associations. I was the sixth generation in my family to be a member and all my cousins were members. Like the Mormons, we believed that all other churches were wrong and that God had to begin again through nineteenth-century prophet Joseph Smith. We disagreed with the Mormons on some key issues of theology and succession (they went with Brigham Young, we went with Joseph Smith's son). Oscar had been a lay pastor of the church for many years and mum was the church organist. I absorbed and believed the RLDS teaching; there really was no option.

Throughout most of the 1960s, Mum and I lived in a two-bedroom home in Braunton Place, Bicton, directly opposite the old Quarantine station. Mum used her black belt secretarial skills to obtain a position teaching shorthand and typing at Fremantle Technical College to support us.

Fred spent most of the five years of their separation in New South Wales (I only saw him during the summer holidays) before eventually returning to Perth. I would spend Saturday nights with Oscar and Nell at 204 High Street, eating home-made Cornish pasties and absorbing my grandmother's philosophy: "Life's not all beer and skittles!", delivered with her trademark giggle. And so, my primary school years passed by.

Two incidents stand out from my time at Richmond Primary. In grade 2, Miss Ranieri told us the story of Bluebeard. By lunchtime, we had just got to the point where we were about to discover what was in the closet. Miss Ranieri asked us whether we wanted to continue the story after lunch. I knew enough about stories to know that I definitely *didn't* want to know what was in the closet. Unfortunately, the vote was to continue, so after lunch, at the age of six, we were introduced to the world of psychopaths and decapitation. For months afterwards, Bluebeard had a vivid presence in my peripheral vision, especially in the vicinity of our garage.

In grade five, our teacher was Mr Judge, whose pride and joy was his new Holden car. One afternoon, we came back into class to the following instruction: "Right class, because you talked too much this morning, I want you to be quiet for the next hour. Continue the work we began before lunch, but I want absolutely no talking. In fact, I won't answer any questions even if you put up your hand, so don't raise your hand. Do you understand?" We did, and duly began work. The problem was that my stomach was becoming queasy and I had that unnerving certainty the problem would get worse, not better. I tried to distract myself with work, but eventually knew that I was going to throw up. Timidly, I raised my hand. Mr Judge saw it, glared at me, and went back to his own work. Cowed, I put my hand down. I was going to be sick very soon. Desperate, I raised my hand again and started shaking it backwards and forwards. Judge glared again and I threw up all over the desk and my work. I'm not sure who supervised the class after Mr Judge cleaned up my vomit and while he was driving me to my grandparents, but I knew that as we drove towards High Street in his now less-than-immaculate Holden, I began to feel better, *much* better.

In these later primary school years, Sunday afternoons were custody visits with my father. Sometimes we would go fishing, sometimes to the beach. When Fred's parents moved from Goulburn, New South Wales to a house in Leach Highway, Melville, we usually visited them. These visits were, at best, awkward. It was even worse if Fred's only sibling, his brother Hope, was there, because the atmosphere was icy: Fred always believed his younger brother had received more favourable treatment; eventually they become completely estranged.

My grandfather Harry had spent all his working life on the railways of New South Wales. He seldom talked to me and spent most of his time pottering in the back yard, seemingly as interested in conversation and relationship as he would have been in the mating habits of Mongolian eels. Fred obviously knew this, so he would sit in a comfortable chair, hold the *Sunday Times* in front of his face, and issue the instruction "Speak to your granny." The message was fairly clear: he had two hours a week with me and would prefer to spend them with the newspaper. All I could see of him above the top of the newspaper was his well-disciplined hair.

The chief exception to this pattern was the end of each term, when possession of a school report made me much more interesting; at these times Fred's early years as a teacher and his genetic contribution to my existence resulted in rhetorical flourishes about my likely future, which always seemed dire. If I'd lived two centuries earlier, the advice would have been much more congenial: "Marry into a rich family, lad, and all will be well." Sadly, History had coquettishly removed overt approval of this option for the academically challenged.

My grandmother Ivy's originally red hair was turning sepia. She was leagues ahead of Harry as a conversationalist, but still only average where children were concerned. Her years in rural western New South Wales in an unhappy marriage with a one week annual escape to Sydney in which she would lock herself in a hotel, watch movies and read feverishly did not give us a lot in common. I think we both worked at it and reading became our common ground. I discovered she was a fan of crime fiction, especially Agatha Christie, so I became a convert, reading dozens of Christie novels to fuel our enforced conversations about red herrings and cyanide.

So I inhabited three worlds: the RLDS world, school world, and the world of my father's family. The differences between them were as obvious as a dentist's bad breath, and I found myself being consistently drawn to the elements I most identified as fun.

In my second last year of primary school, mum and I moved into the house on the hill in Burt Street, sharing a driveway with our neighbours, a family of Jehovah's Witnesses. They had two adult sons, John and Gilbert. Gilbert believed he was Jesus Christ, that his niece was Mary, that the hill we lived on was Calvary, and all its inhabitants were blessed. The second sign we had that all was not well with Gilbert was when he threatened their pastor with a large knife. The third sign was when, one afternoon, he drove his Morris Minor down to Fremantle harbour, onto a wooden jetty, and over the edge. It was a baptism from which he did not return.

A little over a year after Fred and Dorothy's divorce became final, mum remarried. Keith Hill had been in the RAAF in World War II, and after the war, worked on pearling luggers in Broome, and in the Wheatbelt. In his youth in the early 1940s, he had known the future poet and playwright, Dorothy Hewett. He makes an anonymous, but significant, appearance as an early romantic interest in her autobiography, *Wild Card*. Some affection clearly remained, because signed works by Dorothy Hewett kept arriving at our house until at least the late 1970s.

It was one afternoon during 1968 that Keith asked for my permission to marry my mother. I liked him because he looked like the actor who played Ivanhoe on TV, so I agreed. (I've often wondered since what would have happened if I'd declined.) Keith had also been married before, so in August, 1968, shortly before my twelfth birthday, I gained a step-father and two older step-sisters, Susan and Sally. Life became more complicated, but the fun factor also increased. Keith and mum bought or started a string of businesses, including a laundromat, the kiosk at the Fremantle swimming pool, and a receptionist training college. I picked up phrases like, "He's got a head like an outer Mongolian racing tadpole" (code for "that chap looks a bit unusual") and "There's no prize for second place." (code for "I've just got a bigger crayfish than you.")

Dad (as I soon called him) built a hookah underwater breathing device consisting of motor and compressor and we were soon lugging it down to North Mole in Fremantle where it balanced precariously on the rocks, dutifully pumping air through hoses as we dived for fish or crayfish. During the next decade, we owned boats and it seemed as if I spent my teenage years in an amphibious state, with hundreds of hours underwater, with the Five Fathom Bank a favourite spot. Coventry Reef, the southernmost point of the Five Fathom Bank, was isolated and saw few divers. With deep water on all sides, only a small part of the reef is near the surface, but in 1899, the Carlisle Castle was unlucky enough to hit it. It was too far from shore for anyone to survive, and although we never found any of the gold that was supposed to be on board, we did find ballast bricks and old whisky bottles.

I quickly learned to love the strange and wondrous silence twenty metres down, undisturbed by the swell and waves above, in a weightless world where the only sound is your own breathing. School work, teachers, and the expectations of others magically dissolved down there. Diving quickly became my favourite form of meditation. Annoyingly, this subaquatic haven is also inhabited by sharks for which I developed a fascinated terror that led me to read everything I could about them. This helped minimise my terror of most sharks, but focused it very closely on great whites.

One of the oddest looking sharks is the wobbegong or carpet shark. Looking like a hippie's bedraggled rug, it lives on the bottom or in caves and loves crayfish. It's normally quite a sleepy shark, has never killed anyone, and despite possessing a nasty set of needle-sharp teeth, would probably at most take a hand or foot. We'd seen lots of wobbies while diving. "Listen to this dad," I said one day, raising my eyes from my fiftieth shark book, "wobbegongs have to 'cough' – realign their jaw after taking their first bite before they can swallow it." He nodded politely, but didn't seem to be paying much attention.

In order to understand the next story, you need to know how we hunted crays. Back in the late 1960s and early 1970s, it was legal to hunt crayfish with small spearguns shooting a three-pronged spear. We would approach the crays from the front, spear them in the head, then grab the cray's body with a gloved left hand, remove it from the spear and place it in a bag.

One day, we were diving off Rottnest Island hunting crays. Sure enough, there was a promising ledge with feelers sticking out of it. Dad got himself into position, fired, and the sudden twitching of feelers showed he hadn't missed. He reached in and grabbed the end of the spear, slowly removing the cray from the ledge. As he did so, a large set of jaws shot out from the back of the cave and clamped over the cray, which remained on the spear. Dad didn't flinch, but remained in control of his end of the spear, with the wobbegong's teeth a few centimeters from his hand. Seconds ticked by and suddenly, the wobbegong appeared to yawn. Instantly, dad had the spear and cray out of its mouth and a somewhat bemused wobbie began to swallow something that wasn't there. "I remembered what you'd told me about wobbies having to realign their jaws," dad said later. Personally, I didn't know what to be more amazed about – how cool he was or how much he'd trusted what I'd read to him earlier.

Having two fathers on the scene was never easy, but it brought one unexpected benefit. With three very different parents, I realised quickly that it would be impossible to please all of them all the time, and it would be foolish to attempt the impossible. If my destiny was to disappoint at least one of my parents at any given time, the sensible thing was to accept that and to chart my own course. On occasion, these choices were inescapable.

After one of our Sunday afternoon visits, Fred brought me back to Burt Street. We were about to say goodbye when he turned to me and said, "You know, if you were diving with Keith and a shark came along, Keith would let it have you." I realised that my father was struggling with jealousy and bitterness, but I also realised I had a choice to make. I said nothing, got out of the car, closed the door more firmly than necessary and walked away. I was only twelve, but I knew a lie when I heard one.

chapter 3

From Ghost School to Graveyard

The girls at John Curtin hitched their skirts up high enough to launch a thousand careers in gynaecology. The problem, as every high school boy knows, is that the girls in your class are almost permanently unattainable. With the possible exception of the first year of high school when everyone is finding their feet (and which contained my memorable spin-the-bottle-laden thirteenth birthday party), high school girls are fixated on older boys.

This creates the immutable universal law that fourteen year old girls aren't interested in fourteen year old boys, but seventeen or eighteen year old boys with cars and money. Thus the girls in our class remained tantalisingly immanent, but frustratingly transcendent (I was besotted with Marise.) As we progressed through high school, some of us, like Derek, made this work for him and obtained a younger girlfriend, Sue. Most of us though, remained in the classic dilemma: the girls we were attracted to were unattainable; the girls we weren't attracted to may have been attainable but we weren't going to bother to find out. We were adolescent embodiments of Groucho Marx's dictum (which I first heard via Woody Allen): "I don't want to belong to any club that would accept me as a member." [My mother's advice about girls was constant: "Girls don't like boys who are members of the Wandering Hands Brigade", a generalisation that was poor preparation for later encounters with girls/women who proved to be adept WHB members themselves.]

As if this dilemma didn't give us enough to worry about, we were also expected to make progress with our school work. Adults (at least the dominant ones in my life) were preternaturally concerned with my academic progress; it was made very clear to me that my entire future life depended on it. It didn't help that my father was working as a career guidance officer with the Commonwealth Employment Service. Enviously, I noted that some of my friends' parents seemed less obsessed. The first major hurdle was the Junior Certificate at the end of third year high school. Somehow I got through this with all subjects intact, and relaxed… perhaps a little *too* much.

My relief at getting a reasonable Junior Certificate was only slightly lessened by the usual chorus of "but you could do so much better." This chorus had appeared on every single report I had received since finishing primary school, and always seemed more condemnation than encouragement. Excited at having only the Leaving Certificate left to go (and two years before I faced it) I devoted myself to my snooker game which improved dramatically, despite the regular and disturbing sight of Plastic Man's iridescent disembodied head floating through the smoke-filled gloom of the Princess Billiard Hall.

Then the shocks began. My first term report in fourth year was not good and in second term, the Principal wrote on my report "He should consider leaving school." Yes, I had failed a few subjects, but so had others in my class, and they had escaped such comments. Perhaps the fact I'd been caught smoking in the toilets, had my packet of cigarettes confiscated and had the audacity to go to the principal's office and ask for them back had something to do with it (well, it *was* a full packet). The effect of the report on my family was immediate and profound: my mother ran into the front garden, crying hysterically; dad was upset that I had made her do so, and Fred simply exploded. I realised that I was faced with a clear choice: either leave school and live with a trinity of parental disapproval or work hard in an attempt to win their approval. I chose the latter, reassuring myself that I only had to work hard for eighteen months, pass my Leaving Certificate and they would all finally relax.

My snooker game declined, but the plan worked, and at the end of 1973 I gained a solid Leaving Certificate and a matriculation that would allow me into most university courses. I've expressed that in one glib sentence, but the transition between mid-1972 and the end of 1973 represented a comprehensive recalibration of who I was and how I looked at life. At any rate, I vaguely felt I had paid a "debt" to all three of my parents: they had invested time, effort and money in raising me and their main concern was that I would get a good Leaving Certificate, which they saw as the passport to a lifetime of solid employment. I had made a commitment of sorts to keep the peace and to make other people happy, but had paid a price for it; surely making a commitment to keep someone else happy was an ignoble act? Was this what life was all about – lurching from one obligation or commitment to another, in an unending fandango of reactions to the expectations of others? I realised, in a state of mild panic, that this was the last thing that I wanted, but I had no idea if I could avoid it. I had spent eighteen months shaping my life to meet the expectations of others, and I knew I did not want to spend the rest of my life that way.

In the midst of this angst, another major decision beckoned: what to do next? My strongest subjects were English and history. "Why not become an English teacher?" I rejected this proposition instantly. I remembered Shaw standing at the back of the classroom, ridiculed by the students for making animal noises and eventually killing himself. Lack of respect, depression, suicide… no, I didn't want to become an English teacher; in fact, I didn't want to become any sort of teacher. I didn't know anyone who made a living as an historian, nor did I know anyone who made a living as a writer, and artistic poverty was not highly prized in my family. Then I read that the Western Australian Institute of Technology (now Curtin University) offered a major in Journalism. While at high school, I'd had an article published in *The West Australian* newspaper, giving me some confidence I could succeed in this area (although the confidence had taken a knock when I failed to obtain a journalism cadetship). I enrolled and was accepted. However, the summer of 1973-74 stretched ahead before studies began. I had my driver's licence and mum and dad had bought me a 1969 Subaru. I had become the seventeen year old boy with a car that I had envied in junior high school; now I needed money.

My grandfather Oscar was serving as a Fremantle City Councillor and he got me a job at the Fremantle Cemetery in Carrington Street. This was probably a reward for the hours I'd spent walking the heat-hazed streets of Hilton with him, door-knocking every house and handing out how-to-vote cards with a frozen smile. Or perhaps it was compensation for the embarrassing haircuts he used to give me until I finally found enough courage to refuse.

People are polarised about cemeteries: either they're uncomfortable being in them at all (perhaps because they've seen too many horror movies or because they're reminded of their own mortality), or they find them profoundly moving. I'm in the latter group. Even as a teenager, I couldn't read more than a few headstone inscriptions before being overwhelmed by the tsunami of love and loss; could never take a sweeping glance around the thousands of gravestones in a cemetery without sensing the deafening silence of eternity. Too many Gothic novels, I suppose.

On the first day, my supervisor took me to the tree-lined main driveway through the cemetery that wound its way down to the crematorium.

"See how every one of these trees has a name plate at its base?"

I did.

"Each of those name plates is stuck in a small block of concrete not much bigger than a house brick. You can see how, over the course of time, some of them have sunk deeper in the ground than others. Now, when you look down the drive, they go up and down and look very irregular. I want you to dig each one of them up and make sure they're all a standard height above ground."

It seemed simple enough, and equipped with a shovel and a piece of wood marked at the correct height, I began work. I progressed through several name plates, with the work taking longer than I expected. After I'd done about eight or nine, my shovel struck something solid. Intrigued, I dug it out. It was an old black plastic bottle with a red screw-on cap, the sort of container used to hold either motor oil or poison. I was annoyed at the litter and threw it in the nearest bin. Then it was time for morning tea.

After morning tea, I continued work, adjusting perhaps another five or six nameplates when again, my shovel hit something solid. Once more I dug it out and was astounded to find it was an identical bottle to the first. With an uneasy feeling in my stomach, I realised that this bottle, like the first, appeared to be fairly full of sand. At least, I'd *presumed* it was sand. I shook the bottle. It rattled. Slowly, I unscrewed the cap and my worst fears were confirmed: it was full of ash, teeth, and small pieces of bone. I had thrown someone in the bin!

Quickly, I dropped the current bottle back in its hole and raced back to the bin, retrieved the first bottle and then my dilemma hit me: I had no idea which name plate the bin bottle belonged to. I threw it in the hole with the current bottle, filled it in, straightened the name plate, and moved on. As I worked, I wondered why my supervisor hadn't mentioned that the ashes were actually buried in plastic bottles under the nameplates; I worried about whether the dead were actually capable of taking revenge for such posthumous desecration; and I realised that I had quite possibly thrown a spanner into the orderly workings of any future resurrection.

The crematorium was a source of fascination. I was shown how it worked and heard how much faster bodies burned towards the end of the day as the furnace got hotter.

"You've got a mincer there bolted to the bench, what's it for?" I asked.

"For the bones. The heat doesn't actually destroy them and we have to break them up in the mincer."

It was identical to the mincer my grandmother used to make Cornish pasties. Knowing my grandfather's delight in collecting discarded items, I didn't want to think about where hers had come from.

One problem with the crematorium was its location at the southern end of the long driveway: when the sea breeze arrived, it blew ash back over the drive immediately in front of the crematorium. Virtually every summer afternoon, I watched with embarrassed amusement as the "Fremantle Doctor" scattered ebony confetti onto the recently emerged mourners, their faces registering confusion and horror in quick succession.

Grave digging, you need to appreciate, is something of a science, and can't be done by just anybody. You need to know if it's a family grave, how many others are already buried there and how deep, etc. Grave *filling*, on the other hand is relatively simple, or so I thought when one of the grave-diggers asked me to help him. I looked into the grave, admiring the shining wood of the coffin and the simple but efficient way the grave walls were held up by expandable wooden braces.

"Okay," he said to me, "hop in."

"I beg your pardon?"

"Hop on top of the coffin and take out the wooden supports so we can fill it in."

Now by this stage, I'd worked at the cemetery long enough to know that everyone there had a very dark sense of humour. I was sure that this was some sort of bizarre initiation ritual. Besides, I'd read Edgar Allan Poe and learnt that no-one in his right mind *ever* stands on top of an occupied coffin. But the gravedigger didn't seem to be joking.

"Are you sure it can hold my weight?"

"Yep."

I was highly suspicious of this monosyllabic encouragement, finding it very unlikely that coffin-makers - who were designing a product to a price - employed teams of engineers to make these calculations. But I looked around: it was broad daylight… even if the coffin lid did collapse the worst that would happen was that I could get some nasty splinters as I fell through the lid, there would be an unpleasant squelching beneath my boots, and my colleague would be deafened by my screams. I decided to risk it, and the lid held.

chapter 4

Travel, Tequila and Punk Rock

The 1974 tertiary year began in a Whitlamesque dream of free education. Excited campus activists encouraged us to lean further to the left during the orientation camp at Walkaway, near Geraldton, but most of us were more interested in a baptism of hedonism than one of ideology. To dive into the Walkaway swimming hole and surface next to the girl who was the love of your life for the next forty-eight hours, to wash off the rigid residue of high school and leave it to sink in the brackish waters, to relish the crystalline moment of transition between commitments – these filled every moment to overflowing.

By the end of my first year at WAIT, I completely abandoned the idea of becoming a journalist. The main influence on this decision was a Journalism lecturer called Howard. Howard was a short, skinny, forty-ish, chain-smoking divorcee with a drinking problem. At the beginning of the year, I thought he was an opinionated eccentric with a mind like a plastic bag full of epileptic dugites; by the end of the year, I thought he was something more. You see, Howard *really* didn't appreciate it when somebody disagreed with him.

During one lecture, Howard was enthusiastically telling the class how popular he was.

"In one of my other subjects, a student cycles all the way from Mandurah just to sit in my class."

"That's total crap," replied Steve, a student.

Howard looked less than impressed. The following week, Howard waited until he saw Steve approaching the classroom, at which point he closed the door and nailed the door into the doorjamb, effectively barring Steve's entrance.

I decided that if Howard was being spotlighted by WAIT as a sterling product of the journalism profession, then the last thing I wanted was to be a journalist. Perceptive readers will no doubt notice that my logic wasn't water-tight (nor was my previous logic about teachers), but at the time, my decision was final. By this point however, I had completed one year of a three year course. My options were either to pull out of the course completely, or change my major from Journalism to something else. Abandoning the course would have felt like failure, so I changed my major to what I would most enjoy - Literature – and filled the next two years with as many Lit. classes as possible. One of these units must be the most screamingly ambitious educational endeavour undertaken in Perth. In a 15 week semester, it attempted to introduce us to the entire swathe of Western literature and philosophy: we had to read 17 books (or substantial parts thereof) for this one unit, plus do assignments, plus do three other units. The list included: Ovid's *Metamorphoses*, Plato's *Last Days of Socrates*, Machiavelli's *The Prince*, Dante's *The Inferno*, Dostoyevsky's *Crime and Punishment*, Faulkner's *As I Lay Dying*, Marx's *Communist Manifesto*, Dickens's *Great Expectations*, Erasmus's *In Praise of Folly*, Rousseau's *Social Contract*, Mill's *On Liberty*, Kafka's *The Trial*, Camus's *The Stranger*, Orwell's *1984*, plus some Shakespeare, *Genesis* and *Psalms*. It was a typescript tsunami that few survived, but those of us who did never regretted it.

For someone who had completed his Leaving Certificate in one year, and raced off to war, dad would often amaze me with his knowledge. One day he casually referred to Francois Villon, an obscure medieval French poet few Literature students would have heard of, and I wondered if Dorothy Hewett had been the catalyst here (which is still my preferred option), although, years later, I realised his knowledge may have come from the 1927 John Barrymore vehicle, Beloved Rogue.

In these years, my parents discovered overseas travel and took me with them. Mum had never left Australia and dad had only seen the world through the eyes of war. In August 1974, we went on a two week trip to south-east Asia, visiting Kuala Lumpur, Bangkok, Singapore, Penang and Malacca. Mum was in her element: once she led us right past the second-floor restaurant we were seeking and straight into the lobby area of the third-floor brothel, to the bemusement of the loungees. Another time (before I could rugby-tackle her to the ground to avoid the embarrassment) she accosted David Niven in the lobby of the Kuala Lumpur Hilton. One of the highlights of this trip occurred in Penang, where our friends' backyard opened directly onto the beach: dinner one balmy evening was an epiphany of curried king prawns washed down with shots of straight vodka and a tropical sunset chaser. This trip only left us all wanting more and in January 1975 we spent another week in Singapore.

Mum and dad were now in travel overdrive, and the next thing I knew we were booked on a two-month tour of Europe – December 1975 and January 1976 - fitting neatly between my second and third years of study. A coach trip through Europe confronted me superficially with the culture and history of Italy, Austria, France, Belgium, Germany and Switzerland. I fell passionately in love with England and its past. To spend a white

Christmas Day at Alveston Manor, Stratford-on-Avon, the lawns of which had hosted the first performance of Shakespeare's A Midsummer Night's Dream; to ravage countless second-hand bookshops, emerging with centuries-old books for ridiculous prices; to wander in a timeless reverie through Westminster Abbey amidst the fallen heroes of literature and history, all these were experiences beyond compare for this Fremantle boy. I felt overwhelmed by riches.

I was also overwhelmed by Jennie from Five Dock. I never quite understood how anyone who looked like Bridget Bardot and had a fiancé back in Sydney would be interested in me – perhaps she felt a travel romance to be compulsory? – but one Venetian night in my room in the Hotel Concord we melded beneath the blonde rainforest of her hair, her mascara dripping onto my chest. The tour and my nights with Jennie soon ended: she returned to Sydney and marriage and I returned to my final year of study. But, of course, there was poetry…

Deuxieme

Lyon sleeps but we do not
for though the night is old,
Rabelais's town entreats us
to break sleep's sagging hold.

For what? We might ask later
but now we do not care,
excused by youth, chilled wine, warm hearts
and Freedom's garish stare.

Marvell's shy mistress lives no more -
at least not in your skin,
for chastity is not your pride,
nor coyness your main sin.

With clothes dragged on, your makeup smudged,
we whisper, jest, soft-kiss goodnight
in this old town whose ancient eyes
have watched this scene played many a time,
but seldom yet played right.

During my three years at WAIT, the two main social currents in my life continued: my friends in the RLDS Church and my high school friends. I still attended church most Sundays and the rendezvous for John Curtin alumni was a Thursday night card game at Bob's place in Kanimbla Road, Bicton. His mum Wendy graciously put up with us and his sisters Lyn, Sue and Joy were frequently there. We would arrive about 8pm, play cards for four or five hours, drink too much beer, and drive home. This made Fridays something of a challenge. We'd all spun off into different areas of work or study (Bob was working for the ABC, Derek was studying cartography) and there would often be fifteen or twenty of us each week, laughing about high school memories and sharing the intoxication of independence and Emu Bitter.

As I approached the end of my study, the question of future direction loomed once again. A teaching career still didn't appeal and the main advice I was getting urged me to pursue security, which was usually interpreted to mean a Government job. Having neither other options nor valid objections, I sat the required test and was offered several options: I chose the Department of Social Security, Fremantle, starting straight after my last exam in 1976, and just before my twentieth birthday. I had now fulfilled my parents' ultimate goal for me: a secure Government job. It smelled like a commitment masquerading as a career.

Fred had earned a Bachelor of Psychology, so I had now achieved as high an educational level as anyone in my family. Smugly, I reflected on the fact that my high school Principal had been wrong about me leaving school; then it hit me that he had been *right* – it was the fallout from his comment that forced *me* to change. Smugness changed to something approaching gratitude.

Social Security occupied the ground and fifth floors of Crane House in High Street and I would usually walk to work. My job was as an unemployment and sickness benefits continuations clerk: did people deserve to continue getting these benefits or not?

Social Security Fremantle was a steaming jungle of sexual omnivores, prowling through forests of files, skulking behind clouds of cigarette smoke, lurking for prey. There was Les who was lesbian/bisexual/lesbian/pregnant. There was Russell, who began by telling anti-gay jokes to pretend he wasn't gay, but a few months later didn't hesitate to proposition you bluntly in front of other people. There was middle-aged Tony who would eventually ask every woman in the office to pose nude for photographs, and start a fire in the office when he dropped his cigarette butt in the waste paper basket. There was Bob Howard's sister Sue who was going out with Tim. There was the gorgeous Judy, recently married, but with eyes that said she wasn't. There was Geraldine, the very proper Catholic girl who soon had a less-than-immaculate conception courtesy of the sardonically smiling Dennis. There was Lois, who looked like Ursula Andress's daughter and was the ultimate ice-queen with a Sydney-based addict boyfriend and a regular group of male, death's-head, heroin-gaunt minders. Then there were several married people who tried to keep their heads buried in their work and ignore the surrounding hormonal pandemonium and the smell of marijuana in the stairwells. Life had just got a lot more interesting.

Friday lunch was at the National Hotel on the corner of Market and High Streets where for $1.80 you could get sausages and chips and as much salad as you could eat. After work drinks were usually at the closest hotel – the long-defunct Park Hotel in Parry Street. Work filled the gaps between social engagements and we all did our utmost to ensure that work *became* a social engagement. Somehow, none of us got fired.

A small group of us, including Sue Howard, were often at the Raffles Hotel, usually at Lois's instigation. To avoid hefty bar prices, we would smuggle in a bottle of tequila, with some salt and lemons. The only thing we'd buy across the bar would be beers as chasers to the lick, sip, suck routine. Lois may have been unattainable, but a blurred tequila vision of her was better than nothing.

And there was the Suburban Army, the enthusiastic followers of the band Dave Warner's from the Suburbs. We would do a circuit embracing the Raffles, the Victoria, the Shents – any pub within reach where Warner was playing. The lyrics were great fun:

I'm just a suburban boy,
and I know what it's like,
to be rejected every night
and I'm sure that it must be
easier for boys from the city.[1]

Warner expressed who we were, making us simultaneously accept and laugh at ourselves and his confident on-stage swagger also projected some-

---

[1]   Used by permission.

thing we wanted to be. Other bands like the Elks and Dugites supplemented our musical diet: we were primed and waiting for punk rock.

Another favourite haunt was the Stoned Crow wine bar in Stirling Highway, North Fremantle (now Mojo's) which was an intimate venue for local musicians. I remember vividly one night walking back from there into Fremantle after a few too many green ginger wines and Cokes, crossing the old Fremantle traffic bridge by walking along the circular pipe on the outside, fifteen metres above the Swan River.

Bob moved into a high-rise block of flats called High Tor in Mill Point Road, South Perth and the Thursday night card games followed him there. I began to drink far too much at cards and on more occasions than I want to remember, only woke up on my way home as my car bumped over the curb of Canning Highway near Wireless Hill.

Swanny was the proud owner of a 750cc motorbike, which he would usually bring upstairs in the lift. One night at about 2am, a hapless resident of High Tor returned home and pushed the button for the lift. When the doors slid open on the ground floor, she was greeted by the terrifying sight of a huge motorbike doing a wheelstand, behind which was a leather-clad, raven-haired Viking.

Then there was Jim Baker, a friend of Bob's from the ABC. Heavily into rock music, he returned from a trip to Europe and America, having hung out with the New York Dolls and auditioned as a drummer with The Clash. With a Brian Jones choirboy hair cut and boyish grin, he emptied a pile of singles on the table, and we were introduced to the Ramones and the Sex Pistols. A little while later, Jim joined a band, The Victims, and we went to their first gig in the ramshackle old house they were renting, "Victims' Manor", near the train line in North Perth. The audio assault was so loud that the only place to be was on the front lawn. Girls danced with drugs in plastic earrings. Mark D, future writer for *Rolling Stone* magazine, leapt over the fence and crashed on the grass, his bottle of Blackberry Nip intact in his hand. It was an historic night for Australian rock and roll; The Victims had a residency at the now-defunct Governor Broome hotel in Northbridge and key members of the group later became the Hoodoo Gurus; Jim was with them until after their first album.[2]

One night at cards something terrifying happened, although I only know because I was told about it later. I'd had a lot to drink and when I woke up, I was looking at some concerned faces.

"What's the matter?" I slurred.

"You tried to kill yourself."

"What? Don't be stupid."

But they weren't joking. Apparently I had been so out of it that I had attempted to jump off the balcony of Bob's tenth-floor flat. It had taken four or five of them to restrain me. I had absolutely no recollection of the event and what I found particularly unnerving was that I wasn't suicidal: I had an income, a supportive family and a solid group of friends. Okay, I didn't have a regular girlfriend, but that was hardly a terminal condition and I had never even *thought* about killing myself. I also knew my friends weren't lying. Yet I certainly didn't possess sufficient physical strength to challenge four or five of my peers. And if I had tried to kill myself, but had no intrinsic motivation or desire to do so, then where had the motivation come from? In this case, alcohol had not liberated a suppressed desire, but opened a door. I felt convinced that I had encountered something super-natural, and it was neither friendly, nor playing fair.

This experience did not slow down my drinking however, and when I wasn't drinking beer, my favourite was Stone's Green Ginger wine. My

---

2   Jim Baker has remained in rock, winning a WAMI award in 2006. These days, he prefers to be called James. His current band is The Painkillers.

standard routine was to bring my own 750ml bottle to a party. I would drink it straight from the bottle and forty minutes after arriving at the party, the bottle would be empty. I would then look around for something else to drink. I began to realise that I had a problem.

chapter 5

The Offer I Couldn't Refuse

It happened on 17 August 1977, the day after Elvis Presley died. Derek phoned and said he had something to tell me. He came around after dinner and we sat in our sunroom looking upriver across the lights of the new traffic bridge towards Mosman Park. Derek and I caught up regularly at Bob's, so a request for a separate meeting was unusual.

"Sue's just broken up with me. She's going out with Bob now," he said, and his voice was not quite steady.

Sue had been going out with Derek since he was fifteen and he was now twenty-one. As Bob was a close friend to both of us, I understood Derek's shock and muttered something ineffectual.

"Yeah, so it's over," he continued, voice firmer. "I hadn't ever asked her to marry me, but I'd been planning it, saving money, and I'd even bought the engagement ring."

"So what are you going to do now?"

"Well, that's why I'm here. I've got money saved and obviously now I'm not going to be married anytime soon. So I've decided to travel the world for as long as the money lasts. Do you want to come with me?"

My mind began to race. I'd only been at Social Security for nine months so I didn't have as much money saved as Derek, but my twenty-first birthday was four months away and I could ask for gifts of money. I didn't have a girlfriend, so there were no emotional ties, and much as I enjoyed my social life, I suspected it was eventually going to kill me. My parents wouldn't be excited about me leaving a secure job, but they should be optimistic about me getting back into the public service on my return. These thoughts and others flew through my brain and within thirty seconds, I said "yes".

One of my other reasons for wanting to go was more complex, involving some of the processes within the RLDS Church; most of the adult males were in the "priesthood", alongside their secular jobs. Becoming a member of the priesthood involved receiving a "call". The process went like this: the pastor of the church would receive a "call" from God for a particular person and present it to them. It was possible to decline, and some men did, but I knew that the longer I remained in the church, the more likely I was to be approached. When my younger cousin Greg was "called", it seemed even more likely that I would be next; the delay was probably because dad was now the pastor and he suspected something of my social life.

The key issue for me was that I wanted to assure myself of the truth of RLDS teaching. I didn't want to accept it just because everyone in my family believed; I didn't want a second-hand faith. I needed to investigate the nineteenth-century beginnings of the church before accepting a life-long priesthood responsibility; it was, after all, a commitment, and therefore to be approached warily. Derek's situation was proof that romantic commitments were also unreliable, and I started to wonder whether commitments should be completely avoided. At any rate, Derek's invitation gave me the opportunity to escape the immediate pressure of the RLDS situation and also the possibility of visiting America to do research: avoidance of commitment and an adventure - irresistible.

I soon discovered that there would be a third person traveling with us. During his years of dating Sue, Derek had become good friends with her brother Dennis. Dennis, lanky, laconic and twenty-eight, had spent half his life risking death by inhaling fumes in the family drycleaning business – reason enough to leave town. I didn't really know Dennis well, and I was wary of traveling with a virtual stranger. It was also difficult to imagine having a travel companion who was seven years older than Derek and myself. I think Derek realised this and he developed what he probably thought were bonding sessions but were, in my opinion, thinly disguised attempts to kill us.

Derek's idea of bonding was running. We began on that much-haunted John Curtin High School oval, four laps of which equaled a mile. As I jogged in bonding, if not blinding, agony around the track, I could not avoid the irony of how often Derek and I had skipped sport for snooker, and here we were, inflicting it on ourselves voluntarily. I was panting so hard the smell of the grass hurt the back of my throat, and I was certain I had appendicitis. But Derek didn't want to do this just once; it became a thrice-weekly event; four laps a night became twelve. Then, for variety, we would run from my home in Burt Street, Fremantle, east along Marmion Street to Stock Road, north along Stock until Canning Highway, and then west to Dennis's home in East Fremantle. This is the documented evidence of the first time that Derek Taylor tried to kill me.

We set January, 1978 for our departure, but we still had to determine exactly where and how we were going to travel. A key figure in this was a workmate of Derek's, John O'Brien (Obie), who had traveled from Kathmandu to London on an organised coach tour. We visited his Willagee home, saw his slides, and the decision was made: we would do the same.

Few of my RLDS friends understood my desire to travel. At the time there was a TV campaign with the theme "See Australia first". "Why don't you see Australia first?" they parroted.

"Think about it for a minute. It makes no sense for me to see Australia first. I'm twenty and single with no responsibilities. No wife, kids or mortgage. It's the perfect time to see the rest of the world. When I come back and lock into responsibilities, I can see Australia in the four-week chunks of annual leave that an employer will give me. This bus trip from Kathmandu to London alone will take two and a half months – how on earth can I do that with a normal job? If I don't take this opportunity now, I probably won't get it for another thirty years if I have kids. And how many people do you see bumming around the world in their fifties? It's now or never." I saw the advertising campaign as a vampyric attempt to suck the wanderlust from the youth of Australia. My RLDS friends weren't convinced, although to me it was clearer than crystal. If I didn't seize this opportunity, it would never come again.

Not long after Derek's fateful visit, Angela started work at Social Security. Her Birmingham accent and cheeky smile were attractive, but then I discovered she was seven years older than me – the same age as Dennis – obviously too old to be a possibility. However, we discovered common interests in music and one day at work, she spoke to me amidst the candy-coloured files of unemployment recipients.

"Pete, Blondie and Iggy Pop are coming to town and I've got front-row tickets to both concerts. Would you like to come?"

"I'd love to, but you know I'm going overseas soon, so I'm trying to save all I can. I really can't afford it."

"You don't have to. I've paid for them. You'd be my guest."

I probably had a look of amazement on my face, and she sheepishly added:

"Look, I don't want you to think that I'm asking you out for the same reason most guys ask girls out."

"Umm, sure, thanks. It's very generous of you," I replied, feeling somewhat confused, but determined not to miss free concerts.

In the end, the Iggy Pop concert was cancelled, but we got to Blondie, pogoing furiously within sweat-dripping distance of Deborah Harry. After the concert, we headed to a party Angela knew of in an old house in Mill Point Road, a block away from Bob's flat. David Bowie reverberated through the walls, and we wandered through the house, observing partygoers in various stages of wastage, unable to talk because of the volume. Eventually we headed out to the front verandah, where the party noise competed with late-night animal noises from the zoo across the road. I searched for a conversation starter…

"It can't be a very good party, there's nobody making love on the front lawn."

"We could go back to my place."

"I thought you said you didn't ask me out for the same reason guys ask girls out?"

"I lied."

Angela lived with a few friends in an old house in Mounts Bay Road at the foot of King's Park, where the King's Tower apartment block now stands. At 2 am there were no cars driving by and as we lay on her bed smoking rolled cigarettes, the view from her bedroom window was pure, dense equatorial jungle – dark green foliage tumbling down the hill. It seemed as if we could be anywhere in the world at that moment, except Perth, Western Australia. In my heart, I'd already left.

chapter 6

Departure Bay

The weeks dragged by towards January. I'd received a promotion at Social Security with a welcome pay rise. I was now a New Claims Assessor with the power to determine just how sick and unemployed people really were. One of the highlights was the "de facto interview". Single people were paid at slightly more than half the married/de facto rate, and if individual claimants were found to be de facto, their rate would automatically be reduced to this lower rate. Unsurprisingly, not every de facto couple raced in to tell us their new living arrangements.

"Right," said my supervisor, "these de facto interviews can be a bit tricky. Our goal is to find out if the two people concerned who are both on benefits and sharing the same address are actually living on a de facto basis, but we can't ask them the question outright."

"Why not?'

"It's illegal. Invasion of privacy, that sort of thing."

"So we can't simply ask, 'Are you sleeping together?'"

"Absolutely not! It would get the Department into a lot of trouble."

"So what *do* we ask?"

"Questions that skirt around the issue, like, 'How many bedrooms are there in the house?' 'Do you go out together socially?' 'Are you known by others as a couple?' 'Who does the laundry?' That sort of thing."

I looked at him, appalled.

"So you want me to ask these sorts of questions and based on their answers, determine whether they're living de facto?"

"That's it. Then, if you're suspicious, but they don't admit it, we send a Field Officer out to their home to check it out."

"And this is all legal, but asking them the direct question isn't?"

"That's right."

In reality, my own version of the de facto interview went something like this:

"Hi. Thanks for coming in. This is what's known as a de facto interview. What we'd really like to know is whether or not you're living on a de facto basis. However, I need to make it very clear that for legal reasons, I am not allowed to ask you this question outright. So is there any information about your living arrangements that you would like to *volunteer* to tell me?"

For some reason, this seemed to work well, and elicited a degree of honesty that left little work for the Field Officers.

Mum and dad went overseas for a couple of weeks in early January and I had the place to myself. At the time, my cousin Greg was going out with Cheryl, Angela had gone back to Birmingham, and I was solo.

"I don't suppose Cheryl has any unattached friends?"

"I'll check it out."

A couple of nights later, Greg and Cheryl came around with Vicki. We chatted and drank until it was late. Greg and Cheryl made noises about leaving and taking Vicki home. My eyes met Vicki's and I offered to take her home later; it turned out to be much later. We made love the first night we met; we made love more times than we met; but our relationship ended as soon as it began, we both knew it would only last three weeks. I was severing relationships before they began. No commitment, no pain.

There is a well-known equation in the minds of young people: parental absence = party. I was no exception to this rule. It was vital to have as big a party as possible. I invited at least a hundred people, ordered two kegs of beer, arranged minimal food, and waited. Soon the backyard was a throng of people, throbbing to the music of the Clash, the Jam, the Sex Pistols and the Ramones. Suddenly, Lois materialised, and it was all I could do to keep my lower jaw attached to my face. As usual, she was braless, but this time, her blouse was nearly completely transparent, her breasts clearly winning the fight against gravity that my jaw was losing. The usual death's-head remora followed in her wake. We drifted together and kissed a greeting, the first time we'd ever kissed on the lips, as my mind raced to thoughts of her boyfriend in Sydney and Vicki somewhere in the immediate vicinity.

Later, I was talking to Vicki, who mentioned Dave. Dave was another high school friend who had introduced me to the fantasy novels of Michael Moorcock and the music of Hawkwind. He'd come up to Vicki at the party a little earlier:

"Hey Vicki, guess what Pete's doing?"

"I imagine he's kissing Lois," she'd replied, completely unperturbed, thereby pre-empting the news Dave was about to deliver. I was unsure whether the main point of this short exchange was to show how transparent I was, how much of a dag Dave was, or how unflappable Vicki was. And yet, in just a few days, she would disappear from my life forever.

On the night before I left, Greg, Cheryl, Vicki and I drove to Cottesloe beach, heading separate ways in the sandhills. It was late on a Thursday and no-one was around. Aware that our time together could now be measured in minutes, Vicki and I made love for the last time on the windswept dunes before the Guinness-dark sea.

The afternoon of Friday, 27 January 1978 saw Derek, Dennis and myself board the Turkmenia, a small Russian passenger ship. It was the cheapest way of getting to Singapore, from where we would travel by rail to Bangkok, then fly to Kathmandu to join the tour. Family and friends had gathered at the wharf to make their farewells. The moment we had been planning for five months had finally arrived and I now had mixed feelings. Whereas Derek was leaving behind a broken romance, and Dennis was escaping from the servitude and fumes of the family drycleaning business, I was now leaving someone behind. From deck height, looking down on family and friends, Vicki appeared like a pygmy version of herself, all thick dark hair and generous cleavage. What would happen if I stayed? It was too late to turn back now. Grabbing the railing a little harder, I committed to avoiding commitment.

Eventually, the time of waving and streamers passed, and the Turkmenia pulled out of Fremantle heads, turning north, past the Cottesloe dunes.

chapter 7

Fremantle to Penang

We thought that we had a four-berth cabin to ourselves, and gleefully began throwing our stuff around. Suddenly, the wallpaper blinked, and we realised we were not alone. When he wasn't doing wallpaper impersonations, Ian's main interest was drinking, and he set himself the task of eliminating as many of the twenty-five cent cans of Swan Lager as possible, rarely being seen away from the bar. By comparison, I felt like a teetotaler. In fact, I had never been fitter. Derek's grueling jogging regimen had trimmed me down, and I was drinking a lot less, although we discovered that the surly Russian crew was unrestrained when it came to catering. It was obvious that if we ate all the meals provided we would need bigger clothes when we arrived in Singapore.

At breakfast, Dennis told us he had gone for a walk during the night and seen someone take a flying leap onto the net stretched across the still-empty swimming pool. A genial, boulder-sized Russian crew member dryly suggested that if he removed himself from the net, there would be water in the pool in the morning. He was true to his word, and the pool remained a focal point for us for the rest of the voyage: if we weren't in it, we were lounging next to it drinking cheap vodka and bitter lemon. Or in the disco bar underneath the pool, which offered porthole viewing of the swimmers.

Onboard entertainment included movies and bingo games. The only problem was that these took place in a room whose designer had won first prize in the "Design a nautical room in which all elements are combined to make the inhabitants violently sea-sick" competition. Apart from being right at the stern and therefore more subject to movement and vibration, the floor sloped, and the carpet featured a continuous pattern of brown, orange and silver sine curves. A bar ensured that alcohol was factored into the mix. We saw movies such as "Bring me the Head of Alfredo Garcia" and "Burn", during which Ian ran out to throw up.

On the last day of January, we passed over the deepest water of the journey, 6000 metres, on the way to the Straits of Java. I was surprised that such deep water didn't look absolutely black; from its colour it seemed much shallower. Flying fish were plentiful and Derek enthusiastically identified two gold-tailed tropic birds.

At dinner, Sally from New South Wales was among the group at our table. With a couple of other girls, she was holding forth about the evils of the male ego. We didn't rise to the bait and eventually she changed topic.

"You know one of the other things I hate? It's how people pigeonhole you. Now one thing I'm really good at is cooking. You might think that's boasting except it's not just me saying it – everyone who eats my cooking tells me how good a cook I am, so it can't be boasting. Anyway, the minute after they've told me I'm such a good cook, the thing that makes me really angry is that they say 'You'll make someone a good wife someday.' I don't want to make someone a good wife!"

Just as I was trying to get the courage to reply, "You don't need to worry. There's no chance of that," she saw me looking at her.

"Stop staring at me – what are you looking at?"

"You read my mind – that's exactly what I was wondering."

There was laughter from the guys, and even some of the girls, and the mood lightened.

Later that night I celebrated nearly winning at bingo by having my first beer in three days; Den and Derek stayed up until 2 am, downing ten cheap vodkas each.

Customs at Jurong showed an interest in our cases, but when they saw that Den's contained about a hundred yellow drycleaning bags, they gave up. A friend called Soon didn't materialise; we phoned his shop, and discovered he thought we were arriving the following day. His colleague Johnny collected us in a microbus and helped us find a cheap hotel, the Hai Chew in foodstall-laden Purvis Street, near Beach Street. For $19 Singapore per night ($7 AUS) we had a plain but clean third floor room with one double bed and one single. Den won the dice throw for the single bed.

We headed past the Raffles Hotel and into Orchard Road, changed money ($2.61 Singapore for one Australian dollar), and took the lift to the thirty-sixth floor of the Mandarin Hotel for the view. Derek discovered he had walked all the way from the Raffles with his fly undone: "And I thought people were staring at me because I was good-looking!" Lunch was a $2 curry, and I realised that if the cost of living was going to stay like this, I would be able to stay away from home for a *very* long time.

That night we paid our first visit to Bugis Street, wandering past a shop selling gigantic vibrators to a foodstall in Albert Road where we ate pork and chestnuts from a stall, drank cheap beer and watched a performing magician. We ended up walking back to the Raffles where we bumped into some guys from the boat, including Ian. We definitely lowered the tone of the place in T shirts, shorts and thongs, so didn't stay long.

Out on the street, a tri-shaw driver offered "Nice girl – good for you" and a little later a taxi driver offered us a woman for $50 S per hour. We had barely passed this offer when yet another tri-shaw driver flashed a business card which read:

"(1) You want a have a fun with a nice girl?
(2) Lesbian love act"

Option (1) was the same cost as the taxi driver's offer. Eventually we escaped this marketing frenzy and embraced a coffee instead.

The following day began with toast and coffee from a food stall outside the Hai Chew. It cost a total of 0.75 Singapore – less than 0.30 AUS – if food got any cheaper, they'd be paying us to eat it. Then Johnny collected us and dropped us at the train station where we were bemused by the queues. Hedging our bets, Derek got in one and I got in the other; it turned out that his queue was for air-conditioned carriages and we ended up buying second-class tickets to Penang.

When Johnny returned, it was with another couple and he took us to Sentosa Island, via cable car, and then to Jurong Bird Park where Derek kept accurately identifying every bird call or glimpse of feather and I developed skills in dodging copious amounts of earth-bound guano.

We had the weekend left in Singapore. Johnny took us for a long drive and we ended up in Singapore 15 in a seedy bar. Now to the best of my recollection, I don't believe we ever asked Johnny, "Please take us to a dingy bar in the middle of nowhere where we can sit in almost total darkness and have ugly middle-aged prostitutes stick their hands down our shorts." Somehow, we managed to get out of there with our shorts relatively intact; unfortunately, the women followed us to the door and we saw them in broad daylight.

Shortly after Johnny dropped us at the train station early on Monday morning, I realised we were about to be given a demonstration of frustrating inefficiency. Our previous ticket-buying experience had provided an appetiser: confusing queues which only seemed to shorten at glacial speed; now came the main course.

The game: start off in an orderly queue, which quickly dissolves into a frantic free-for-all in which mutual courtesy is the first casualty. Show your ticket at the gate, run to the queue saying "Other Passports" where the barriers are too narrow for your obese baggage. Curse yourself and anyone remotely responsible for your over-packing, show your passport, run up to the next attendant who also wants to see your passport, which of course you have by now completely stashed away in your money-belt; he also wants to know how much money you have and when you tell him he writes it incorrectly anyway. Then, clutching your passport in case you need it again (which of course you don't), you run to the next guy who fortunately doesn't want to look into your baggage or ask why you let his mother put her hands in your shorts the day before. Then it's a simple quarter-mile dash to carriage M. All of this framed in the menacing context of guards armed with truncheons and .44 pistols who periodically flexed their authority by insisting the Chinese New Year crowds move wherever they wanted. For a moment, the Department of Social Security in Fremantle seemed almost sane.

However, the carriage proved comfortable, the airconditioning functional, and we settled in for a journey through Lenek, Batu Anan, Bating Melaka, Kuala Lumpur and Ipoh, where clouds perched serenely on mountain peaks, before arriving at Butterworth at 9.30pm.

Disembarking, we pushed our luggage through crowds of pressing faces, up the slope and onto the free ferry. As we sailed into Penang at 10.30pm, fireworks heralded the beginning of Chinese New Year, but unfortunately, did nothing to lighten the stench of the city. Obie had recommended the Chung King Hotel in Chulia Street, so we fended off the tri shaw drivers' offers. We located Chulia Street, then realised that the hotel was still nine blocks away. It was late, our bags were chafing in our hands, and patience was in short supply. We dragged ourselves to the next set of lights, dodging huge cockroaches that were running between piles of rubbish in the street, then made the next set of lights, and gave up. We hailed a taxi which took us straight to the Chung King where the desk clerk asked us to pay $40 Malaysian each. It was far too much. I suggested the beach in desperation, then the taxi driver took us to two more Chulia Street hotels, which were full.

Finally, we found a triple room in the Nam Wah Hotel for $15M, but had to be out by 10am. There was no problem with that request, because the hotel was disgusting. The floor was so dirty that your feet stuck to it as you walked. The pillows were rock hard, the toilet indescribable, and you began itching as soon as you lay down on the dirty sheet covering the semen-stained mattress. Despite all this, we slept like dead men.

chapter 8

Penang

We rose early and staggered up Chulia Street with our luggage. The next hotel was full, then Derek spotted the Oriental Hotel, on the corner of Chulia and Penang Road. It looked expensive, but we were desperate. Den and I waited outside with the luggage, watching a rat cavort in a gutter, while Derek checked the price. A few minutes later, Derek reported that the rooms were luxurious and only cost $43M. We jumped at it.

Showered and breakfasted, we spent time in the room relaxing. We were on the seventh floor with a great view: the beach to the right, the harbour to the left and Penang hill straight ahead. The shops along the street included Chan Yew Loong Electro-Plating, Weng Loong Watch Store, Taj Mahal restaurant and Chan Kong Chan Opticians and Watch Service. Noting the last one, Derek joked "They probably wait until some poor sod is going blind and then sell him a watch." Directly across the road, the Odeon was screening "Imperial Sword".

Rejuvenated, we walked down Chulia Street to the ferry terminal in search of a Tourist Bureau Dennis had glimpsed earlier. When we couldn't find it, we walked to Beach Street then north until we came to the clock tower erected in honour of Queen Victoria's Diamond Jubilee. Outside the post office was a derelict who hadn't washed in five years: he was wearing a torn grey shirt, his hair so matted together with grease it had curled up in revulsion at itself.

On a more aesthetic note, in the basement of our hotel we discovered the Hana bar and its friendly, red-swathed hostesses whose job description was to spend most of their time with the biggest-spending customers — which certainly wasn't us. However Leez and Sovya were gorgeous and for some obscure reason seemed actually to prefer to hang out with us rather than the overweight, overspending, middle-aged Japanese the bar manager kept directing them towards. We would spend most of our Penang nights in the Hana, drinking cheap beer and chatting with the girls.

We located the Thai embassy, filled out the necessary forms, only to be told that we wouldn't need a visa for Thailand as we would be staying for less than fifteen days. Yet a little later, the Tourist Office (we eventually found it) woman told us that it was wiser to have a visa. At the sight of three Australians rapidly losing their tempers, she reassured us that it would probably be okay because we had confirmed bookings to leave Thailand. So, with fingers crossed, we booked first class, airconditioned sleeper tickets from Penang to Bangkok.

With that accomplished, we visited the snake temple where Derek and I submitted to various serpentine embraces. It was reassuring to be told that the snakes were drugged into a stupor, but the faces of the locals indicated that there was still an element of risk to the process. Dennis, older, wiser, already poisoned with drycleaning fumes, declined.

Later that day, we checked out a bar called the Green Door and as soon as we walked in, knew it was a mistake. Cigarette butts littered the floor, small cubicles skulked around the edges, and drifting through the Marlboro miasma was the most grotesque collection of women in the world. We were out of the door within seconds and ran back to the hotel to count our fingers and toes.

We soon sallied out again, this time to the Hong Kong Bar which we'd noticed right next door to the atrocious Nam Wah. It looked promising because quite a few Europeans patronised it. It turned out to be a sailors' bar, featuring photos of ships that had visited the port, buoys from Glasgow, and calendars covered with graffiti. It had cheaper beer than the Hana, and the jukebox had a good mix of music, including one of my favourites – Rod Stewart's Maggie May. As soon as you ordered a drink, a girl appeared with a camera and took your photograph to place in their large collection of photograph albums. We began talking with a couple of Aussies from Queensland who were in the Army. They talked about some of the local pornographic shows and where to find them. They also told us about their favourite brothel, the Ah Chew (yes, really!) in Kimberley Street. A "short time" with one of the girls there only cost $M16 (about $4AUS).

We headed to the Ah Chew, hesitating for a moment at the entrance before pushing through the crowd of tri shaw drivers. We were motioned down to the bar at the back, which was surprisingly clean, with aquariums on the walls. Arthur asked Derek if we wanted girls and within a minute there were three girls with us. A quick beer and some fondling ensued. Then Arthur directed Derek and his girl to a room. Then Annie and I headed off to room 38 after I gave Arthur the required funds. This was a significant departure from my RLDS upbringing, but I felt little hesitation. I had already travelled a fair distance along that road. I was also reasonably sure that Annie wouldn't be seeking a commitment.

As we undressed, I discovered Annie was twenty-four and had been married. She wanted to know where we were staying to come back to the hotel with me. Then we were both naked, and for a minute we just stood there.

"You are so clean," she said.

Now if I'd been thinking straight at that moment, I would have dressed and raced out of the room, but as most of my blood had already left my brain, the implications of her statement simply didn't register. When we re-emerged, Derek was already there and Dennis soon joined us. We managed an ice cream on the way back to the Oriental where we collapsed.

We spent the following day at Batu Ferringhi, lazing on the beach with the Rasa Sayang hotel in the background. This was the Penang I'd seen with my parents back in '74: luxury hotels and shark fin soup, not trashpits like the Nam Wah and rats the size of wallabies.

While lying on the sand, perhaps encouraged by the gentle movement of the sea, I had an intense feeling of being adrift. We'd been away from home for two weeks and I was floating away from all past certainties and relationships; both physical and metaphysical moorings had been left behind, and I was following the tide in an unknown direction. My departure was also a complex rejection: it was a rejection of locking into a forty year public service career; a rejection of what so many saw as security; a rejection of a regular income as a major priority; a rejection of the concept that Australia was the centre of the universe; a rejection of a whole set of commitments that people around me held dear. My lifestyle was increasingly moving away from the morality of the RLDS church. I had sailed beyond those values and certainties: it was unnerving and thrilling at the same time. I was without a compass on shifting seas, with no idea of my final destination. I was embodying the existentialist path my Arts Degree had fostered.

Leez spent time with us during the day showing us around Penang, visiting Fort Cornwallis on the seafront and the Botanical Gardens. It was amazing how her presence with the three of us inspired taunts from the locals wherever we went. When we asked Leez what they were saying, it was clear that they were accusing her of sleeping with all three of us. In fact, she didn't sleep with any of us, but Leez, whose father was an ex-police commissioner, was not fazed by any of it, giving as good as she got. When an Indian yelled something particularly annoying from his shop, Leez chased and abused him, told him her father's position and wrote down the name and address of his shop.

On our last night in the Hana, Leez and Sovya dedicated a song to us "When will I see you again?" The answer, of course, was "never".

chapter 9

Bangkok to Kathmandu

On the train to Bangkok, I finished the Hesse novel I was reading and began something about Rasputin. At the Thai border, they dragged me off the train. I suspected it had something to do with the large radio (purchased in Singapore) I was carrying to deliver to a friend of John O'Brien's in Bangkok – the unfortunately-named Mr Porn. Three heavily-armed guards inspected the radio while I waited next to a guy with a big ledger book and a cat. No-one asked me anything or wanted me to sign anything. After a few minutes, they decided I'd delayed the train long enough and with a sigh of relief, I re-boarded. As I did so, a soldier (who I'm sure was Idi Amin's ugly brother) spotted the radio, dragged it down and took me to the end of the carriage where he spoke to the man who had first taken me off the train. I had no idea whether they were trying to determine if the radio was really a bomb, or whether it was worth enough to kill me for. Finally, it was all over and we continued towards Bangkok.

As we were arriving in Bangkok, the train stopped outside a flour mill and a shifty-looking guy in a blue shirt drifted down the corridor. He found Derek and Dennis first, and it turned out he was Mr Porn Jr. He had a taxi waiting and with just a ticket check and completely by-passing customs, he whisked us off to the Reno Hotel.

Our room at the Reno was air-conditioned, clean and only cost US$3 each per night. After settling in and cleaning up, we headed to the Rose Garden, where everything was over-rehearsed and sanitised. The best part of the afternoon was when a group of schoolgirls who could speak a little English gave us flowers they had surreptitiously picked in the gardens. They made us write down our names and addresses. Dennis took a Polaroid photo of the girls and gave it to them. Perhaps they thought that any foreigners as scruffy as we were *had* to be rock stars.

Porn took us that night to one of the famous shows in Bangkok that are named after him. Suffice to say that Fanta, ping pong balls and a banana featured prominently, but I was bored as soon as I walked in. There were some married couples present, and I spent more time watching their reactions than watching the actual acts on stage.

Afterwards, Porn took us to an upmarket brothel called the Nana Flower where all the girls were dancing with plastic numbered discs around their necks; you simply picked the number you wanted. Back at the Reno, Derek and his girl had a room to themselves, while Den and I shared a room with our girls. My girl was called Dan, a former professional masseuse.

Sometime later, all four of us convened on what was normally Derek's bed because Den's girl, Mit, had some pot. She expertly hollowed out a filtered cigarette, refilling it with a mixture of pot and tobacco. I'd smoked pot before, but it was Den's first time; it was probably a lot healthier than drycleaning fumes.

With our passports awaiting visas at the Nepalese embassy, we had dinner the next night at Mr Porn's. On the way there we passed a scabrous dog that lingered in front of moving cars, inviting death; this fortunately didn't dull our appetites for the mountains of prawns, mussels, rice and Singha beer Porn provided.

With the night still young, Derek and Dennis were keen to repeat the activities of the previous evening, and a little later, we were back in our room at the Reno with three women. Derek and Den had the same two girls from the night before, but I had chosen someone else, Lina. After some more pot from the obliging Mit, the lights were out and each couple went to their separate bed, but all in the same room. It was then that disaster struck. Everything had been going well, and then suddenly… it wasn't.

"I've got brewer's droop!" I called out in frustration and there were giggles from the darkness of the other beds. I tried showering, had a cigarette, but nothing worked. I sent Lina home in a taxi and spent the rest of the night listening to Derek and Dennis getting more than their money's worth.

The next day, Derek tried to jolt me out of my black mood.

"Look, it's hardly the end of the world. It's happened to me before too; it's no big deal, if you'll excuse the pun! Anyway, how many times did you get it off with Dan the night before?"

"Three."

"And you didn't get any sleep then either, right? Okay, so you were exhausted and shagged out, so it was perfectly understandable that you really weren't up to it last night."

It all made sense of course, but I wallowed in self-pity and humiliation a while longer.

Floating market tours were canoes with attitude zooming over filthy water against a background of golden temples. At the temples there were photo opportunities with gilt-encrusted dancers, but you had to pay. We soon figured out how to stand behind the group of women and take photos of each other without them realising what was happening, so I think we invented photo-bombing. Every dollar counted. We collected our Nepalese visas and were on our way back to the hotel, when suddenly our car was surrounded by police. They took one look at Derek and Dennis and searched them, ignoring me due to the aura of cherubic sanctity I was projecting. After they left, our driver told us that they had been convinced Derek and Dennis were carrying dynamite and drugs.

Our flight to Kathmandu left early on February 20, and while we were waiting at the airport, we met a young Japanese guy called Chi-Chi. His English was basic and I think he attached himself to us for security. The plane stopped at Rangoon where rice paddies stretched to the horizon, embraced by wide, serpentine rivers. Derek drew on his knowledge of geography to inform us that the area was created by deposition. At least, that's what I *think* he said, because with free alcohol on board, we were knocking back quite a lot of Carlsberg and brandy. The chill air of Kathmandu found us in high spirits as we turned our thoughts to finding a hotel. Our coach tour left from the Blue Star Hotel, but all thoughts of booking in there were shelved when we discovered from Chi-Chi's guide book that double rooms cost US$20. A taxi driver persuaded us to check out the centrally located Hotel Gainda. The price was US$1.00 each per night for a triple room, so we were prepared to compromise on luxury.

Arriving in Kathmandu was like traveling five hundred years back in time. In some obscure way, the architecture of the city reminded me of parts of old Florence. Shopfronts opened directly onto the street with living quarters above; chickens scratched about on heaps of refuse at the end of the winding corridors between buildings; people in rags dawdled through streets dotted with excreta, spittle and vomit, oblivious of the cars swirling around them. I was entranced by this time travel, but I was about to exit my trance with a jolt.

It happened just after we had eaten at Jamaly's (French onion soup, sweet and sour pork and rice, chocolate pie and coffee for US$1.00) and returned to the Gainda. I was standing at the toilet and felt … strange. I looked down and my worst fears were confirmed:

"Hey guys – I've got a dose!"

Derek raced in and confirmed it.

It was late afternoon. I was in a country that had been untimely ripped from the Middle Ages (and presumably had a similar standard of medical care), we were about to embark on the world's longest bus trip, and I had just contracted venereal disease. Things could have been better.

Derek and I sped into the street in search of a doctor. Someone pointed us in the direction of New Road where we eventually saw a sign for a military doctor. Thinking he should know a thing or two about venereal disease, we dashed in.

"Unfortunately, you're not going to be in town long enough for us to get results from a blood test. What are your symptoms?"

I told him and he wrote out a prescription for six shots of penicillin of twelve lacs each, and pills called Pyridium, which would ease the stinging sensation. Back on the street, we had no luck finding a chemist who had six doses of twelve lacs, and eventually went back to the doctor who changed it to a single shot of twenty-four lacs. Two chemists later, I'd had the injection.

One of the bonuses of the Hotel Gainda was personal butlers, on call twenty-four hours a day. It was a family-owned hotel, and the two waistcoated boys, aged about eleven and fourteen, were fascinated with us, wanting nothing more than to hang around and run errands for us. We only had one errand – to run to the nearest shop and buy us some Chukri rum (US$1/bottle) and Coke.

By the time Derek and I returned to the hotel from our medical excursion, Dennis had finished the first bottle of rum and started on a second. We each drank a bottle of Chukri, but for some reason, I couldn't get to sleep.

Sleepless, I arose around 3 a.m. to go to the toilet, and suddenly knew I was about to be ill on a seismic scale. Unable to find the bathroom light, I ran back into the bedroom, opened the window and vomited violently into the courtyard two floors below. No sooner was this over than diarrhea struck and for the next two hours, I remained in the toilet. Much later and much lighter, I collapsed into bed. It had been an eventful day.

chapter 10

The World's Longest Bus Trip

The following morning, our butlers brought us breakfast in bed – toast, omelette and coffee for 50 cents, after which we hired bikes for 40 cents per day and headed off. I was feeling lousy: the combination of vomiting, diarrhea, VD, the massive injection in my bum and less than three hours' sleep meant I was hardly at my sparkling best.

Den and Derek weren't feeling fantastic either so we only cycled to the Blue Star, where the tour group was gathering, and met Tony our tour guide who remembered John O'Brien from two years before. I discovered that there was a young doctor on the trip, and, for obvious reasons, fervently hoped he wasn't a PhD in ancient Greek poetry.

The next day, we were feeling a bit more energetic, and cycled out to Swayambuya temple with its all-seeing eyes where we saw a man suffering from elephantitis. It looked incredibly painful: his bloated legs seemed like they belonged to an over-ripe corpse, but rarely has a disease been so well-named. We lunched at the Nepal coffee-house and helped Chi-Chi (whom we had rechristened Fuji) buy an airline ticket to India. After this, we wanted to sample some of the legendary pie shops, and taking a tip from a fellow-traveller, were soon ensconced in the New Style Pie Shop where my choice was a lemon meringue and chocolate pie, washed down with hot chocolate. Bob Dylan was wafting from the cassette player and there was a Faces poster on the wall. I had only a few minutes to ponder the intermingling of east and west before I felt sick.

I made it back to the hotel and during the next two hours threw up six times; at the end I think I saw my stomach lining fly by. Surely, something had crept down my throat and scoured my stomach with steel wool. We blamed the deep-fried cheese balls I'd had for lunch. I couldn't eat or move for twenty-four hours and lay immobile the following day while Den and Derek cycled madly around the city and environs, discovering marijuana growing wild. I consoled myself with the thought that this had to be the physical low point for me – surely things could only improve from here on. This was later to prove to be a wildly unjustified presumption.

Kathmandu was the first place on our trip I hadn't visited before and its alien nature enthralled me. I knew I could never fully understand this culture even if I stayed for years. A man was drinking milk out of the gutter using a leaf as a scoop; men walked hand-in-hand in the streets; beggars were present, but not prolific, and didn't keep pestering after the first refusal. The child beggars were the worst, adopting depressed and world-weary expressions as you approached, swearing at you after you passed. Did childhood exist in Nepal, I wondered? The local concept of hygiene seemed medieval, with rubbish often being emptied in the street, and people casually spitting out of upper-floor windows; on one occasion, there was a horrified scream in my ear as the punctilious Fuji found himself suddenly sporting a mucous beanie. Experiencing Kathmandu was like drinking deeply from the mountain streams in the area; it was an encouragement that the world would have many bracing and unpredictable treats to offer.

Our time in Kathmandu was coming to an end, as was our time of completely independent traveling. We were about to commit to ten weeks in the company of total strangers and to facilitate this we decided to spend the night before departure at the Blue Star.

Early on February 25, 1978, we boarded the orange and white Pennworld bus to begin the world's longest bus trip. Initial impressions of our co-travellers were mixed: apart from Bruce who was in his fifties, most were a little older than us, mainly English, Canadian, Australian, some married couples and, amazingly, *two* sets of identical twin sisters. We soon re-christened them. The austere, barrel-shaped, blond twins who kept to themselves, always wore scarves in their hair and had perpetual looks of thin-lipped disapproval were immediately labeled the Gruesome Twosome. In a similar vein, the other twins, who actually were much more personable, became (unfairly) the Grim Sisters. I've no idea how people referred to us.

Our first night's camp was at Pokhara, by the edge of Lake Fewatal. Although the surrounding poles and barbed wire created a concentration camp ambience, this was overwhelmed by the beauty of the place at dusk, with mountains dominating the nearby hills that sloped in ridges down to the lake.

The provided two-man tents were excellent, and the air mattress and sleeping bag kept out the evening chill. Staggering out in the morning, it wasn't the cold that took my breath away, but the incredible view of the Annapurnas. Breakfast was oatmeal and a cheese pancake at the Snowman Restaurant and we were soon off on one of the most tortuous roads in the world, with precarious drops to one side.

Tony Courier and Dave Driver were our crew members. The more Tony told us about the trip as we drove along, the more we liked it. We had paid the upfront cost of the trip – AU$750 – before leaving Australia. We knew that there would be an additional contribution for a food kitty. The bus contained a cook tent and we would be rostered on for cooking and cleaning. Tony told us that this was his seventh (and probably last) time leading this tour and therefore, it was his goal to make it the cheapest trip to date (groans from some; cheers from us). One implication of this was that we would be camping wherever it was safe to do so, only using hotels when necessary for security.

As we drove to our second night's camp at Gaida, Tony Courier shared some information about Nepalese customs. The Sherpas particularly caught my attention. Adult children often bring their lovers back to their parents' home and have sex in the same room as their parents. Trial marriages are quite acceptable, as are two brothers marrying the same wife, apparently because the men are away for large parts of the year tending flocks in upper fields; this system means that the wife has a chance of having at least one husband around. Jealousy is unknown in these situations, but divorce is also easy. If a wife wants a divorce and the husband doesn't, she gives him a token of one rupee towards what he paid for the wedding expenses and the divorce is finalised. In the case of one of the marriage partners taking a lover, the offender merely has to pay the hurt party a set fee, everything is forgotten, and the now-friendly trio proceed to have a meal together. It occurred to me that these arrangements were probably the reason I hadn't seen any lawyers' offices in Kathmandu.

While Tony was sharing this information, there were two enormous thuds on the roof of the bus. Looking out the back window, we saw local kids on the rise who clearly had nothing better to do than throw the biggest rocks they could at us.

At the edge of a river, we loaded the tents and cooking gear into a Land Rover, and walked, following it, onto a ferry, which crossed a swift current to a small dusty, rubbishy town where a local bus was waiting. We bought a couple of bananas each and thirty oranges (the three of us had eaten a dozen oranges each in the previous two days) before boarding the local bus for the one hour trip to Gaida. Derek, Dennis and I sat on the roof of the bus with a few others for a dusty, bum-numbing ride. Often, the bush was reminiscent of Australia, and the villages seemed to be both clean and friendly as we bumped our way towards Chitwan National Park.

After pitching our tents and showering, we headed into the bush on foot in search of rhino, but after stalking the grasslands on the far side of the river for a while, discovered nothing but kingfishers. An English girl called Jean walked with us for a while, but stayed behind at the bend in the river. Later, crossing by herself, she came face-to-face with a rhino and headed into the nearest tree, from which she observed it for half an hour. We were having fun of a different sort, swimming in the shallow river in our underwear and trudging through swamps before returning to camp and starting a reluctant fire. A wild boar appeared on the far side of the river while we were eating minestrone soup and farmhouse stew washed down with Chukri rum.

"Who wants to go hunting in my Land Rover?" The speaker had drunk far too much rum and there were valid reasons to doubt his sanity, but most of us still wanted to go. Because the vehicle could only fit a few, we whittled it down by choosing numbers, and soon nine of us were climbing aboard. Suddenly, we were speeding through the Nepalese night in an open four-wheel drive in search of rhino or Bengal tigers, holding on with whitened knuckles lest we became jungle jetsam and hence something's supper. The rhinos and tigers were wisely hiding, but rabbits and a fox obliged and we stopped at an elephant camp where cheese, rum and gin were freely passed around. If nothing else, the manic drive helped me to get to know some of the other tour members better as we inadvertently spent most of the time in each other's laps.

chapter 11

Snake Eyes

The morning began with two deer speeding past on our side of the river, then bounding across it, pausing on the other side in the long grass to look disdainfully at us before finally disappearing. The three of us traipsed off into the bush after breakfast, spying vultures, peacocks, hoopoe and rolas, much to Derek's delight, before heading back for an elephant ride.

The two and a half hour elephant ride was well worth the resulting pain: we saw five rhinos and plenty of deer before arriving at the river and canoeing in search of crocodiles. This was less successful because other canoes were ahead of us, so all we got to see were three reptilean splashes.

The following day we left Chitwan in the first rain we had seen since Singapore and all three of us had health concerns: Den had diarrhea, Derek had some sort of infection in his toes, and I had serious doubts about whether the VD was lessening. By now it had occurred to all three of us that when we were traveling as a unit, we might be held up by the ill-health of one person; what could happen now that there were thirty of us?

We crossed into India, where I had to surrender my Singapore Airlines pen to a border official as a bribe before he'd let us through, and soon arrived at the Hotel de Paris in Benares/Varanasi. We were initially disappointed when told there weren't enough rooms, but then delighted as we improvised a system that was definitely not going to impose much on the collective kitty. We hired two rooms, one for men and one for women, in which we locked all our valuables, and erected our tents in the grounds. After demolishing a meal of fish, roast lamb and beer (yes, it's a food group) in the hotel, I chatted to Judy until midnight. I returned to the tent I thought I was sharing with Derek that night, but my stuff was actually in Den's tent so I stumbled in that direction, leaving behind a now awake and unamused Derek. I remained awake myself: the tent was stifling and the mosquitoes ferocious – swatting them with a Gideon's Bible didn't work - and I eventually headed into the communal hotel room. The resulting lack of sleep lent a rather hallucinogenic quality to a dawn visit to the Ganges River.

The sun rose angry red as our group stood almost reverently on the steps above the ancient Ganges, where pink-brown buildings descended to the water's edge. Corpses were being burnt on river-side pillars and bones were thrown to the waves; crows were picking choice morsels from the human barbecue as all around us people were spitting, washing, praying, cleaning their teeth, beating clothes against the flat slabs or contorting into yoga's pretzled peace.

"Toto, I have a feeling we're not in Fremantle any more."

Pink forts, former homes to maharajahs, towered above the squalor as they had for centuries as we took our lives in our hands, boarded narrow canoes, and pushed out into the holy river. We floated in stillness as the morning worshippers garlanded the fluid hair of mother Ganja with flowers and immersed themselves three times facing the rising sun.

"The Ganges river has a high level of mineral purity and a lack of bacteria," our chubby Indian guide assured us. A porpoise surfaced. A dead pig bloated by, surrounded by grey foam.

"Bodies sometimes float into the morning bathers," our guide continued, "but they simply push them away back into the river. Anybody who dies in Benares goes straight to Nirvana."

And anybody who gets in the Ganges is going to Nirvana a whole lot quicker than they otherwise would. Our stillness in the canoe was not reverence; it was terror of falling in.

Before departing the next day, a few of us made one more quick trip down to the ghats at the edge of the Ganges. In the middle of watching a cremation up close, I got propositioned via sign language and replied in kind. A scorched onion of a head gazed towards us; only the toes remained unburned and absurdly pink, defiantly pointing at the sky. I felt someone tap my back, turned, and nearly gagged. The fingerless hands of a leper had prodded me, brown skin peeling to reveal white beneath. His noseless face looked like it had been beaten raw with a brick. Suddenly, it was time to leave.

About 90 kilometres out of Varanasi, the bus broke down. We spent several hours stranded in the middle of nowhere while Tony Courier hitched a ride on a truck back to a small town, survived being propositioned by the crew, and returned with a local bus mid-afternoon. We got back to Varanasi in the early evening and had to re-pitch our tents in the middle of a lightning storm.

The bus situation remained uncertain, with the option of continuing by local bus and Driver Dave catching up to us when our bus was fixed. On the front lawn of the hotel, entertainment took the form of snake charmers encouraging trained mongooses to attack and decapitate live snakes. A black-mascaraed monkey man was also there, smiling and cruelly beating his monkey if its parody of a human dance was less than perfect. The cruelty of the animal shows simply mirrored the aggression of the roads where the law of the jungle seemed to rule: cars threatened rickshaws and were in turn threatened by trucks. In the background, a dramatically reluctant bridegroom rode an absurdly decorated horse, accompanied by firing shotguns and hovering crows. India offered nothing but the unexpected.

The decision was made to continue to Delhi by train. Fortunately, Den had recovered from the runs, losing half his body weight in the process, but several others had succumbed. The train trip was the perfect occasion for a long rum-fuelled card game and when we arrived in Delhi early the next morning, a Sundowners Bus took us to the Ranjit Hotel. The fact that the hotel had no rooms for us was the breaking point for a few, and loud complaining noises continued as we headed to a campsite in Ali Asaf Road.

We all had limited clothing as most of it was back with our luggage in Varanasi, so I shivered through the melodramatic but spectacular sound and light show at the Red Fort. More exciting was the drive back: we paid our motorcab drivers to race each other, with the winner getting an extra rupee. The drivers made an instant decision that for an extra rupee it was worth risking the lives of everyone on the cabs, including their own. Later, as the hypothermia and adrenalin overload subsided, I drifted off to sleep with the Stones' Sympathy for the Devil wafting through the campsite.

Next day, Tony Courier descended from his hash haze and took us towards Jaipur in another Pennworld bus. As we drove out of Delhi, it reminded me of Paris (if you could overlook the beggars), and demonstrated that India was much more industrialised than Nepal. Our temporary driver wasn't impressed as he hadn't had a day off in three months, but he drove us to the Amber Fort, which was encircled by mountains; signs advertised Kwality icecream that the stores didn't sell, and the hot item on the streets was coloured slides of the sexually athletic carvings at Khajaharo.

In Jaipur, mountain-flanked home of maharajahs, painted pink by royal decree, I sat next to an emerald pond, watching parrots chasing jackdaws through the trees, marveling at the jangling difference that was India.

While thinking about the Indian art of staring - how to return a half-smile to curious stares and how to outsole insolent ones - my reverie was interrupted, initially by a peacock with five peahens in tow, and then by a turbaned astrologer with a gravity-defying moustache.

"You have snake eyes," he said. "You watch everything and listen to everything. You please yourself in what you do. You also have bad habits." I eventually got rid of him, which became easier when he discerned that one of my bad habits was not paying money for unsolicited astrology readings, which you think he should have known to begin with.

From Jaipur it was back to Delhi, via Fatehpur Sikri, sixteenth-century capital of Mogul emperor Akbar, and Agra. There were the obligatory photos at the Taj Mahal, where we learnt that the four corner towers were angled outwards at six degrees (so in the event of earthquake, they would fall away from the main building) and marveled to learn that the original plan was to build a matching tomb in black marble across the river, connecting the two with a solid silver bridge.

On our last night in Delhi, a group of us, including Doctor Dave and his wife Barbara, had dinner at a Tandoor restaurant. Dave and Barbara had just spent nine months stationed with the airforce in Penang, where they had learnt scuba diving. We made a date to dive together in Aqaba.

The next morning, I woke feeling like the dregs of an Indian gutter: sore throat, snotty head, rampant VD and diarrhea. The next two days disappeared in a daze of discomfort: eight hours each day on the now-repaired bus, during which my sphincter became the biggest muscle in my body.

chapter 12

Kashmiri Daze

Although we spent a night at the Picnic Hotel in Jammu, life was far from a picnic. As we rolled into Kashmir, using self-pity as an anaesthetic, I realised that I had been suffering from VD for a month. The mountains around Srinagar were covered with snow, which was the first time Dennis had ever been in it, and there was an obligatory snowball fight before we continued our descent down to Dal Lake.

Srinagar in mid-March existed in beautiful black and white, and we had long been looking forward to our stay on the famed houseboats of Dal Lake. Beautiful in their rectangular wooden plainness, they each had several bedrooms and a balcony facing out into the lake. Each was family-owned and run like a private hotel. Transport between houseboats was on canoes called shikaras. Our boat was Pearl Ship and the crew was Judy, Lorraine, Alison, Dennis, Derek, Dave Driver and myself. Derek and Lorraine had become an item in Delhi.

The houseboats were total luxury compared with tents or even hotel rooms. Floors, walls, roof: everything was made of wood and its aroma was all-pervasive. Rugs were underfoot, a wood fire was in the corner, and the family provided meals and round the clock service. *This* was camping!

I dropped out early from the evening's hash-fest and woke to the stunning view of mountains reflected in the lake. Perfect …except I was still worrying about my dose. After breakfast, Judy wanted to get a pack of cards from Scarlet, the boat Doctor Dave happened to be on. I seized the chance to shikara with her and managed to grab a moment alone with Dave.

"Dave, I've got a case of galloping gonorrhea." I gave him all the gory details.

"Well, they didn't have a chance to test you properly, so there are a couple of possibilities. First, is that you could have a strain of gonorrhea that is immune to penicillin. Second, you mightn't have gonhorrea at all, but non-specific urethritis – NSU for short - which has identical symptoms." After advising me to have a blood test in London, he wrote me out a prescription for Amicillin.

The next morning the world seemed brighter: I'd had the prescription filled and it seemed to be working. I started engaging my "snake eyes" and paid a bit more attention to my fellow travellers: Judy and Dave Driver were playing Mastermind; Dennis was worrying about when and where he'd cashed a traveller's cheque; Tony Courier was hitting it off with Lee; Charlie and Lois seemed to be having difficulties; Derek and Lorraine's relationship was weird. In fact, Lorraine was aloof from everyone most of the time, even Derek, until she dragged him to bed at night.

That night, while Derek and Dennis shikaraed off to Buckingham Palace for another hash fest, the rest of us remained behind reading, writing and dozing. Suddenly, Dave Driver commented that I was looking "distinguished", and Alison agreed. I certainly wasn't feeling distinguished, but was feeling mellow and I realised what lay behind their comments: from the time they had met me I had been carrying VD and obviously worrying about it; now that it was in retreat, there was a tangible difference. From the houseboat balcony, I watched the pine trees bristling their way up the

Kashmiri hills, chasing a mist that was gradually rising from the river. I had been away from home for seven weeks, and realised I wasn't really missing people much: perhaps the astrologer was right about me being hard-hearted. How strong was my commitment to home and family after all? Was I really running away from all commitment?

Saturday March 18 started off quietly. Derek and Dennis had smoked so much hashish the night before on Buckingham Palace that they couldn't paddle in a straight line. They had spent about two hours spinning in circles in sub-zero conditions before they eventually made it back to Pearl Ship. So we lazed on board until late morning before undertaking a shikara tour of the lake, which proved much bigger than I first thought, varying greatly in cleanliness and depth. A chocolate-brown kingfisher with a white shirt-front dived in front of me, revealing an electric blue back; Derek later identified it as a white-breasted kingfisher, although I would never have known if he was making up the names anyway.

After lunch, Derek, Den and I decided to head over to town because I was starting to run out of Amicillin. When we crossed the lake into Srinagar, we realised that a lot of shops, including chemists, were shut on Saturday afternoons, so we took a leisurely walk around town, up to the bund, commenting on the British influence on the local architecture. At one point, two shoe-shine boys pounced on us, wanting our business.

While we were talking to them, we heard a noise in the main street, a block away. Looking down the side street, we saw a crowd gathering and marching in the direction we wanted to go. Some of them looked down the alley towards us, and waved their fists at us angrily. One was carrying a black flag, and we recalled we had seen a few other black flags on cars. We had no idea what was going on, but we knew we wanted to get away from it.

Derek took the lead and decided to head along the bund in the same direction as the crowd, outrun them, cut in front and find an obscure way to get to the hill at the edge of town. Once there, we could gain some elevation, see what was going on, and possibly find a safe way back to the edge of the lake. After a short distance, we met a smart-looking Sikh and asked him what was going on.

"It is not a good situation. People are upset because General Bhutto in Pakistan has been sentenced to death within the week." I was slightly relieved by this because I couldn't see what it would have to do with Europeans, but we kept moving quickly anyway to get ahead of the mob.

My relief disappeared when we passed another group who called out: "It's very dangerous on the streets for you now. Get somewhere safe." Had I survived VD only to be dismembered in the streets of Srinagar? We were running now, and for the first time I felt grateful for all that jogging Derek had inflicted on us in Fremantle. We got ahead of the mob, cut across the main street, and realised that our path converged with where the mob was heading - the UN building where an army was drilling in the grounds. We sped up, got behind the UN building and out of sight. We went around the hill, passed behind the cemetery which seemed to serve double-duty as a public toilet, and laboriously climbed the hill. Soon, we were several hundred feet above the melee, but also several hundred feet above the lake and our bus. Our next problem was to find a convenient place to descend which would take us through the maze of houses between us and the lake.

Down we went, boots skidding on wet grass and pebbles. The mob we met at the bottom consisted of friendly kids and we went through them and a barbed wire fence to find ourselves in a street that seemed to run parallel to the lakeside. But should we go right or left now? The minute we had started our descent, we had lost sight of the angry mob and had no idea how close they may be. Dennis assumed command and we headed left. Half an hour later, we were at the lake; if we'd turned right it would have taken us ten minutes. A quick shikara paddle and we were back at our houseboat. There were no parties that night.

chapter 13

Afghanistan to Iran

After a short delay the next morning due to frozen petrol, we were on the road, retracing our path to Jammu. Landslides had wiped out sections of the road, and after a couple of hours spent negotiating the bus around semi-cleared rockfalls, we came to a complete stop. Ahead of us, as far as the eye could see, stretched an unbroken line of TATA trucks, moving at a snail's pace, if at all. It seemed we were not destined to spend the night in Jammu after all.

Tony Courier disappeared and was gone for two hours. He reappeared at dusk and we saw a miracle begin to unfold as at least one hundred trucks pulled over to the cliff-face so that we could pass. I have no idea how many rupees changed hands, but Tony clearly felt it was a better option than being stuck in a bus on a mountainside overnight with thirty people, no toilet facilities, and hundreds of truck drivers in the immediate vicinity.

We moved forward slowly to the head of the queue, but our problems weren't over yet. The real hold-up was the condition of the road: the landslide had completely washed the road away, leaving a mixture of rock, sand and mud. We watched a bulldozer making last minute repairs in the dwindling light. All of us except Dave Driver and Tony Courier got off the bus and stood on tortured earth with hundreds of TATA onlookers: would the makeshift repairs take the weight of the bus? Dave started the bus, drove forward at a moderate pace and crossed successfully, accompanied by loud cheering. We re-boarded and arrived back in Jammu just after midnight.

We were up early to drive to Amritsar, where we visited the Golden Temple and attended a lecture on Sikhism. It took us more than two hours to cross the border into Pakistan, and at the Holiday International Hotel in Lahore, six of us shared a room (the houseboat crew minus Dave). Initial impressions of Lahore were of a well-laid out city, lots of Japanese cars, and a high consumption rate of Coke and Pepsi.

Our morning tour of Lahore was nondescript. We saw the local fort and the mosque which was supposed to be the world's largest, although it had been rebuilt after raiders and centuries of neglect had taken their toll. We later found out that our guide for this tour was a registered alcoholic, no mean feat in Pakistan, which, being Muslim, was "dry".

The afternoon saw us drive through mesas and valleys to Rawalpindi, which seemed amazingly clean: we arrived after dark and settled into a campground. From there to Peshawar and the Park Hotel, and a side trip to another world called Darra. A local bus took us there and, on the way, decided to race another bus, running a car and an old man on a bicycle off the road in the process.

Darra had its own "mini-border" and industries: drugs and guns. We wandered around the small open factory units where turbaned men, often missing eyes or fingers, made everything from pens that fired .22 calibre bullets to sub-machine guns. We posed with the guns - Craig fired a pistol and remained intact - and then strolled over to the hash shop.

Various tour members were sampling the goods and Steve was excitedly waving a slab of hash. It was about thirty centimeters long by twenty centimeters wide and seven millimeters thick.

"Look at this, you guys! Do you know what this would cost on the street in Australia? Three thousand dollars. Here it costs twenty dollars!"

The next day we left Darra and Peshawar behind and began climbing through the Khyber Pass. We passed through several miles of mountains, caves and hills, all custom-designed for ambush, and forts which we were told not to photograph, but did anyway. The country was the stronghold of the Pathans, who officially lived under Pakistani rule but in reality lived by their own rules. Revenge was a major factor in their lives; no murder cases ever reached the courts because revenge was pursued privately until whole families were annihilated or one family leader groveled to another. Clearly, it was not a place to make confrontational eye-contact with the locals.

We passed Kochi caravans with their camels and earless dogs – owners cut off the dogs' ears and fed them to the dogs to make them vicious. Seemed to work. Another two hour border crossing and we were officially in Afghanistan, a country with the distinction of having been occupied at various times by Darius the Persian, Alexander the Great, Genghis Khan and Tamerlane.

The Hindu Kush proved even more awe-inspiring than the Khyber. We climbed three hundred meters in altitude in three kilometers of intestinal road; similar terrain to the Khyber but compressed and twice as high. Then it was down to the plain, past snow-capped mountains to Kabul, where we shared a room at the Metropole Hotel with Judy and Alison. We headed out to the Miami restaurant where vegetable cutlets, yoghurt, honey and a rich chocolate pudding seemed a sensible meal. I was about to miss Friday.

I woke with a stomach ache that soon transformed itself into a fiesta of bowel movements. Derek and Dennis wisely fled the room, climbed the mountain above town, and explored old Kabul. I forced myself out of bed in the late afternoon (the sulphur tablets I had been taking had eased my stomach) and cruised down Chicken Street in search of flick knives. The

Afghan street-sense reminded me of the Nepalese – wandering, wondering, oblivious. Donkeys overladen with garlic stopped in the middle of the foot-path as the smell of fish and nan pervaded the streets.

The riot in Kashmir had shown we had no guarantee of safety just because we were traveling with an organised tour. Political and social issues of which we were unaware could intrude unannounced, with a distinct lack of courtesy and possible grievous bodily harm. It seemed sensible to be at least vaguely aware of what was going on in the world, so I started the habit of picking up a copy of *Time* magazine in a newsagent and flicking through it (actually *buying* it would have been extravagant). It was the end of March and Aldo Moro had been kidnapped by the Red Brigades in Italy.

During some free time the next day, the three of us walked eight kilometers to the Museum and were busy wandering around, looking at artifacts as old as 50,000BC. A local bus brought us back for 2 cents, but if local transport was ridiculously cheap in Kabul, some things weren't: beer was more expensive than anywhere else so far - $4 – for the same sum you could buy four meals.

That night, I awoke to the noise of somebody staggering around our room. A burglar? I focused on the thick, woolly silhouette, and eventually realised it was Lee. She put down her handbag, started talking to a lump of blankets on Judy's bed, used the loo and then demanded of us in general, "Where's Noni?" We kindly informed her that she was in the wrong room on the wrong floor, at which there was an outburst of hysterical giggling which vanished down the corridor and continued in the room underneath us for half an hour. This wasn't the end of the evening's entertainment however: sleep came to an end a couple of hours later when Judy and Alison, both well-pickled from a party in room 309, arrived bearing Easter eggs for us.

Although I wasn't feeling 100% the next morning, the variety of scenery helped me ignore the stomach rumbles: we climbed level with the snow as we left Kabul, and then descended to arid plains. Our morning chai stop was Ghazni, a city razed by Genghis Khan, and perhaps not the best choice considering the circumstances. Two weeks before our arrival, the driver of another overland tour bus had run down and killed a local woman and child. He was facing a large fine and a jail sentence, and the bus had been impounded. His tour group was stuck in Isfahan as they awaited a new driver and a new bus.

Despite this tragedy, the locals were friendly and I spent a lot of time with a small child and his animal book. He would point to a picture and tell me the animal's name in Pashto, and I would give the English, discovering that the Pashto for kangaroo and platypus bore no resemblance to the English equivalents.

At Kandahar we checked into the Aria Hotel. Appropriately, a wave of sickness of operatic proportions rolled through the group: Bruce threw up all over the carpet and got diarrhea; Peggy threw up and had a fever; Derek had cold flushes and stomach cramps; Den and I got diarrhea. This is perhaps the moment to mention we were traveling before the Pennworld people had thought of putting toilets on their buses. If we'd been on the road for a few hours and were in the middle of nowhere, we would simply stop the bus and the guys would go to one side and the girls to the other. I found myself wondering how many sick people were required to halt the bus altogether?

As we drove off the next day, the first disaster was not the sort I expected: a few kilometers down the road I discovered I'd left my moneybelt in the hotel, under the mattress. We drove back, and it was still there, untouched, but it was a stupid thing to do and I felt embarrassed at the inconvenience I'd caused. Back on the road, I began to feel better and I had bread and an orange for lunch. The orange was a mistake. Thirteen kilometers out of Herat, I was desperate for a toilet, but determined not to gain the honour of being the first person to stop the bus for this purpose. I gritted my teeth, grasped the edge of the chair and broke into goosepimples as we passed one possible toilet after another. Finally, we were in the centre of Herat, Tony pointed out the hotel, and we drove past it! I nearly collapsed as we drove to the end of the street and did a U-turn. I was in the hotel's nearest toilet before Dave Driver turned off the ignition.

Lomotil and sulphur tablets later, we hit the streets. We headed east from the Super Behzad Hotel towards the shrine and antique shops, pestered numerous times by locals asking us if we had jeans for sale. Despite checking out various knives and guns (and always unsure if we'd get them past customs in Britain), we ended up with more mundane souvenirs: Derek bought an English penny from 1799 and I bought a solid silver coin which had been made into a medallion. It cost me the grand sum of $3.75 and as soon as Derek identified it as silver, the shopkeepers tried to talk me out of buying it.

As we drove towards the Iranian border, we met a Top Deck Travel bus heading in the opposite direction and a fellow diver assured me that diving in Aqaba was great. The border itself took record time, despite sniffer German shepherds and officious officials, and we arrived at our campsite in Meshed, a short distance from the blue and gold domed mosque. The night was freezing: clothes refused to dry, showers refused to stay hot, and airbeds refused to stay inflated.

As we drove through Gorgon, making mental notes to avoid women with unusual hairstyles, we hit and killed a dog. On the way to Shasi, we passed a statue of the Shah and Margaret the snob exclaimed:

"Oh, I must write Rodge, he hates the Shah!"

"Does he know him?' one of the Grim Sisters aptly inquired.

"No, but he reads a lot."

A little later, Alison, who was wanting to share a bottle, called out:

"Are there any empty cups on the bus?"

"Yes!" responded Judy.

"Don't be modest," I replied. Well, it wasn't going to be a romance anyway.

Les was singing a lot as well; so it wasn't a great day, but worse was to come – we were about to encounter our first Rotel tour. Now I really have no idea how Rotel tours were marketed in Germany, but I suspect the advertisements went something like this:

"Are you old, obese and incontinent? Then consider leaving your mark on another continent. Join a Rotel tour to Asia and we will layer you like sardines inside a claustrophobic sleeping trailer, give you lots of dodgy food, and get you to campsites early in the day so that you will find the toilets in a pristine condition. You can then defecate endlessly, block the sewer lines, and leave the toilets in a disgusting condition for the poor sods who arrive later in the day."

Clearly, this marketing drive worked marvelously, and the first thing we did on driving into a new campsite was to scan the area for the iniquitous presence of the black Rotel bus and trailer. If they'd arrived first, there was no defence. Honestly, hadn't Germany heard about nursing homes?

chapter 14

Tehran to the Dead Sea

On the way to Tehran we drove through a nameless town that sold vodka and stuffed birds. Derek wanted to cram the latter into his luggage, but knew he'd never get them into Europe. We compromised with Smirnoff for $3 a bottle. Les liked the Smirnoff as well; in fact, it inspired him to climb (and slide down) a date palm in the middle of the night. He woke with no memory of the night before, and no idea how so many splinters had become embedded in his hands.

Tehran loomed as a concrete monstrosity with few parks or natural attractions, and litter blowing everywhere. We climbed the Shahyad Monument, took illicit photos, and pondered just how unattractive this city really was. It also had one of the world's most dangerous airports, awarded a black star because landing there involved flying low over the city.

Isfahan was much more appealing than Tehran, exuding a well-dressed confidence which expressed itself in an obsession with dressing young boys in suits. The tree-lined main street, Sharabagh, oozed European ambience. We also made friends with a group of Americans stationed in Isfahan, visited their place in Karneh, and demolished their hamburger and beer supply while the Rolling Stones' album Love You Live played in the background.

History beckoned through a hangover mist and we visited the tombs of Darius, Xerxes and Artaxerxes before wandering around the impressive ruins of Persepolis for two hours. Just across the road from Persepolis were some much newer buildings which the Shah had built to celebrate the 2,500th anniversary of the Persian Empire in 1971, a celebration he delayed for nine years because he didn't think the economy was healthy enough. All the crowned heads of Europe were invited to the star-shaped tent city he built for the party. Each wore a specially-made costume containing a kilogram of gold and the catering was arranged by Maxim's of Paris. I could only imagine what Rodge would have said. At the other end of the catering scale, we did the cooking that night in the campground at Shiraz, and I must say I think our tomato soup and hot dogs were quite well received.

Leaving Shiraz, we drove through Dogonbadan and camped off-road behind some hills in the middle of oil country near Al Qumah, surrounded by gas flames illuminating the hilltops like multiple sunsets. After helping with the breakfast next day, I wandered off, tried to shut out the background noise of the dismantling camp, and concentrated on the arid beauty of the Zagros mountains and their unearthly shapes. A Titan had ripped up the earth with a hoe: scattered scalene triangles of earth were everywhere.

After an abrupt end to the Zagros, we descended onto the Ahvaz plain, on through bird-filled marshes to Bandar-e-Shahpur and our first glimpse of the Persian Gulf. Crossing from Iran into Iraq, we passed the meeting place of the Tigris and Euphrates, and headed towards Babylon, previous capital of the world. We had been warned that Babylon was the "wash-out" of the trip, and it lived down to expectations. Most of the original city was being excavated below ground level, with everything significant above ground being reconstruction. The original ruins were far more interesting.

When we returned from Babylon to our campsite at Faruq in a Baghdad suburb, we emitted a collective groan – a Rotel tour was there. Yet again, it contained a truckload of Germans from the generation that had lost the War; yet again, they remained true to their motto: "The world may have beaten us, but we can still crap all over it." Alcohol seemed the only solution and we discovered the local date-based liquor, Arak, for less than $1 per bottle. Although it tasted more like shoe polish than icky-sticky pudding, it was just drinkable with orange juice, and certainly enough inspiration for an evening spent creating limericks about Germans and their bottoms.

Baghdad was famous for its masguf (seafood) restaurants, so the three of us bussed back into town and walked down Raschid Street to the banks of the Tigris. We eventually found the masguf restaurants, but were shocked to discover that they wanted the equivalent of $12 per fish. We walked back up Raschid, ate two 60 cent hamburgers each, followed by ice cream, feeling incredibly smug that the masguf munchers had paid ten times as much for their meal. Culinary sacrifices sometimes had to be made on the altar of nomadic longevity.

From Baghdad, we drove straight to the Jordanian border, which consisted of two sections: the Iraqi section at Al Rutbah and further on, the Jordanian customs and immigration at H4. We reached Al Rutbah at noon and struck two problems. The first was that the toilets were indisputably the worst we had encountered, which was no mean feat. The toilet block was a rectangular building with no windows and only an open door. The only light entered through the doorway. As soon as I stepped inside, I was stopped in my tracks by the smell and, glued to the spot, saw toilets full and overflowing onto a floor covered with excreta and used tampons. I turned and ran out. Shortly afterwards, someone took a high-pressure hose to the place and it became almost usable.

The other problem was Maurice's passport, which the Iraqi officials noticed had not been stamped on entry. One official, intent on making an impression, suggested that Maurice should go all the way back to the Abadan border to get it stamped (illegally of course, as theoretically, he hadn't ever entered the country). Tony asked why they couldn't stamp both entry and exit at Al Rutbah. This concept was beyond them, and when Tony suggested that the whole affair was a result of Iraqi inefficiency in the first place, he was told to shut up. It wasn't going well. We ended up spending three and a half hours at Rutbah until a superior official returned from his siesta and stamped us straight through. The delay meant that we couldn't get through H4 that night, so we camped in the middle of the desert in a dust storm.

The unfortunate souls who had to use the toilets at H4 said they made Rutbah's look like a centerfold in *Bathroom Monthly*, so it was with elation we quickly cleared H4 the next morning. The countryside changed dramatically as we entered Jordan: miles of broken volcanic rock, often in quite small pieces, covered the rolling hills, presenting us with another landscape we had never seen before.

Amman was a sizeable city in a valley with its own Roman forum and houses scattered at angles up the valley walls. The food was great, and we were soon scoffing roast lamb nanwiches for 50 cents each. We drove past Mt Nebo, (where Moses died after seeing the promised land) across a flat stretch to the Dead Sea, three hundred metres below sea level.

Everyone knows that the excess salinity of the Dead Sea results in a surreal floating sensation, but there are two facts that are less well-known. The first is that the Dead Sea is very slimy as well as very salty: on emerging, you feel as if you have been dipped in olive oil. The second is that in all photographs taken of men floating on their backs in the Dead Sea they appear to have substantial erections.

Once out of the water, I headed straight for the shower block and into another surprise: the shower block was unisex and there were no curtains. I walked past each cubicle and they were all occupied. What I noticed was the sheer lack of inhibition amongst people who had (mostly) never seen each other naked before. They waved, laughed and spoke as I walked by in my shorts. It said something about the bonding power of traveling together. But I had a choice to make: either to join an already-occupied cubicle or to come back later.

I was at the last cubicle, and it was a quick decision, made largely because I knew that to leave would be cowardice.

"Do you mind if I join you?"

"No, come on in." The Grim Sisters, identically nude, smiled a greeting, and suddenly didn't seem very grim after all.

chapter 15

Romance in the Ruins

On the way to Aqaba we drove through spectacular plains with sudden shocks of rock rising from them; it would have been a good place to film a Western. The Park Hotel was on the beach with Jordan Underwater Services next door. Doctor Dave and I quickly arranged to dive the next day at the cost of 5 dinar each ($16) all inclusive.

From the beach, we looked directly across the Gulf of Aqaba to Eilat in Israel. South of us on opposite sides of the Gulf were the Sinai Peninsula and Saudi Arabia. The only sign we had that a war was being fought in the area was that the beach was patrolled at night and no-one was allowed on it.

We had a party on the bus that night and much alcohol was consumed. Lots of local lads descended, bringing beer, nuts and cigarettes. The reason for their largesse soon became clear:

"You Australians are much fun."

"Thanks. You guys are very friendly."

"Can we please borrow some of your women?"

While it was, of course, tempting to point out a couple of women they were welcome to borrow, we eventually felt obliged to admit that as we didn't actually *own* any of the women, we weren't able to lend them out.

Like the rest of us, the local lads were on their own, although at least one of them didn't end the evening that way.

The diving next day was mesmerising. Doctor Dave, the guide and I quickly descended to about thirty metres, a depth at which the coral started to decrease, and were about to go deeper when Dave signaled he was cold. We surfaced, making no decompression stops because we had really only just got down there. Dave was wearing a sleeveless wetsuit vest, whereas mine had long sleeves and a hood. I offered to swap, but Dave didn't jump at the chance, so I wondered if he was suffering more from mild panic than cold. I was busy trying to seem as professional as possible, but it was really only about my fourth tank dive, having dived mostly on hookah. In the end, Lois took over Dave's tank, I gave her the long-sleeved vest, and we went back down.

On the first descent, I had been breathing as slowly as possible to conserve air and my tank still had a lot remaining. On this second descent, I burnt it up as fast as I could, knowing I wouldn't use it all. We didn't dive as deeply the second time because Lois was having difficulty compensating, so we spent time exploring, finding lionfish in caves, breaking open sea urchins to create a feeding frenzy of harlequin colour. Everything was so different from diving off Fremantle: water temperature, water clarity, fish varieties, and I reveled in this weightless, alien, psychedelic utopia. I felt a sense of guilt as I realised that diving back home would never be the same again.

We surfaced all too soon and I refused to believe that my first Red Sea dive had been my last. We climbed into the battered Kombi (about a dozen people had been snorkeling) and drove back to town. Later, Dave discussed the possibility of diving again the following day. I told him my budget really didn't stretch that far, but then I thought of something. Earlier, I had overheard Dave offering to teach Les, Scott and Tony Courier how to scuba dive the next day. Dave had only been diving for nine months, so he had taken on quite a job to teach three novices. In addition, Les was a hypochondriac, and I was sure he'd quit after about two minutes leaving… a spare tank! I went to sleep dreaming of a free dive.

The great plan failed though, because Dave drank so much he slept through lunch. The fall-back was that a few of us went snorkeling, this time further along the coast near the Saudi border.

The following day we drove three hours to Petra, reclusive red rock city. Leaving the bus outside, we passed a double-storeyed tomb on the left, then entered a narrow gorge with seventy metre high red sandstone walls, which snaked downwards for several miles. Walking was difficult as it was on loose stone all the way, but suddenly, around the corner of the gorge, we caught sight of the magnificent Treasury House, a sudden burst of order in the otherwise random stone. After a short rest at the Treasury (spent avoiding locals selling trinkets and over-priced Pepsi) we wandered down to the red warrens and considered camping there for the night. What caught my eye was a classic example of a Greek stage, the first I had ever seen outside of drawings in drama texts. The acoustics were excellent and most of the stage had collapsed, revealing the rooms beneath.

Laziness dictated we camp by the bus rather than lugging our tents into Petra, and the next morning we were off to Jerash, far more fertile than Amman, where we camped in the midst of the ruins of an old Roman hippodrome. Amidst the romance of Roman ruins, Lorraine had moved on from Derek and was now on her fourth guy of the trip, and Derek was starting to focus on Alison. As I realised that nothing much was happening for me in that department, it struck me that I wasn't overly concerned. I also knew one of the reasons I loved diving: it shut out people – there was no noise, no speech, no relationships; you were an alien and alienated. It was a thrill for me to be alone. But if solitude was my drug of choice, were relationships the currency I had to pay for it? I caught an image of a possible future: an increasingly eccentric, eremitic existence - and blinked it away.

After a morning clambering over the Lego block disarray of Jerash, we had a short drive to the Syrian border where we spent three hours. Gary, standing in the money-changing queue, decided to try some humour:

"Well, here we are waiting for the next Israeli raid!" he yelled.

About thirty pairs of eyes stared him into the dirt and he visibly shriveled. Just over the border were squadrons of tanks, and truckloads of soldiers had been passing us for hours. As we drove towards Damascus, another truckload passed us and one of the soldiers caught sight of Peggy's legs. She was wearing shorts and her legs were bent up on the seat in front of her. I realised that the soldier would be unable to see the shorts and in the second it took for the truck to pass us, he jumped to his feet for a better view, striking his head on the luggage rack above him.

Damascus can claim the dual honour of being the oldest continually inhabited city in the world and brewer of some of the most revolting beer I have ever tasted. It was called Palmyra Beer and the people responsible had the grandiose name "Societe Nationale D'Embouteillage – Damas". I'm unsure why they thought it was a good idea to filter their beer through the unwashed underwear of the Syrian Armed Forces, unless it was to limit alcohol consumption, in which case I'm sure they were wildly successful.

We explored the dusty streets of Damascus, discovering that the main street has been called Straight since New Testament times and is now the local bazaar. Traumatised by yet another Rotel tour in our campsite and their ubiquitous redecorating of the toilet block, we were overcome by inertia. Judy cooked the three of us a ten-egg omelette and later we lazed around, playing Chinese patience, Jude lying with her head on my knee as we played. Later that night, an owl made a noise like a small train just before unleashing an unbelievable quantity of guano on Den's tent; we decided it must have been the mascot on the Rotel tour.

When we arrived in the oasis of Palmyra, city of a thousand columns, the three of us looked across the expanse of Roman ruins and focused on one point in the distance. We knew each other well enough by now that we hardly needed to discuss it; we simply had to go there.

Rising on a steep hill in the background was Fakhredin Al Maany, a seventeenth-century Arab castle. Being much newer than the ruins in the foreground, it was in much better condition, but its inaccessibility made it a challenge. The climb up the hill was on loose rock, so it seemed to be one step up to two down, but eventually we made it to the crest and the view back over the plain was stunning: the oasis and date palms of Palmyra were the only visible intrusion on the desert in either direction until it disappeared over the horizon. But there was a problem: we were at the top of the hill, but not yet in the castle, which we now realised was surrounded by a ten metre deep moat. The bridge across the moat had collapsed, so we descended into it, leaving our shirts and Derek's SLR camera at the bottom. I took my much cheaper Kodak camera with me, determined to have some photographic record.

Sweaty and smelly, we eventually made it into the castle. Some of the others made it up the hill, but no-one else made it inside: we had the castle to ourselves. As we entered, I was amazed. I had imagined that there would simply be an empty courtyard inside the walls, but nothing could have been further from the truth. The fort was a stony honeycomb with chambers varying in height from less than two metres to ten metres, dead ends, seemingly meaningless recesses, passages that came to a sudden end, under which stairs went down to a still deeper level. The actual number of levels was indiscernible because of the irregularity of the architecture and the way sand had built up to partly obscure some of the lower openings. I wanted to spend all day there, but we only spent an hour.

This obscure Arab fort was the most exciting building I had seen on the trip so far. The Taj Mahal and almost all the other palaces, red forts, (even Petra) had been turned into tourist attractions with sound and light shows and assorted paraphernalia, or were being restored with the archaeological equivalent of plastic surgery. Here, there was none of that and even the most recent graffiti was not offensive, but somehow served to record the community of those who had shared in this minor marvel.

Then something strange happened. I realised I was looking at an eighteenth century inscription in a seventeenth-century castle above a much earlier Roman city built next to an even more ancient oasis. I felt dizzy as the centuries whirled around me in this stone corridor in an abandoned castle in the Syrian desert. The air was heavy with the weight of long-gone dramas and mystery. Who had lived and fought here and why? What had their lives been like? What had they believed and valued? I was frustrated by my inability to know the answers, by the coquettish nature of History, teasing the eager with partial knowledge. As my feet rearranged the dust; I longed for answers that did not come and I stood there, frustrated and giddy. I realised that History, evanescent as she was, offered depth, maturity, and perspective that was available in no other way. To ignore her siren call was to ignore her gifts - gifts that were offered by no other. Taking complete advantage of the situation, History, flouncing her tresses, grabbed my sweaty shoulders and French-kissed me in the ruins, departing with a winsome over-the-shoulder glance. She may be a tease, I sighed, but she was definitely worth pursuing. I was willingly in her thrall. It was the one commitment I felt comfortable with.

chapter 16

Raki's Revenge

Our tents were pitched on the stony grounds of Palmyra's Hotel Zenobia, just a few minutes from the main ruins. We were even more an object of fascination to the locals than they were to us. In this case, the locals were not only unaccustomed to men in shorts; the very existence of legs seemed to surprise them.

Syria had one more architectural delight in store: the largely-intact Crusader castle Craque de Chevaliers, high on a hill and the windiest place on earth outside of a dust storm. You had to lean heavily into the wind to walk, or even to stand upright. We explored, we leaned, we stumbled, we imagined the grime and carnage of multiple crusades over two centuries of bloodshed in the name of belief. We had the luxury of imagining and moving on, and were soon camped in a rain-soaked pine forest in a corner of Lebanon. This was the first real rain since Srinagar, and it was an aromatic indulgence to have damp pine needles under the tent instead of sand and rock.

In Turkey we discovered "real" bread once again, tore a loaf into thirds and devoured it. Alcohol was also freely available and Derek, Dennis and I quickly downed a bottle of Efes Pilsen each before going quarters with

Tony Tiger in a bottle of raki (the local ouzo). We finished drinking the raki on the bus and insisted that Dave Driver finally put on the soundtrack to The Adventures of Barry McKenzie. We bought another bottle of raki from the Grim Sisters, drank that, and then three bottles of Steve's wine. In between singing along with Barry, calling out car licence plate numbers and attempting the pheasant plucker's song, it became increasingly evident that several of us in the back of the bus were very drunk indeed.

Of the three of us, Derek was by far the worst. The first casualty was his budding romance with Alison: unfortunately when he needed to throw up, the closest receptacle was her carry bag. Later, an on-bus medical examination showed that his pulse had slowed right down and his eyes were rolled back in his head. The following morning, he was still alive, but living in the middle of raki's revenge. We spent the day on the beach outside Silifke in various stages of recovery, culminating in beach volleyball.

Although we wanted to drive to Alanya, a fuel shortage limited the maximum purchase to twenty-five litres. We got no further than Marmu, where I had lunch with Peggy and Steve (stuffed zucchini, sausages and chips for less than $1) and helped Elaine and Louise do the food kitty shopping. Even though it seemed to me we looked very much like the locals, they could spot us easily, and were always keen to initiate conversation. Their first question was always the same:

"Deutsch?" Which of course, could have been a tactful way of discovering if we were emaciated members of a Rotel tour group, and hence about to desecrate their public conveniences.

"Australian," often only brought blank stares, so we had to compromise with "English".

Turkey had a lot in its favour, even if that didn't include Turkish delight and yes, there were some food shortages (meat was hard to obtain and Syria and Jordan were much better for chocolate) but it was green, it rained

(Camelot-fashion, after sunset) and we could camp in places that were shaded by pine trees and alongside streams that ran down into the ocean at our private beach. Derek could pick up the BBC on the bus radio, even if it was only to discover that Crystal Palace had lost (not the best 22nd birthday present for him). It was hard not to contrast Turkey with places like Benares or the Iranian desert. We had certainly made the right decision to do the overland trip from east to west rather than in reverse, because the end of the trip would be more comfortable than the beginning.

Tony Courier had to hitch to a nearby town to buy fuel to get us to Alanya, where there proved to be plenty. On the way to Alanya, we passed a massive amphitheatre in the middle of nowhere. It was not just the simple take-advantage-of-a-natural-slope amphitheatre, but purpose-built with lofty walls. The performers would have had a four-storey high wall immediately behind them.

Through Burdur and Denizli, we arrived in Pamukkale (Hierapolis) and camped in the grounds of the Mistuh Motel. I erected our tent by myself in freezing rain; the others had already beaten me into the nearby hot pool. I joined the game of water polo, until an unorthodox manoeuvre from Derek saw him kick the ball over the motel. The following morning we explored the alien deposits left by the hot springs - albino ledges and waterfalls were everywhere, steaming and calcified – before driving on to Ephesus.

In Ephesus, we wandered past the library which was directly opposite the brothel, past tombs and a 24,000 seat amphitheatre where the apostle Paul had preached. It was the toilets however, that won the award for ingenuity. Designed to cater for a number of people simultaneously, the toilets consisted of stone benches with circular holes at regular intervals. The clever part was that the Ephesians had re-routed a stream to run underneath and carry the waste down to the port. A 2,000 year old auto-flush toilet! The port itself was no more; Ephesus is now ten kilometers inland due to silting (the toilets were probably to blame). I found myself wishing for a greater degree of Biblical literacy: I only knew the little I'd picked up in Sunday School and through sermons.

Twenty minutes past Ephesus was Kusadasi, from which the Greek island of Samos, birthplace of Pythagoras, was clearly visible across the clear, cold and calm water. Greece owned islands close to Turkey and used them for military purposes, in contravention of an agreement. Derek and I walked into town from our beachside camp, uncharacteristically bought a Kusadasi T-shirt each, and strolled back to a dinner of wine, macaroni cheese and rice pudding. Elaine and I discussed punk rock and the future of the world into the night. As I was going to bed, there was a sudden noise of panic from Elaine and Louise's tent. They had discovered that the lump under their ground sheet was not only inconvenient, but also animate. We made various adrenalin-pumping guesses as to the monster's identity before Maurice shone a torch under the ground sheet to reveal only a pile of dust. We ruled in favour of the uninvited guest being a mole, which led to a few unkind jokes the next morning at Elaine and Louise's expense.

The following morning, we passed the sole remaining pillar of the Temple of Artemis, one of the wonders of the ancient world. A stork was nesting on top of it. Apparently the temple was destroyed on the day Alexander the Great was born; legend has it that Artemis was attending Alexander's birth and her absence from the temple meant she was unable to defend it.

Izmir (ancient Smyrna) was the third largest city in Turkey (after Ankara and Istanbul) and the main export port. The city had been destroyed three times. Firstly in 1883 by an earthquake; secondly in 1922 as a result of war with the Greeks; and thirdly in 1928, just as it was being rebuilt from the 1922 destruction, by another earthquake. It was the most European city we had seen so far and in Pergamon we tasted our first draught beer since Penang.

Troy and its fake wooden horse were unimpressive. However we did manage to discover a blue tit's nest in a hole in a wall and a dead snake with which Derek terrorised Judy. We camped that night near Canakkale, on the eastern shore of the Dardanelles. We were about to cross into Europe. The world's longest bus trip was coming to an end.

chapter 17

An Englishman Never...

It was a short drive from Canakkale to Eceabat, the ferry departure point, which was crowded with goats. We kept dodging around the goats, which got on the ferry with us, and we launched out into a tricky current. Apparently, the top layer of water flows one way and the bottom layer flows in the opposite direction. It was the possession of this knowledge that enabled Ataturk, in World War I, to predict correctly where the Allies would be landing. After the half-hour crossing, we lunched at Gallipoli (Galibolu) and contemplated the tragic outcome of currents and topography at this place when our grandparents were teenagers.

Istanbul, formerly known as Byzantium and Constantinople, immediately showed itself worthy of much more time than we could give it. We toured the huge gloomy-green underground cistern which was once the city's water supply, grabbed a quick Efes Pilsen, and passed the Eye of Sofia (once the biggest church in the world) on our way to the Topkapi Palace. We spent two hours there, fascinated by the exhibits: amazingly well-preserved porcelain from various Ming periods; an 86 carat diamond on a revolving black velvet disc; metre high candleholders with 6,666 diamonds symbolising the verses of the Koran; hairs from Mohammed, as well as his bow and Koran; 1,200 year old books; and various parts of John the Baptist. Starring in The Pink Panther movie was another of Topkapi's cultural achievements.

After another Efes in The Pudding Shop to overcome the desiccating effects of culture overload, Den and I headed to the Old Turkish Bath. We chose the standard "self-service" bath (minus massage) and for $1.20 we washed and steamed off 63 days' worth of ingrained dirt before meeting up with the others and bussing back to camp. More aquatic fun awaited Dennis however. During the night there was a terrific thunderstorm and our cook tent began to slide off into the night. Den, usually the lightest sleeper amongst us, raced out in his underwear to save it.

The following day we crossed into Greece on the first day of the Greek Orthodox Easter, which meant most shops were closed for three days. This propelled those on the tour who reveled in opportunities to complain into a state of ecstatic gloominess. In reality, there was nothing to complain about. Kabala was hilly and geared for tourists. Record stores stocked Jethro Tull, Uriah Heep and Ten Years After; food was cheap and beers cost 50 cents. After dinner in the town, our group split according to inclination: one group for beer, another for chocolate cake. Den and I were in the latter group and soon we were back in the square, chocolate-covered sponge in hand, watching Elvis Presley in Girls, Girls, Girls with Greek subtitles.

While we were chewing and watching, the news spread that Dave Driver was unable to open the bus door as the lock was jammed. A second wave of gloom descended on the drunker group as they contemplated walking back to the campsite. A few minutes later, the lights in the bus came on. Derek had hit the side window, releasing the latch and, with a boost from Tony Tiger, had climbed inside. Everyone rushed over and Derek started the bus in triumph.

The following day was spent at the beach, swimming and playing volleyball until the afternoon. Such idyllic pleasures were soon interrupted however. Tony Courier and Brian had discovered the wonders of retsina, the local fortified wine. Earlier on the trip Brian had declared:

"Do you know the difference between an Englishman and an Australian? When an Englishman gets drunk, he never vomits." Needless to say, Brian was English.

Maybe it was the retsina, which, of course, is hardly your normal English tipple. Suffice to say that both Tony and Brian spent most of the afternoon thrashing around on the beach, baking lobster-red and (although far be it from me to contradict an Englishman) there was, by the end of the day, some pretty hard-core dribbling going on.

Remaining at Kabala the next day while Tony and Brian reassembled themselves, we discovered a large snake, and Derek was elated to discover a nightingale's egg, which he assured us was very hard to find. The decision was made to eat out again that night: a beer, spaghetti bolognaise, two cakes and half a litre of milk for $2.60. In the bus on the way back from town Noni, Judy and Alison began singing, "I wish I was a fascinating bitch, I'd never be poor, I'd always be rich..." There was no doubt about it: this tour was a bargain – 75 days, two continents *and* free entertainment.

We all knew that the last few days of the tour would pass in the blink of an eye. This was partly because of Tony Courier's vow to make this the cheapest trip he had led: Europe was more expensive than Asia, so time in Europe was minimised. Through Thessalonaki, we crossed into Yugoslavia at Gevgelija, passed through Belgrade, of which we saw little except that the river divided the old city from the new, and headed to Zagreb. In Zagreb we camped near the university campus and suddenly began seeing significant quantities of highly attractive women. I'm unsure whether this was something to do with the local gene pool, the proximity of the university, or my own perception, but if it was an hallucination, I wasn't the only one affected.

The countryside was captivating, with green rolling hills interspersed with occasional thickets and swamps. I reflected on the huge variety of landscapes we had experienced on the tour, and it struck me that I had never once been bored with any of it. As we rolled along to Al Stewart's Year of the Cat and Abba's Dancing Queen, I worked on a theory of boredom. I wondered if boredom was experienced mainly by people who didn't choose to engage with their surroundings. Boredom was the default position of non-engagers. I was working on this theory and feeling pleased with it when Les made a comment in the dinner tent:

"You know I found the road between Nis and Zagreb boring."

"Really? I think things are only as boring as people let them be."

"That's a pretty cutting comment." And of course, he was right. But I didn't think I could back down because I was confident of the essential truth it contained. Nevertheless, I felt a little ashamed, and found myself with a new subject to ponder: the uncomfortable nexus between truth, tact and respect for the feelings of others.

From Zagreb we passed through Ljubljana to the Austrian border. While we were changing money, I overheard Barbara saying:

"You know, I've heard that some people on the tour are living on as little as $5 a day. I couldn't possibly live on such a ridiculous amount!"

Well, she was a doctor's wife; I didn't have the nerve to tell her that we were living on $3 a day.

Entering Austria on the 70th day of our 75 day trip, it struck me that this was the first European country I had visited before. We had really been covering the miles, traversing virtually the whole of Austria (Klagenfurt-Salzburg) in one day, so Tony's decision to spend a rest day in Salzburg was welcome. The group split up according to interests: some raced up to the castle on the hill; others scoured the town in search of Mozart's birthplace; others bought tickets to a Mozart-Dvorak concert. The three of us simply hit the streets.

We headed out from our camp in Bayerhamer Strasse down to the city through the sensory overload of a local market crammed with cheeses and smallgoods, to spend an hour in a pub lingering over a beer and trying to translate German magazines. Dennis was excited: Austria was the first country he felt was really Europe. He was so excited he decided to figure out our overall financial position, announcing that taking our total expenditure into consideration so far (fares, food kitty,etc) we were averaging $20 per day. We knew that this would skyrocket once we hit London, but expected it would drop once we hit the next phase of our journey: we had decided to cycle around northern Europe.

chapter 18

Lager Monsters in London

The German border crossing, like the Austrian, was easy. In Munich we were dropped at the Olympic Stadium. David Bowie, Queen, Jethro Tull, ELO and Thin Lizzy concert posters were everywhere. We found a small pub, had half a litre of beer each and ogled the barmaid. Dennis launched an unsuccessful attack on the condom machine.

Our campsite had its own supermarket: Germans might have to answer for Rotel tours, but they certainly got some things right. We were soon back in the centre of town where the three of us split from the rest and wandered down New House Street. There were two main attractions: the first was a record shop with eight huge windows full of record covers: one was devoted to the Beatles, both pre-and post-split; one contained almost every Dylan album; another almost every Stones' album. To top it off, there were four video screens showing clips from concerts, including Queen and Bob Seger.

A few yards further on, there was a shop showing porn films for three minutes per deutschmark. It was a waste of a deutschmark and after a little more wandering and eating, we ended back at the Mathaus with the rest of the tour group where we each bought a huge beer. We quickly realised that virtually all the group was drunk and as soon as she saw me, Elaine (well under the weather) came straight up to me and instantly, we were kissing. It was clear how the evening was going to end and Derek and Dennis, popping up in my field of vision over Elaine's shoulder semaphored their approval.

After too many lagers, Dennis talked Derek into stealing one of the huge beer steins. Derek stuffed it under his jumper, but by the time he'd got to the door, it had moved around to the back and he appeared to be auditioning for the part of Quasimodo. The doorman instantly assessed the situation and in one swift motion, retrieved the stein and punched Derek in the back of the head.

After Elaine left my tent in the early morning, I managed a couple of hours' sleep before waking light of head and light of wallet. We were getting to the end of the trip and crossing borders almost daily, so it was pointless changing much money. I had $5US left.

Our last night of the tour was in Bruges. We had to clean everything out of the bus, repacking the tents and our bags, ready for our final disembarkation in London.

"Well," Derek said, "this clean-up's going to be a major operation. We're going to need everyone's help to do it."

"I have absolutely no intention of paying for a holiday and then actually have to do work on it," replied Brian.

"So I'd noticed," retorted Derek, "but it'd be great if we *all* took that attitude, wouldn't it?"

Brian said no more.

The cost of our last evening meal together in Bruges was paid from the food kitty. It was the day we read that Aldo Moro's body had been found in the boot of a car.

The four hour crossing from Ostend to Dover was smooth, the sky was hazy and the water dirty brown. We had lunch at Canterbury. I had Les's running commentary in my ear for two hours, which I considered suitable penance for my previous "cutting remark". We drove past some cows. "Cows," said Les. We passed a flock of sheep. "Sheep", said Les. I clenched my fists until my fingernails dug into my palms. Penance wasn't meant to be easy.

Then we were in Stepney, passing Whitechapel Tube and a left turn brought us face-to-face with the Tower of London and the bridge. We dropped some people off outside Thomas Cook, saw Telly Savalas walking down the street, dropped some more off at a small hotel called Lord Jim and then we were at the last stop. It was a cul-de-sac and we grabbed our luggage, walked down the lane and took one last look back at the bus that had taken us halfway around the world. It was 10 May, 1978 and we had spent 75 days sharing a cloistered intimacy with thirty strangers. Would we ever see any of these people again? It had been a commitment of sorts, these 75 days, but no more. "West Wittering 3139!" Fiona called her phone number to us as she and Craig jumped into a cab; it was another friendship we would never pursue. The world's longest bus trip was over.

Derek the black-belt cartographer was always the navigator. I'd told him that the hotel we were going to stay at was in Kensington Square Gardens, but he had taken that as Kensington *Square*. So off we trekked, trusting completely in Derek's navigating ability. Give him his due, we did eventually end up in Kensington Square, only to discover that we'd actually been very close to our hotel at the original drop-off point. By the end, I was carrying Derek's bag as well as my own but then, through the mist of exhaustion, I recognised two landmarks from my previous trip: the Antique Hypermarket and the Goat Tavern. We found the hotel and collapsed in luxury – our first proper bed since Afghanistan and our own private bathroom and toilet with no Rotel tour in sight! We cleaned up, watched Liverpool beat Bruges 1-0, drank an unimpressive pint of Wetney's Bitter, ate egg fried rice and satay, and collapsed again.

I wanted to spend most of the next day between Virgin Records in New Oxford Street and various second-hand bookstores, but Derek and Dennis kept dragging me out of them. We withdrew £1,000 each from the Bank of New South Wales in Sackville Street in preparation for the next stage of our journey. A quick check on the current state of the world in *Time* magazine showed an emphasis on God: articles on Latin American liberation theology; God had told Oral Roberts to build a large medical centre; and a young woman in Germany died of starvation at the end of lengthy Roman Catholic exorcism procedures. None of these seemed to require hibernation on our part, so we confirmed the plan of purchasing bicycles and camping gear and spending about three months cycling around northern Europe and Scandinavia.

Significantly, Derek's parents had moved back to England while we were travelling overland. It had always been their goal to make money in Australia and return to settle in Selsey, West Sussex; they were currently staying with Derek's uncle Ro and aunt Shirl, which became our initial home base.

We left Victoria Station in a train bound for Chichester: pheasants, rabbits and Arundel Castle whizzed past. Then it was the twenty minute bus trip to Selsey where Derek's sister Teresa was the first to spot us. Greetings over, bags dumped, we inflicted serious damage on the local laundromat: after three and a half months of our minimalist approach to handwashing, our clothes got their first thorough wash. Surprisingly, the machines didn't break down.

The next day, the doctor sent us to the special clinic in Chichester. Blood tests showed that we were all seriously dehydrated, that I still had

NSU and that one of the lads had scabies. And that was just the preliminary result. I was immediately placed on a 14 day course of tablets, so we needed to stay in the UK at least that long. "And have at least a pint of beer each as soon as you leave here – you guys are so badly dehydrated your blood's almost solid!" It seemed an appropriate time to begin reading Orwell's *Down and Out in Paris and London.*

We spent a few days assembling our cycling equipment, buying Peugeot bikes in Bognor Regis, one-man tents in Portsmouth, and wet weather gear in Chichester. For medicinal purposes, we patronised The Stargazer and The Neptune in Selsey, The Ship in Chichester, The Lamb in Bognor and The Anchor in Sidlesham.

One night at The Neptune, we met several of Derek's old school friends including Steve, who had been to Australia twice. At closing time, we went back to Lorna's and drank some more. I checked out her record collection, several locals got very drunk and fell over, and Dennis and Lorna (who was getting divorced) seemed to be hitting it off very well. A few joints were rolled and passed around. At 2.30am, Lorna's nearly-ex came home, at which point Dennis hastily removed his arm from her and we left. We drove through a pea-soup fog to Church Norton, wandered through the graveyard, did a circuit of the church, paid our respects to the stony grey lady and raced back to the car, as it was freezing.

Blood test results the next day showed no more problems. The doctor said that I should be fine in a fortnight and I discovered that the incubation period for NSU was anything from five days to three weeks, so I probably got it from Annie in Penang. We bought fishing rods and knives and realised that after a week of "home life" we were all beginning to get restless. We all had a virus that didn't show up in bloodtests – the AMT virus – we were addicted to movement and transience. It was a conscious addiction and I wondered if I would ever be able to return home and settle down.

Was it even possible to settle down after a trip like this? I was avoiding commitment of all kinds, even geographical ones – could life really be lived like that? Our futures were being framed by the choices we were making, but it was impossible to tell how.

We had a fairly serious practice cycle before heading out in earnest. Derek, being our navigator and in his home country, marked out the route. What should have been a mild introduction to our cycling marathon became a baptism of fire. We cycled up the A27 to Arundel, past the castle and out of town on the A29, turning off to go through Storrington and Washington to Bramber. We were on the absurdly named South *Downs*. Whoever named them should have been required to cycle them because there are far more ups than downs. Derek had a puncture on the flinty surface and we camped in the middle of nowhere. The next day we passed Chanctonbury Ring, Washington again, Pulborough, Five Oaks and Horsham. By the time we hit Ashington, we had achieved 200 miles, aching anuses and, on my part at least, serious doubts about my ability to handle three months of this.

chapter 19

Of Cycling and Bush Smells

It was 30 May 1978 when we cycled out of Selsey, leaving 80% of our luggage behind. The freedom of the open road, the ability to determine our own schedule and speed, and the fact that we were virtually self-contained in terms of accommodation and transport appealed greatly. An obvious downside was that we could be brought to a complete halt if one of us got sick.

We made it to Brighton for lunch, but before Peacehaven we struck three steep hills in a row, on the last of which Derek strained a leg muscle. Dinner was a cheap Chinese in Eastbourne before continuing to Pevensey. We camped near a castle which had been used as headquarters by William the Conqueror and made it into our tents at around 10 pm, having covered 61 miles on our first day.

Let me make a frank admission at this point. It's beyond my talents as a writer to magically transform large amounts of cycling into riveting reading. Our legs went around in circles, large hills were dreaded, we sweated copiously, and ate obscene amounts of food to replenish energy. This went on day after day, week after week. So if you'll indulge me by imagining this happening continually in the background, I'll do you the favour of simply mentioning the major incidents.

We cycled through Rye to Folkestone, having decided that the road to Dover looked too hilly. Our last experience before crossing the Channel was being thrown out of the True Briton pub in Folkestone simply because the manager didn't like the look of us. After a smooth but sleepless night crossing during which I somehow still managed to fall off the lounge, we arrived at Ostend early in the morning and cycled twenty kilometers to Blankenberg where we spent a couple of hours collapsed by a stream. Over the border, Sluis was a cheery introduction to Holland: brass bands marched through the streets and the town came alive in the evening when all the shops remained open.

Through Vlissingen to Domburg, over the Zealandbrug to Ouddorp, where we made a serious mistake. If I can save you from making this same mistake, it will certainly be worth the purchase price of this book. When you're cycling long distances, you always carry some food with you, and naturally, it's lightweight and nonperishable, so we had some instant potato sachets. We made this up on our small portable camping stoves and put it between slices of bread to create mashed potato sandwiches. Dear reader, please learn from our experience – do not try this! Approximately ninety seconds after you've finished eating, you will suffer from ICAS (instantly concreted abdominal syndrome). Symptoms include: severe abdominal pain, inability to stand or even sit upright and large amounts of groaning. Symptoms can be expected to last for an hour or more.

Having recovered, we sped through Rotterdam via the Maas tunnel, a cold and clammy passage under the river, through Delft to the Hague, where I needed to get some answers. At the tourist information centre, there was, of course, an attractive girl in attendance.

"Excuse me, can you direct me to a VD clinic?" I could have taken the easy way out and simply asked the way to the hospital, which was where she ended up sending me anyway, because apparently, Holland didn't have separate VD clinics. It was just around the corner.

"Excuse me," I said to the receptionist, "I would like to make an appointment to see a doctor."

"What sort of doctor?"

"A VD doctor."

She directed me with some sense of urgency and in due course I arrived at another reception desk attended by a middle-aged blonde woman who was talking to an attractive younger woman. The above conversation was repeated almost word-for-word with the added difficulty that the older woman didn't appear to understand what VD was. I was saved from a grotesque sign-language explanation by the younger woman who suddenly realised what I was talking about. Six people in the Hague now knew about my problem (the girl in tourist information had discussed it with two men) and I still hadn't seen a doctor! The middle-aged woman dashed around and made an appointment for the next day, following which we spent some hours in the Mauritshuis, which was famed for its Rembrandt collection, although I preferred the paintings by his contemporary, Jan Steen, which seemed to revel in a messy domesticity.

The following day, the doctor thought I was over the VD and the symptoms I had were something else: more pills and five days to fix it. We were on the road again, passing posters advertising concerts by David Bowie, Elvis Costello and Ian Dury, and began talking about setting ourselves up in a London flat for the winter. Meanwhile, *Time* magazine told us that conservative Islamic forces in Iran were becoming restless under the Shah.

Gouda boasted the oldest Gothic town hall in the country and was, of course, cheesy. On arriving in Oudewater, we asked a policeman for directions to the campsite and he drove ahead of us as an escort, proudly point-ing out a stork and its three young; clearly, the crime rate in Oudewater was low. The following day we packed wet tents, skirted Utrecht and lunched in Amersfoort, where in a remarkable feat of agility Derek managed to drop his milk *and* ride over it. Five minutes after eating lunch, Derek was keen to be on the road again. Dennis and I were much lazier.

"Come on you guys. Let's hit the frog and toad."

"Give us a break. Movement is over-rated and not necessarily a sign of life."

But of course, we were soon moving again through Nykerk to Ermelo, where we camped for the night. A glimpse of an evening meal: bread, cheese, krakowurst, coconut marzipan in custard, milk, Mars bars, and strawberry wine.

Over breakfast the next morning, a strange aroma filled the air.

"What's that smell?"

"Is that you?", repeated three times, with three negative answers. The unpleasant odour remained.

Finally, Derek concluded, "It's just a bushy smell." Dennis and I looked at each other, unconvinced.

A few minutes later, as we got up from breakfast, all was revealed. Derek had sat in, and placed his bike pannier in, a large pile of steaming squirrel excreta. As he reacted with suitable horror and intriguing dance moves, Dennis and I assumed sage expressions:

"We think we've discovered the source of the 'bushy smell'".

Bushy smell jokes continued for the rest of the day and pretty much for the next thirty years.

chapter 20

Brondbyoster Blunder

It was somewhere between Ommen and Coevorden that I wondered if I was starting to feel uncharacteristically homesick. Then I realised that it was something else. It was a combination of anxiety over whether the NSU had gone, the thought of how long I'd actually been suffering from it, and the realisation that I had no-one to blame but myself. At a deeper level, I understood clearly that the years of youth and innocence had passed: at twenty-one, I felt old. The feelings were unnerving and I had no idea what to do with them, except keep cycling. The road could be a demanding and all-consuming mistress, and there was some comfort in distraction.

The Hutterheugte campsite at Dalen was the most complete we had seen: restaurant, supermarket, laundrette, snack bar, pancake parlour, indoor heated pool with saunas, bowling alley, and bar with colour TV. The contrast with some of our overland campsites could not have been greater. Dennis demonstrated great skill on the pinball machines and was christened the "pinball gizzard" by Derek as an unexpected nil-all draw between West Germany and Tunisia played out on TV.

Unmanned oil pumps bowed slavishly as we cycled to the border at Twist; it was June 11 and suddenly we were back in Germany. In the

Meppen campsite we shared coffee and cake with a Dutch couple who had spent ten years in Canberra, and met a guy from Queensland who had spent a year driving and working around the continent. From Meppen we cycled mainly back roads and continued through Werlte to camp in the middle of a forest.

The next day was the longest so far. We cycled 115 kilometres through mainly rural land: Garrel, Dotlingen, Delmenhorst, Neustadt, Bremen (where we sadly missed the eleventh-century cathedral with the five hundred year old mummies), Lilienthal to Tarmstedt.

Erratic weather as we cycled through Zeven and Steddorf saw us sometimes in T shirts, sometimes jumpers, sometimes raincoats. A rumoured Buxtehude campsite proved non-existent. Wet and unenthused, we ate in a bus stop outside a cemetery and camped on some vacant ground for the night. From there it was Hamburg, founded by Charlemagne 1200 years before, and sunshine, and the Reeperbahn.

We were amazed at the efficiency of the Hamburg transport system. Outside our campground we could catch the 182 bus to Schlump, the underground, from which we could access the whole city. Initial impressions of the Reeperbahn were as a more intense version of London's Soho. Continuously screening blue movies competed with the Davidstrasse ladies outside the Hotel Stein. From Davidstrasse we strolled past Friedrichstrasse to Herbertstrasse and behind the wall, inspecting the merchandise. A few of the women approached us, but we weren't buying.

We visited the Hamburg Natural History Museum and the Kunsthalle, but there were conflicting claims on our loyalties: Hamburg had a lot going for it, but our first loyalty was to the road; moving on was our only commitment. Despite differences in personalities and interests, we had all become chronic transients, seduced by the mystery around the next corner, beyond the next hill; the unknown always valued above the known, the uncertain above the secure.

After an evening in the Logo club in Hamburg's university quarter where an abominable skiffle group was at odds with on-campus posters of The Runaways, we had a short cycle the next day to Pinneberg. We hadn't struck any severe hills in Germany so far and we'd been told that we should be able to cycle as far as Oslo with few topographical challenges. The mileage we had cycled was beginning to look impressive on the map; we estimated we had covered about 1500 kilometres since buying the bikes.

After Pinneberg, our next camp was in the idyllic Rendsburg state forest. Idyllic for maybe three minutes, until the ants began to eat us alive. When we finally found an ant-free spot to camp, the flies descended, smashing our illusion about Europe being fly-free. In the morning, we got up before the insects, riding through Schleswig, Flensburg and crossing into Denmark at Krusaa, camping on the coast at Kollund.

Riding through Sonderborg to Fynshav, we caught a ferry to the Odense peninsula, working on our tans on the top deck. After landing, we rode to Faborg, and for the first time passed a lot of other cyclists who were kitted up for camping. Faborg was fascinating with Tudor-style architecture everywhere, mainly behind modern shop fronts. At the Faborg campsite, Derek discovered a hedgehog. It played dead for some time, then promptly bolted towards where I was lying on the ground writing a letter, and dived into my armpit.

"Well, there we have it," quipped Derek, "scientific proof that hedgehogs have no sense of smell."

We continued to Nyborg on the other side of the peninsula and caught a ferry to Korsor on the main island. As the 84 kilometre day progressed and we passed through Slagelse to camp at Soro, I noticed my temper fraying. I was getting frustrated with being unable to make my own decisions.

When we were on the bus trip, all the main decisions were made for us, which was the only viable model for thirty people traveling together. The three of us had looked forward to being more independent and heading off on our own. Yet if Derek and Dennis wanted to do something or ride in a certain direction, I was obviously outvoted and Derek's skill with maps meant that his voice usually prevailed. This was an obvious and inescapable dynamic arising from three people traveling together, but I started to look forward to traveling solo. I was also uncomfortable with this: I had left everyone and everything behind except my two travelling companions; now I was planning to leave them behind also.

The twin spires of Ringsted's cathedral looked promising from a distance, but up close the town was fairly grotty and reminded me of Stepney. It started to rain as we headed to Roskilde and we raced to the shelter of a motorway bridge to eat a lunch of bananas and yoghurt, seated on leftover bricks. When the rain showed no signs of easing we had little choice but to don our rain gear and cycle on to Copenhagen. We arrived at Absalon Camping about eight kilometres from the centre and the rain suddenly stopped as soon as we'd pitched our tents. The attractions of leisure time in a capital city beckoned, and we booked for four nights and checked on the state of the outside world: *Time* informed us that the Mormon church had just decided to admit the previously-excluded blacks into their priesthood. Women remained on the banned list. The RLDS Church had no ban on blacks, but shared the exclusion on women.

The Tivoli gardens were unimpressive: restaurants, pinball machines, one-armed bandits and uninspiring live music. We got back to the campsite about 11pm to discover a party happening in celebration of midsummer. Derek and Dennis joined in and amazingly met a girl who used to live in Petra Street, East Fremantle, just around the corner from Den's parents. I chose bed instead and drifted off to the sounds of people singing "Waltzing Matilda".

We met a nude Brigitte Bardot at Louis Tussaud's waxworks museum, and at the Royal Arsenal museum wandered through three floors crammed with weapons from the fifteenth century to the present day, leaving only when the museum closed, aiming at the fixed-price smorgasbord in the train station.

What followed was, quite simply, gluttony on a grand scale. I can offer little by way of excuse, except to say we had been living on a very basic diet while cycling. Marinated herring and pilchards in tomato sauce, caviar, ham, beef, salami, chicken, salads, veal, sausages, casseroles, meringues, torta, blanc mange, pastries – the temptation to overindulge was irresistible. I think the real problem was the carton of milk I drank afterwards.

We staggered out of the smorgasbord and onto the train for the trip back to camp. As the stations flew past the window, I knew I was about to be violently ill. The train was full of people, the windows were fixed, and of course, the doors only opened at stations. I was using all my willpower not to throw up. I tried not to think of food; I tried not to look at things that moved; I tried not to look at Derek's and Dennis's faces. More stations passed and the struggle became intense. Finally, our station, Brondbyoster, arrived and as the doors opened, I flew out of them. I think I had only taken about two steps before I sent a massive projectile vomit bouncing along the platform like a stone skimming along a pond, horrifying hordes of well-mannered and respectable Danes.

As Derek and Dennis collapsed into hysterics, I ran to the toilet to continue throwing up more discreetly, while shocked Danes headed for the nearest phones to lodge complaints with the Australian embassy. Derek had his "bushy smell", now I had my "Brondbyoster"; I could only hope Dennis's turn would come soon.

chapter 21

The Copulative Imperative

After a slightly slower start, we caught the train to Kobenhavn H and headed straight for the Ny Carlsberg Glypotek, which proved outstanding. Etruscan, Greek, Roman, Syrian and Egyptian art jostled for attention in an elegant classical building. Glass, brass and marble were everywhere. We spent two hours wandering around and still didn't get upstairs to the painting section.

We emerged at lunchtime and walked through Nyhavn, past bars and tattooists, up to Langelinie and the Danish Freedom Museum. After discovering the nearby medical history museum was closed, we returned to the Freedom museum and spent some more hours inspecting the pamphlets and weapons of the Danish resistance. Encultured and sore of foot, we returned to camp.

The following day was rainy, so we lazed in the morning and in the afternoon headed to the Carlsberg Brewery tour, during which we met an Aussie called Peter who was driving around Europe with his sister and two other girls. Afterwards, we saw Saturday Night Fever and then headed to Daddy's Dance Hall where we stayed until 1 am, only to discover we'd missed the last train home. We ran around frantically, fluked a bus back to

Valby, and walked 3.5 kilometres to the campsite where we arrived shortly before 3am, in the mist and early dawn of a Danish summer day.

A more subdued day followed: we hooked up with Peter and his group in their van, toured the Tuborg brewery, and visited the Zoological Museum which we awarded top marks because it featured a stuffed okapi. Back at camp, I had a cold and there was a sauna in my head, so I headed straight into the cocoon of my tent. And that, I imagined, was the end of the day for me.

As I was dozing, I could hear the voices of Peter and his group, as well as Derek and Dennis. But there were other Scandinavian voices, both male and female. I tried to block them out and sleep, but then realised that Derek and Dennis were trying to encourage one of the girls (who sounded slightly drunk) to come over and wake me up. Great.

A few seconds later, I was roused by a Swedish beauty at my fly. I pulled on some clothes, got out of the tent, and within minutes Diane and I were embracing like old friends (just because I was sick didn't mean I couldn't be friendly). Derek and Dennis suddenly stopped smiling; I found out later that they had assumed that Diane, Caroline, Ingmar and Steven were two couples. All of us headed to a disco that night, returning at different times. After two brewery tours in two days, a bad cold and several hours in a disco, I was trying hard to pretend I wasn't dead on my feet. When Diane and I got back to the campsite, we went to the tent she was sharing with her sister Caroline. Steven was there, which was a surprise; it turned out that Ingmar had returned first and locked Steven out, so the logical thing for him to do was share with Caroline. Which left the question of Diane.

Caroline looked at Diane, then me, and said in the most matter-of-fact voice: "I thought you'd be sleeping with Peter anyway." Obviously, somewhere, I'd missed something. Somewhere in the literature given to

Australians heading to Scandinavia there must have been a paragraph something like this:

"It is required of any Australian male, lying sick in a tent in Scandinavia, to greet any overtures by slightly inebriated Scandinavian women with an appropriate sexual response."

I'd obviously missed this paragraph and after Brondbyoster, exhausted and sick as I was, I could hardly afford to risk any more outraged phone calls to the Australian embassy. I took Diane's hand: "Let's go". As we walked towards my tent, it was already getting light.

The National Museum of Fine Art the next day did not impress like the Glypotek and we were soon back at camp, with Diane wobbling around the campground on my bike. Diane invited Derek, Dennis and myself back to their home near Kristianstad in Sweden, and we accepted. Peter, desperately trying to seduce the gorgeous Caroline, got their vanload invited as well, although the girls in his van were not impressed. The next morning, the others departed in their cars and the three of us followed on our bikes, catching the ferry into Sweden and camping in a forest next to a quarry about 20km from Malmo. Before going to sleep, we set rabbit traps in the woods.

About 4.30am, I woke to the sound of Derek and Dennis outside talking, but in unusual tones. As I surfaced from sleep, I realised that they were talking about the rabbit trap.

"What is it?"

"Dunno. Looks like some sort of weasel."

"If that's a weasel, it's on steroids. Looks like some sort of small bear to me."

"Maybe it's a polecat?"

Various amounts of scuffling, anxious sounds, swearing, thumping and grunting followed, the sum of which convinced me that nothing was going to coax me out of my tent until all this was over.

"Hey look, it's snapped the string." Good. Whatever it was had gone and I went back to sleep.

Subsequent discussions and examination of local fauna books revealed that the lads had temporarily caught a pine marten, a particularly nasty creature which, as it happens, does look remarkably like a cross between a small bear and a weasel on steroids. Part of the scuffling and a lot of the swearing was due to them being attacked by bees in the middle of the exercise.

We saw a death adder on the road the following day, and Derek enthused about the birdlife – buzzards, kites and eider ducks – before we camped in the forest at Linderod. Then it was through Kristianstad to Nymolla, where the girls lived. Peter and his crew were still there, which made everything rather crowded; we pitched our tents on the front lawn, then headed to a party in a block of flats where both vodka and Status Quo were never-ending, and danced and drank into the night. The Swedish penchant for drinking vodka became more excusable when we realised that the latest sensation on TV was I Love Lucy. After a few vodkas, Marie, one of the girls traveling with Peter, announced her intention of sleeping with men of as many different nationalities as possible.

"Did I tell you I'm actually Lithuanian?" quipped Dennis.

Our second night there was a barbecue with many of the girls' relatives attending to observe tame Australians at close quarters. The next day, I took Derek and Dennis aside.

"Guys, I've got a problem."

"Yes, we know," they replied, "which one are you talking about?"

"Look, you know I'm sleeping with Diane right?"

"Yes, there's no need to brag. We're the bozos who sent her to your tent, remember?"

"I'm not bragging – I can't keep up the pace. She wants to have sex continually, not just every night but *all* night. It must be something to do with the long summer: I think these Swedes hibernate all winter and have sex all summer. If we don't leave this place soon, I won't be able to cycle out of Nymolla, let alone to Oslo." They made deeply insincere noises of sympathy. "Well, it's just like I've always known," Derek said with a sage expression, "familiarity breeds in tents."

We left a couple of days later, and there were no goodbyes. Diane made a sudden decision to leave my tent extra early to pick strawberries on the morning of our departure; she was gone when I woke, leaving me a note in Swedish. I felt momentarily guilty I was glad there could be no farewells, but the guilt soon passed, another relationship was jettisoned, and I committed once again to the siren call of the open road, which asked so little of me.

A few kilometers after Nymolla we rode onto a plateau and a continual tableau of pine forests, lakes and rivers, through Olofstrom and Alsmundsryd to a mosquito-infested forest camp near Tingsryd. As we quickly broke camp the next day in a vain attempt to outrun the mosquito hordes, we vowed not to camp in the vicinity of a lake again unless it looked eminently fishable.

As we progressed, the scenery changed. We were continually gaining altitude as the forests became more frequent and the landscape rockier. Dennis found a 100 kroner note (£12) on the road and shouted the day's food as a result. We had three successive forest camps, near Vaxjo, Eksjo and Rimforsa. It had been forty days since we left Selsey.

chapter 22

The Delights of Amnesia

The hills were getting bigger, the roadside was often garlanded with wild strawberries, and we heard moose in the forest at night. As we passed through Linkoping and Norrkoping (a large, drab port in which we nearly lost our way following the E4 and dodging the parts that were autobahn) we clocked up 2,000km since leaving Selsey.

Through Norrkoping and Bjornlunda we arrived in Södertälje, a high-rise town with a large population of Greeks and Italians; two days later, we were in Stockholm. We spent a week there, based at the Sätra campsite, a converted sports ground near the Fruängen train station. We had our first hot shower since nine days before in Nymolla and collected letters from the poste restante: my father was bitter about life in Western Australia and thinking of getting a job in Adelaide; he was also thinking about meeting up with me somewhere in Europe. I had reservations about this, not wanting my cherished independence to be invaded. I had left Western Australia behind; the thought of it following me to Europe was disconcerting. I had little enthusiasm about being hunted down by commitments and expectations of any sort, let alone my father's. I hadn't lived in the same house as him since I was five years old, and I knew his expectations were stratospheric and rigid.

We had already noticed the high proportion of street drunks in Sweden: young and old, at any time of the day or night, sprawled across park benches or in shopping arcades. Drinking seemed to be the national sport. It was, therefore, ironic when police moved us on when we were completely sober. We were having a perfectly respectable alfresco lunch in a churchyard.

"You can't eat here."

"Why not?"

"It's a graveyard."

The logic escaped me: the resident dead had once known what it was to eat. How could the presence of food now offend them? Personally, I thought they would have appreciated the visit, but we obediently moved on.

As we wandered around the old town, visiting the Magnus Ladulas club a couple of times, Stockholm seemed vaguely Parisian. There were free open air concerts at the Rälambshovsparken where hundreds of people drifted through a haze of hashish; enormous ice cream cones on Skansen; mouldy stuffed animals in the Biological Museum; and the impressive Wasa museum, with preservative constantly being sprayed over the hull of the ancient ship which sank on its maiden voyage in 1628. One night at the Engelen pub, we met two Swedish couples who invited us to visit them in Karlstad; they also translated the note Diane had left for me:

"By the time you get this translated, you will probably be a long way from Sweden. I know I was not the right girl for you, but some day you will find someone better than me. When you do, please let me still be your friend."

I tried to make allowance for the translation, but the note of self-pity irritated me. Beneath the irritation, there were further disturbing thoughts:

was I impossible to please? How had I given Diane the impression that she wasn't good enough for me? Was I even capable of a lasting relationship? Was it better not even to try? I knew I didn't have the answers (and suspected I didn't want them anyway); fortunately I was distracted from melancholy by a huge woman who was unsuccessfully trying to chat up Dennis.

On our last day in Stockholm, we went to see the movie The Last Waltz, documenting The Band's farewell concert. It was great to see so many rock heroes sharing one stage, although Neil Young was completely off his face and Ronnie Wood definitely needed more camera time.

We found a quick way of leaving Stockholm, through Södertalje to the picturesque lakeside town of Mariefred. While Den slept, Derek and I circumnavigated Gripsholm Slott, a sixteenth-century castle that jutted into the lake, complete with immaculate gardens and a large art gallery. After a forest camp just before Strängmas, we headed into a rainy day during which we only cycled a little north of Enköping. Our next major stop was to be Uppsala, but we were destined never to make it.

The following morning we packed up our forest camp and started cycling. After a few minutes, I noticed a large piece of grass protruding from the hub of my front wheel. I remember thinking about pulling it out and then everything went blank....

Slowly, I began to wake. I was alone in a room, which I gradually realised was some sort of hospital. There were no other people in sight and no noise. I didn't know who I was or where I was; I had absolutely no memories at all – it was complete amnesia. I was conscious of two simultaneous feelings: a low level of anxiety and a transcendent sense of freedom and purity. I had no past. I was reborn. The slate was clean. Even though at that moment I couldn't remember anything of my life, I knew with certainty that I had never felt this pure before: part of me was anxious, most of me was soaring.

Lying there, I tried to force my mind to remember things, but it didn't work. Was I sick? Had I been in an accident of some sort? I looked at my body: I was dressed in shorts and a T shirt and there was a bandage around my hand. Everything else seemed okay. Slowly, I moved into a sitting position on the bed, then stood. There was still no-one in sight, and no memories were emerging.

Opening the door, I stepped into an eerily empty corridor. There was no-one visible in either direction, but the linoleum on the floor seemed to confirm that I was in hospital – but a hospital with one patient? Who was I? Was this some sort of mental institution? Had I lost my mind in both senses of the word?

At one end of the corridor, a long way away, I could see a window, and beyond that, a garden. I was on the ground floor. I headed towards the window, moving slowly, and eventually heard a voice I didn't recognise. It was a woman's voice, and I didn't recognise the language either. As I came closer to this voice, I entered a reception area and saw a woman sitting behind a desk. I opened my mouth to speak to her, wondering if I could speak, and if so, whether she could understand me. At that moment, I glanced out of the window and saw two small, green tents pitched in the hospital gardens. There was a flash of recognition, and, gradually, memories began to return, pieces of the jigsaw puzzle fitting together until it was all there. I was back; the sense of anxiety had gone, but so had that euphoric sense of freedom. The price of regaining my past (and therefore my present) had been the loss of transcendence; later I would often wonder whether it would be worth losing myself again to regain that sense of soaring purity. I decided that it would.

chapter 23

Oslo

Derek and Dennis reconstructed the events of the day for me with a mixture of shock and hilarity. I had reached over to pull the grass from my wheel, but in doing so, had turned the wheel onto my hand. My hand had gone into the spokes and then into the fork, bringing the bike to an instant halt, sending me flying over the handlebars onto the road. Hitting the road, I had an epileptic fit with all the trimmings: eyes rolled back, foaming at the mouth, body in spasms.

Derek and Dennis had flagged down some plain-clothes police who had phoned an ambulance which sped me back into Enköping. Apparently, I had regained consciousness around 11am in the hospital while doctors and nurses were busy taking my blood and doing heart tests, although I had no memory of this. The doctors had told Derek and Dennis that I might have to be kept under observation for several days, and for this reason they were given permission to camp in the hospital grounds. As it turned out, I awoke in the early afternoon and was discharged by 2 pm. We remained camped in the hospital grounds that night, surrounded by determined joggers.

The epilepsy puzzled me: I had never been epileptic. Further investigations revealed that under conditions of dehydration and stress, anyone can suffer a fit. We were cycling many kilometers a day, sweating profusely, and not drinking enough; combined with the shock of suddenly being thrown from my bike, the explanation was clear enough. There was no reason why I should experience another fit. I realised how terrifying it must have been for Derek and Dennis to be miles from the nearest town and have to deal with me in that condition. They had earned the right to milk the experience for jokes for years to come.

After my bike had been repaired (my hand had bent the front fork) we cycled only a few kilometers to Bredsands where we camped by a lake, lazed, rowed out and caught and ate some pike. I knew that Den and Derek were checking me out to see if I was fit to cycle. I was, so we covered 80 kilometres the next day through Vasteräs, to Fagersta. The ride into Fagersta was both hilly and wet. We were caught in the worst downpour of the trip so far, and took refuge in the forest, which proved insect-free. By contrast, the next day was the best we'd had in Sweden. The temperature was about 30 Celsius and we cycled all day with our shirts off before camping in forest near Hjuisjo.

The following day, spent riding from Hjuisjo to Filipstad, was July 27 – exactly six months since we left Fremantle, but it felt much longer. We had no luck fishing, but standing on rocks in the lake at Filipstad, with mist rolling in on the left, a summer house on the right and capercaillie flying by, it didn't matter much.

We had a long day cycling to Grums in weather that reminded us of Perth, complete with a sea breeze (probably blowing off the Vänern) and flatter, crop-filled countryside. Our acquaintances in Karlstad were sick, so we didn't linger, but fought our way through a mass of autobahns to find our way out of town on a back road.

In Grums we discussed future plans. We considered cycling around France, Spain and Italy the following summer, but on opening the map and discussing distance, we realised it was too ambitious to attempt to cycle through these three countries in one summer. We toyed with the idea of rail travel, but eventually decided that the best thing would probably be to buy a small old "bomb" that we could also use for touring England. In the middle of this discussion, a Volvo spun into the campsite and dropped off a French hitchhiker, Jean-Eurne, who was from Angers. We spent most of the evening talking to him and smoking his Gauloises, while he recommended the Dordogne region and the west coast of France for castles and beaches.

As we were cycling off the following morning, I heard something rubbing on my front wheel. I couldn't see what it was so I stopped. Derek and Dennis had cycled ahead, and by the time I discovered that the tyre was pulling away from the rim and rubbing the brakes, they were out of sight. Before I could start unloading the bike, the tube exploded like a shotgun. The lads returned (probably thinking I'd been shot) and we changed the tube for an old one and swapped the tyre. We cycled for about an hour down the road when I had a flat tyre again. I patched this and was blowing the tyre up when it blew another hole. I fixed the second hole and then the pump came apart in my hands, rusted from the inside. We decided the Fates were against us.

I pushed my Peugeot to a lakeside rest stop while the others rode. We considered camping there until one of us could ride back to the cycle shop in Grums the next day to buy tubes and a pump, but after fixing the tube, decided to walk to a nearby house to see if they had a pump. They didn't, but directed us to someone who did, and suddenly, we were on the road again. We managed to cover 61 kilometres and camped in forest near Sillerud.

On a hot Scandinavian summer's day we rode through Töcksfors and then hit a range of hills that climaxed with a monster that forced me down into third gear, low range. At the top, we all plunged into a lake, before riding the last few kilometers to the Norwegian border. No-one even looked at us as we rolled through the border and then into Őrje on the E18 where we camped on a farm where no-one spoke English.

Momarken and Askim passed and we cycled uneventfully into the outskirts of Oslo. The fjord broke into view and shortly afterwards the Norwegian equivalent of a beach – hundreds of people clinging like limpets to large, sloping rocks. My bike tyre got caught in a tram rut, nearly flipping me into oncoming traffic, as the road into town skirted the fjord, then took an abrupt uphill right hand turn to Ekeberg camping. This hill was the steepest I had ever attempted and it kept going forever. When we finally reached the summit, my stomach sank: the campsite bore the sign "Full". Perhaps sensing potential violence, the attendant wisely let us in "because you are cyclists". Tents pitched, showered, we were ready to attempt our human being impressions once more.

Oslo was the furthest we would cycle. Our plan was to leave our bikes there and catch a train to Bergen, so we bought our tickets and spent the evening trying to sleep while drunken tourists kept walking into our tent ropes. I wasn't sure which was more disconcerting: the violent shaking of my small tent as they tripped on a tent rope, or the thud as they hit the ground a few inches from my head.

The next day we checked out the Henrik Ibsen exhibition at Club 7, watched street pastel artists, and I spent the afternoon in the library reading Quentin Bell's *Bloomsbury* while the lads lolled in a sauna. Rain evolved into a thunderstorm and suddenly being in a sleeping bag in a tent seemed the best place to be. Somewhere in the early hours of the morning, I was woken by various strange noises in the midst of which I could discern Dennis swearing. I followed the precedent of my pine marten policy and stayed exactly where I was, knowing all would be revealed next morning.

I didn't have to wait long: in fact, I really only needed to stick my head outside my tent to know what had happened. Dennis had pitched his tent at the bottom of a small hollow. The heavy rain had run towards his tent, the ground had become very muddy, and eventually, the tent pegs had come loose. Den's tent then collapsed on him in the middle of the night in the middle of a thunderstorm. Surfacing from nightmares of suffocation, he had fought his way free from his shroud-tent, wisely decided to abandon it in the circumstances, and forced Derek to share his tent for the night.

Drying out the next day, we snuck into the Kon Tiki/Ra museum and bought something to eat, only to discover we were surrounded by imbecilic Americans. Now I am aware there are some very nice and extremely intelligent Americans, but many of them obviously choose to take their holidays at home, rather than overseas. We were subjected to loud conversations, most of which could be described either as "stating the bleeding obvious" or "saying absolutely everything that comes into my head because I'm labouring under the mistaken impression that you'll find it fascinating."

Eventually, it became too much for Derek. Jumping to his feet next to the worst offenders, he assumed a loud and highly exaggerated American accent: "Look Martha, they've got banana trees in Norway!" and simultaneously threw his banana skin over a nearby bush. I looked at their faces, and none of them got it. It was really very sad.

A little later, Dennis was similarly inspired. Near the train station, he pointed at a piece of rusty pipe, adopted a high-camp accent, and declared, "Ooh, Cyril, look at this ancient cannon!" Dennis thought I was the one standing next to him, but in fact I'd moved a short distance away, and he'd shared his high-pitched exclamation with an unsuspecting and terrified local.

chapter 24

From Bergen to Britain

We left our bikes at the local RLDS church, and after a smorgasbord feast at the elegant Hotel Norge, where I felt distinctly out of place, boarded the train for Bergen. The train climbed through treeless, but snow-covered high country. We passed through 220 tunnels and an altitude of 4,600 feet above sea level. It was a luxury to see scenery passing by without my legs being locked in continual circular movements.

Bergen had been founded by King Olaf in 1070 and we spent a couple of days there, fascinated by the fish markets and tortured by the size of the trout we hadn't caught. Our short time in Bergen was, by common consent, a time of recuperation. We lounged in the town's main square, read newspapers in the library, and smoked Camel cigarettes. Back in Oslo, *Time* magazine celebrated the arrival of Louise Brown, the first "test-tube baby". We retrieved our bikes, and boarded the Oslo-Frederickshavn ferry.

Our ferry fare was a bargain. They considered our three bikes as a car and gave us the special deal for four people with a vehicle – our own sleeper cabin. This was our first night in a proper bed for over ten weeks, but was of limited encouragement to one of the lads who was afflicted with a penile rash. After several unsuccessful charades attempting to communicate the nature of the problem in various Oslo and Bergen Apoteks, stopping just short of willful exposure, he determined to solve the problem himself. He decided to crush a large number of salt tablets in a glass of water and immerse his penis in it. He was thus engaged when I burst in through the cabin door; alarmed, he spilt the solution everywhere and made comments that were less than welcoming.

We cycled from an overcast Frederickshavn, avoiding a thunderstorm, to Ălborg. We were back in yoghurt country; it was not unusual for us to eat two litres of yoghurt each per day. Hobro was the next stop, virtually on the same latitude as Edinburgh. Just outside Hobro was Fyrkat, the site of a 1,000 year old Viking fort. Nothing remained of it except the surrounding earth wall, but the shapes of the buildings were known from the post holes left by long-rotted timbers. From there we rode to a "sinkhole" on a farmer's property, and then to another property to inspect a burial mound. For a small admission fee, the farmer gave us a torch and pointed the way. Hunched over almost double, we wormed our way through the mound's passages into the burial rooms at the end. It was an eerie sensation to stand in a place where the dead were buried 5,000 years ago, in a tomb that was older than the pyramids of Egypt.

Back at the campsite we lunched on mackerel and boiled spuds; then the lads had a kip. I was in no mood for a nap. History had entranced me once again. What was it about her? Omnipresent, but elusive; romantic, but reticent. Was the pursuit of her really worth the effort, or was it a fool's errand? Would she ever deliver a fraction of what she promised? Regardless, I realised that everyone is produced by, produces, and becomes history: why not pursue that from which there is no escape? The pursuit of that which cannot be escaped seemed like wisdom. There appeared to be no real down-side to this commitment to History; I suspected it was the only kind I was capable of making.

With two of us awake, we decided our companion had slept long enough and we threw back the flysheet on his tent. He was awake, and kneeling in his tent with his penis in one hand and a can of fly spray in the other.

"What the hell are you doing?" we chorused. He looked somewhat abashed.

"Well, you know I've been suffering from scabies for a while. It's driving me crazy. I know it's caused by some sort of parasite, so I thought if I just sprayed my penis with fly spray it might help."

The two of us looked at each other and shook our heads: "That Kashmiri hash has a lot to answer for." And we left him to it.

Ărhus was the second biggest town in Denmark and looked a lot like London; in fact, much of Denmark was reminiscent of England. After camping a short distance from town in the Marselisborg woods, we visited the prehistory museum where the highlight was the Grabaulle man. More popularly known as the "Bog Man", he was remarkably well preserved due to tannins and other chemicals. The analysis of his stomach contents was fascinating. Unable to restrain ourselves, we all bought postcards of him to send home, assuring our families that we were in much better shape by comparison.

From Ărhus to Vejle to Kolding to Toftlund, the country gradually got flatter, but the wind became a major obstacle, keeping us to about 50 kilometres per day. We had covered 3,300 km since leaving Selsey and were all complaining about our kneecaps. It was August 17, exactly a year since that fateful day Derek had told me about breaking up with Sue and revealed his plans for traveling. One decision that changed so much: like a rock thrown in a lake – do the ripples ever stop?

In Toftlund, Anne Bancroft seduced Dustin Hoffman, but with no attractive and determined non-celluloid older women in sight to distract us, we cycled on through Tonder to the German border, and beyond to

Niebŭll, where poor signage made it difficult to locate the campsite, which was on a farm. We rejoiced to see prices hadn't increased since we were last in Germany, and dined on ravioli, Mars bars and cheap wine.

In Husum, we could tell by the stares that we weren't what this touristy town was used to, nor what it wanted. Dear Husumites, it's just a bit of honest sweat, dirt, body odour, and a penile rash. Please remember, you live in a country that unleashed Rotel tours on the world. People who live in glass toilets shouldn't throw stony stares.

Meldorf was our next stop and then, on a hot and windless day, we had three ferry rides, crossing two tributaries of the Elbe and then the Elbe itself. An Aldi store in Gluckstadt provided quantities of fleischwurst, sauerkraut and peaches and we cycled on to Osten where Den collapsed, exhausted. Out of sympathy for our aching bones, we made a slower start the next day, and discovered a strange metallic noise coming from Den's rear wheel. We never did find out what it was, but it lessened as we rode on.

Basdahl gave way to Bramstedt, Hagan, then Sandstedt on the banks of the Weser. Unfortunately, the only campsite in Sandstedt was for permanent residents, not transients like us. We had cycled 150 kilometres in two days with no shower. We hesitated only a moment before walking in as if we owned the place and showering. I also washed my shirt because Derek and Dennis had begun apologising to the locals on my behalf, so I knew things were bad. No-one said a word: it was either an exercise in Teutonic tact, or they were terrified of us. We camped on vacant land next to the ferry we wanted to catch the following day.

After crossing the Weser, we negotiated a sluice of large black slugs on the cycleway, and continued to Bad Zwischenahn, over the Ems, through Bunde to the Dutch border, where we met an older American cyclist (at least thirty-five) called Jake. The quintessential hippie with long hair and beard, tinted glasses and colourful head scarf, I'm sure he was frisked for drugs at every border crossing, but he had some anyway. He continued with us to Nieuweschans where we camped and listened to his travel tales. Some seemed far-fetched, but he made central America sound fascinating and I wondered if we'd get there later. Jake provided us with a model of someone ten years older than us who was still on the road, and showed no signs of slowing down. So it *was* possible… Elsewhere in the world, so *Time* informed us, Evita opened on the London stage, Anglicans were celebrating the ordination of women; and Catholics were awaiting the appointment of a new Pope (probably not a woman).

As we headed in the direction of Groningen the following morning, the windy conditions seemed to affect Jake more than us. We stopped at a small town called Scheemda and joined Jake in his ritual morning coffee, realising it was the first time we had paid for coffee since Turkey. Then on through Hoogezand Sappemeer, past canals and ship building yards towards Groningen. Initial impressions were unfavourable as we approached through the industrial area, but near the centre, beautiful towers came into view and we entered a city filled with people, mostly young and on pushbikes, jostling with cars for street space and dodging pedestrians who were crossing to the carnival in the centre of the square. We were all impressed. Saying goodbye to Jake who had friends in the town, we found the campsite and spent the evening with two French girls who gave us their Paris address.

The following day, a market had replaced the carnival, with a background soundtrack of Dire Straits and AC/DC. Then it was on to Leeuwarden, through the windiest weather we'd yet experienced, to Franeker. From Franeker we rode to Harlingen across the Afsluitdyk for 30 km to Den Oever, where the entire town was drunk for some obscure reason, then through Wierengerwerf to Hoorn. Our campsite was called de Hulk, but was guilty of false advertising as the requisite Marvel character was nowhere to be seen.

From Hoorn, it was a short ride into Amsterdam where we spent hours wandering around malls, record shops and availing ourselves of the free ferries. It might have been my imagination, but the red light Amsterdames seemed more attractive than their Hamburg equivalents and we discovered that the Heineken brewery tour was a most helpful precursor to the Van Gogh museum.

Because I hadn't embarrassed myself for a while, I decided to visit the tourist bureau and ask an attractive young woman for directions to the nearest VD clinic. Blood samples and a painful scraping followed and I couldn't believe the verdict – I had NSU again! I had been given the all-clear before Diane – had I picked it up again from her, or worse, had it not gone in the first place, in which case I'd probably given it to her? I was banned from alcohol for a week and put on pills.

Distraction therapy was called for, so we visited Anne Frank's house, and the Ryksmuseum where the Nightwatch was just one of many impressive paintings. The cultural roundup was completed that evening when we caught two punk rock bands called The Filth and Speed Twins at the Paradiso nightclub. The next day we caught a train to Vlissingen, a ferry to Breskens, and then it was only a short cycle to Sluis.

On September 5 we rose early and sprinted the 25 kilometres from Sluis to Ostende in an hour. We had no idea of the ferry timetable and arrived to discover the 11am ferry about to leave, a long queue in front of us, and a three hour wait for the next ferry. We walked straight on board and told the guy checking tickets that we'd been told we could buy them on board, so he sent us to the purser. We bought our tickets and headed into a rough crossing.

We had planned to get as far as Rye that evening but cycling in England proved as difficult as we'd remembered, although we seemed to have a few more downhills in our favour this time. The hilliest stretch was from Dover to Brighton – the extent of the White Cliffs and the place where the South Downs meet the coast. It was a triumphant feeling to soar down the very hills which had wrung the sweat out of us on our first two days. Just west of Newhaven was a hill which nearly finished us. After climbing a series of hills through the town we saw this monster rise in front of us and lost the battle before it had even begun. Our hope of not having to walk our bikes in England was dashed. As it turned out, we almost couldn't even walk up it. Our bikes, laden with about 25 kg each, seemed incredibly heavy. To bend over too far was to strain your back; to walk erect put too much strain on calf muscles. I tried walking on tiptoes, the balls of my feet, flat-footed, but nothing eased my calf muscles, which felt like perished elastic at full stretch.

The monster hill meant we only reached New Romney where the three of us shared a double room at the Old Stone Lodge (dating from 1251) for £3.80 each. Both heartened and slowed down by a huge English breakfast the next morning, we rode through Rye to Peacehaven.

The cycling trip was coming to an end and, as had been the case towards the end of the overland bus trip, the end of a major voyage tended to be an anti-climax. I realised that for the last few days I had almost been willing the cycling trip to end, wanting to cycle into Selsey, unpack the bikes for the last time, and launch out on the next journey. Restless activity had become mandatory, it seemed, and it flashed through my mind that I was now probably doomed never to succeed in the public service. In the back of my mind, I sensed questions forming that I didn't want to consider, questions that wanted to nag me for answers: can you be happy doing any-thing? Will this restlessness ever come to an end? Can you ever find a sense of purpose or a relationship that will endure? I closed the questions down before I could fully consider them because I knew that the honest answer to them would probably be "no".

chapter 25

Playing with Fire

From Peacehaven, it was four and a half hours of solid cycling to Selsey, with a ten minute break. Bognor Regis, Chichester, the signposts to Selsey, the Blacksmith's Arms, The Anchor at Sidlesham, the ferry with its bird-watchers, the turnoff to Church Norton where we'd hand-fed the birds and wandered through the cemetery one misty morning, a left-hand turn at the newsagent and a right into Holford Green (Derek's parents now had their own place) and it was all over. It was September 7, 1978: the cycling trip had lasted 101 days and covered about 3,000 miles (4,800 kilometres).

During the next few days, while Begin and Sadat were chatting at Camp David, we visited Chichester a couple of times, went ferreting for rabbits (unsuccessfully) with Derek's granddad, set our own rabbit wires between Norton and the ferry, and caught a Blondie concert in Portsmouth. I had to pay for my own ticket, wasn't in the front row, and didn't get propositioned. Debbie Harry was a platinum speck in the distance.

A serious note crept into our discussions. In Amsterdam, Dennis had become concerned about the responsibilities of the family dry cleaning business because his father hadn't employed anyone to replace him. On arriving back in Selsey, Dennis heard that his mother was "nervous and "worried" about his absence. After mulling this over, he declared his intention of being back in Perth for the next southern winter.

As the Shah imposed martial law in Iran, and Keith Moon died of a drug overdose, we returned to London in the back of a butcher's van, sitting on four slaughtered pigs. Nobler entrances have been made into this great city. We found a triple room (with bath) in the Camellia Hotel near Queensway for £3 each per night and our first full day in London featured sixteen miles of walking, including a guided tour of the Tower, and an evening production of The Passion of Dracula at the Queen's Theatre. It was the first play either Derek or Dennis had ever seen, and the mixture of eroticism, humour and horror won them over.

The next month alternated between London and Selsey, drinking in everything both could offer. I drooled over the Gutenberg Bible and the 1623 Shakespeare Folio, we visited the Planetarium, bookshops and record stores, and watched numerous movies, including Star Wars, Last Tango in Paris, Annie Hall, Sleeper, and Everything You Wanted to Know about Sex but were Afraid to Ask. I emerged a confirmed Woody Allen fan. At Madame Tussaud's (much better than her Danish counterpart) the best fun was standing still, rigid and unblinking, and having tourists look down to see your identity plate! In Oh! Calcutta, watching the naked women on stage was nowhere nearly as enjoyable as watching the octogenarian next to me who had turned up expecting a play about the British Raj.

In Selsey, Derek introduced us to the magic of trot line fishing. At low tide, we would go down to the pebbly beach, and hammer two metal pegs into the ground. Between the pegs was a fishing line strung with numerous hooks, each baited with a whelk. As the tide rose, the line would submerge, and hopefully some fish would discover the whelks. We would return at the next low tide to see if we'd caught anything. This gambit proved very successful and each morning we caught at least a cod or a bass; sometimes several.

As September headed into a cooler October, we planned the next phase of our trip. Deciding to avoid a UK winter, we booked an apartment in Malta for a month, after which we would go to the United States and Mexico. Dennis received more pressure from home. His parents wrote asking when he would be returning and if he still wanted to be in the business, which they would sell if he didn't want to continue. His reply was vague, but indicated he would return by winter. I felt sorry for him: he was taking his first real break after 14 years of drycleaning servitude and his parents were putting pressure on him. Commitment, obligation, expectation, duty – to me it was the language of enslavement.

On the way back from a night's drinking at The Neptune, where Lorna was looking like death, and Evelyn was maintaining an ersatz effervescence, Dennis admitted that the only time he was ever happy staying in one spot was when he was working because it filled in the time. I wondered if I used books in much the same way, reveling in the thoughts of others to avoid considering ultimate issues of meaning and purpose. A commitment to a book was comfortably finite. I decided to review my reading list since returning to the UK. In a month I had read: *Plain Tales from the Raj*, John Keel's *Our Haunted Planet*, *The Once and Future King* by T. H. White, *The Undiscovered Country* by Stephen Jenkins, two books by Carlos Castaneda, *Behold the Man* and *The Dancers at the End of Time* trilogy by Michael Moorcock, *Do What you Will [A History of Anti-Morality]* by Geoffrey Ashe, *The Projection of the Astral Body* by Sylvan Muldoon and Norman Cohn's *The Pursuit of the Millennium*. Hmmm… a heady mix of the occult, history, radical religion and fantasy; I was not so much avoiding ultimate issues but looking for answers … everywhere. All I was certain of was that I was entranced with history, and that one day, I had to investigate the RLDS church fully.

As usual, with plans made, we were keen to move on, and events began to blur. Before leaving the Selsey region, we reveled in the intactness of Arundel Castle, lunched at the Black Rabbit pub on the river Arun, and Dennis, a Beaujolais-bearing beau located a temporary haven with Helen. In London, we saw Mickey Dolenz at a screening of Grease, drank too much to celebrate being on the road for nine months, caught up with some of our fellow overlanders, saw a group called Doll by Doll play forceful and intelligent music in the Nashville Room, and flew to Malta.

Our choice of Malta had been determined largely by price: it was cheap to fly there (£77 return) and cheap to stay there. And of course, being an island tucked neatly between Sicily and North Africa made it a great place to spend part of the winter. We arrived on Malta at 1 am and were driven the fourteen miles to St Paul's Bay through light drizzle. The buildings all looked biblical to me – flat-roofed and made of local stone. Our apartment was on the third floor and so new that the building was still being completed. We were only a short walk from the clear waters of the bay, with bars and restaurants nearby: we had made an excellent choice.

Bar crawling the following evening, we ended up in the Tartan bar and met a young couple from Leeds, Janette and Tony, aged 21 and 22 respectively. Jan was pretty and extraverted; Tony was more reserved. In view of their youth, it was a surprise to discover they had already been married for three years. Tony was a soccer freak and hit it off instantly with Derek. Lubricated by the cheap local wine, Jan and I got on *too* well, and I found myself stroking her knee under the table.

Over the next few days, we spent a lot of time with Tony and Jan. Jan's flirting with me in front of Tony became rather blatant:

"Well, I need to smoke – I have to have *something* to do with my hands – after all, this is a public place." Strangely, he didn't seem to mind.

We also discovered Bunny and Jackie, both from the UK, who were in the ground floor apartment. They had hated the two weeks they'd spent on Malta, because it was too laid-back after the UK punk scene. They joined our group and we spent a night drinking at our place, then at the Tartan, and then the Incognito, where Jackie's ample cleavage and multi-coloured cigarettes undulated through the haze. When we eventually surfaced the following afternoon, we drove past Mellieha Bay to Marfa Point, which faces Comino and Gozo, discovering a sheltered and aptly-named Paradise Bay. Paradise threatened to be short-lived for me, however, for a letter from my father informed me he was planning to join us in Malta! I was shocked. He'd virtually invited himself without asking, and although he had written of possibly meeting me in Europe, it had been vague up until now. My mind ran through the possibilities and I felt a little relieved; it had been quite difficult for us to get tickets to Malta, so perhaps my father might only get as far as London.

That night after dinner, Tony, Derek and Dennis were engrossed in a game of cards and Jan asked Tony's permission to have a drink with me. He agreed, we went to Chez Francis and she told me the story of their marriage.

"It was two weeks before the wedding. I began to have second thoughts about marrying Tony, but I didn't tell anyone."

"Why not?" seemed the obvious question.

"Because I didn't want to upset anyone and because my parents had already paid for everything. They had too much money invested in the wedding and the reception. I didn't want them to lose it all." I kept my thoughts to myself, but losing a lifetime to save some money seemed a poor exchange.

"About three weeks after we got married, everything just clicked into a routine and it hasn't changed in the last three years. We don't make love anymore. I can't even remember the last time Tony kissed me."

Jan was fun, slim, attractive, with shoulder-length sandy/ginger hair and blue eyes. I couldn't understand. It felt like there were pieces of the puzzle missing.

"So if Tony's not interested in you, what is he interested in?"

"He loves sport, so he's always either playing it, training for it, or watching it on TV. He lets me go for drives with his mates and they're always trying to get it on with me, but I've never let them."

In the middle of our conversation, we met an unsober officer from the British aircraft carrier, the Ark Royal, which was docked in Valletta harbour on its final voyage before decommissioning. He arranged for the two of us to have a tour of the ship. We moved on to the Incognito, by which time we were kissing.

The next day, Derek, Dennis and Tony headed off to the football and I stayed in the apartment. Jan arrived, and we spent the afternoon in each other's arms. Embracing in the kitchen, we knocked over a wine bottle and were innocently picking up the pieces when the others returned.

Our first attempt to visit the Ark failed, and another was scheduled. As we made our way to the harbour, Jan told me she and Tony had just had a major argument and she'd told him she wanted a divorce. I started to feel distinctly uncomfortable and I was glad of the distraction of Dave, the sailor who'd arranged our tour and was suffering severely from a hangover. He met us looking incredibly ill and steered us to 6 Delta mess where he abdicated in favour of Fergey, who took us all over the Ark. We spent eight hours on board, visiting John in the fire office, seeing the rugby trophy, the poltergeist picture, and drinking free beers before catching a dice-boat back to town with Fergey and hitting the first bar on the right off Republic Street.

Inside, we met two sailors who knew Fergey and proceeded to demolish some vodka with them. I spent a lot of time talking music with Jimmy. Finally, after enough vodka, Jan produced her wedding ring and told them the story. Fergey was incredulous:

"This Tony must be a right toss-pot then." I found myself trying to defend him.

Jan and I taxied back to the apartment block. Somewhere our lips parted long enough for her to say:

"I love you. Come back to Leeds with me." I felt like a piece on a chess board; she was using the "L" word already. Initially, I had thought that paying attention to Jan might make Tony jealous, and all would be well, our relationship simply a Malteaser. Now she was talking about divorce, implying she was leaving Tony for me.

"Of course I'll visit you in Leeds." She noticed my rephrasing.

"You promise?" and although it was dark, I knew one eyebrow was raised, along with her expectations. My shoulders sank under the weight of even a slight commitment.

"I promise."

chapter 26

A Fatherly Visit

Tony and Jan flew back to Leeds, and Derek, Dennis and I spent the next couple of days lazily snorkeling and doing a circuit at night between the Swiss Chalet, the Mona Vale, Eros, the Tartan and the Incognito (where Jan and I had become regulars). Steed, the guitarist at the Tartan, had formerly played with David Essex and took requests, dutifully trotting out Maggie May for me every night.

News came through that my father was awaiting a cancellation and still might arrive in Malta. As I considered the possibility, it became less daunting. It would be quite good to see a family member after being away for ten months, and my father was usually so gloomy about everything; perhaps being in unfamiliar territory would cheer him up.

One night at the Tartan was livelier than most. The "Yorkshire cowboys" were there with a guy from Jersey and they were the butt of innumerable jokes from Steed:

"See that guy there? He's Jewish. Only trouble is, when they circumcised him, they threw away the wrong bit."

Someone dropped his trousers to reveal an eye tattooed on each buttock; a drunken English Literature professor, off to the Middle East the next day, fell backwards onto our table.

In the early hours of November 28, my father arrived on Malta. I'm sure he was more shocked than I at our meeting. He looked exactly as I expected: neatly dressed, smiling under his obedient hair, with three cameras around his neck and too much luggage. I now had hair below my shoulders, a moustache and beard, the latter demonstrating a blonde/ginger tendency that betrayed the original plain brown.

We talked until 4.30am. After a few hours' sleep, I drove him into Valletta where we visited the palace armoury, and Fort Elmo where we were nearly blown off the battlements. The further my father was from home, the more desperate he was to take photographs. Some of the most ingrained memories of my childhood are my father positioning me for innumerable photographs: I always had to be facing the sun, and he was always yelling "Don't squint!" as if a child looking into the sun has a choice. He never grasped the creative potential of shadow, either in photography or life.

I knew he would want to take dozens of photos on Malta. He took photos of St Paul's catacombs, views from the barricades of Mdina, the Roman baths and Golden Bay. Despite drinking a fair bit of my father's brandy that night, we headed off early the next day to the Hypogeum (similar to the catacombs, but used as a temple, not for burials), the Tarxien temples and the cathedral at Tarxien cemetery where Fred's shutter finger went into overdrive. In short, I took him anywhere and everywhere I possibly could that he might want to photograph and he was, it seemed, happy.

The four of us flew back to London together. After a lightning trip to Selsey with Derek and Dennis (mainly to unload duty-frees as gifts for Derek's parents) I headed back to London with Fred. Fred passed me an envelope with an early birthday present from home – it was a cheque for £145, but I could only cash it at the National Westminster Bank in Threadneedle Street. I decided this was as good an opportunity as any to show the old boy a bit of London, so we headed up Bayswater Road, Oxford Street, High Holborn, Newgate Street, Cheapside, Poultry to Threadneedle. There was a moment's panic when they weren't going to cash the cheque because I didn't have my passport with me as ID, but then my old student card came to the rescue.

Then it was down Queen Victoria Street, to St Paul's (photo stop, naturally), Fleet Street, Strand, Trafalgar Square in fading light and into Piccadilly Circus before heading home via Bond and Oxford Streets where news of the Jonestown cult murders of 900 people in Guyana was just breaking. After covering so many miles on foot (a real London baptism), Fred and I had no plans to head out that evening. He retired to his room, and I headed to the room I shared with Derek and Dennis, who, having had a quieter day, headed out to the movies.

They never made it to the movies. Just before midnight, they both burst into the room, blind drunk, Derek on all fours. Dennis was shouting about tanks, boots, and ducks. Gradually, it emerged that they had met some people in the Shakespeare, downed eight pints of cider each, and were now drunk enough to donate several vital organs each, without anaesthetic, and without missing them.

The room was soon a mass of crawling, chundering, naked human flesh. They hadn't been this drunk since Turkey. I left them in bed in tatters the following morning as Fred and I headed to the US embassy to collect my visa; later in the day, Derek and Dennis were supposed to collect our tickets to Houston.

Fred and I tubed to Paddington and caught a train to Plymouth, where we booked into the YMCA. Not only did we each have a private room, but the YMCA also had two full-size billiard tables, a pool table, table tennis, a cafeteria and squash courts. As I walked around, I discovered lessons in judo, typing, and French occurring simultaneously; this wasn't a YMCA - it was a small village.

Plymouth was quite modern, and Fred speculated correctly that it had been heavily bombed during the war as we launched into a full-scale walking tour the following morning. He clicked away happily at the lighthouse, and we walked past the citadel into the Barbican area of old Plymouth, visited the spot from which the Pilgrim Fathers had left, inspected the Plymouth tapestry in progress in Prysten House and continued to the bomb-gutted Charles Church, left standing as a monument to the Plymouth war dead. We spent one more night in Plymouth, celebrated my twenty-second birthday, and returned to London to join a short coach tour.

One of the reasons I was uneasy about traveling with my father was that we had not lived under the same roof since I was five years old, and therefore I had no memories of what it was like to be with him for an extended period. I was nervous. So my plan was three-fold: to keep him busy; to give him lots of things to photograph; and to surround us with other people – hence the tour we were about to start. My theory was that the proximity of other people would (for both of us) relieve the constant cloister of each other's presence. I knew that my father was easily angered by other people; the tour would provide them, and lessen the chance he would be angry with me. Ignoble, but a good plan.

We downsized our bags, left excess luggage at the Camellia Hotel and joined the tour at the Tower of London. The short tour was designed to hit all the well-known English tourist spots, allowing about twelve and a half minutes at each: on the first day it was the turn of Oxford and Stratford, via Warwick Castle. At Warwick Castle, I was devastated twice: firstly, by the twelve and a half minutes allowed to inspect such a vast and overwhelming structure, and secondly, by a pair of eyes.

As we were walking down to the Castle, a family passed us on their way up: mother, father, daughter. The daughter was slightly younger than me, and for no more than three seconds our eyes met, and my uncastellated heart was undone. In that unguarded heartbeat of visual communion there was an almost tangible sharing, a sensing of possibilities. She passed me and for a giddy moment, I thought of grabbing her hand, introducing myself, abandoning my father and the tour. Of course, I did nothing of the kind; I didn't even look over my shoulder in case she wasn't looking over hers. Later, I would write mediocre poetry about her and try to blame it all on the romantic gravitas of the Castle and my addiction to Elizabethan poets, but decades later, I have still not forgotten those eyes...

WARWICK

These castle walls have seen far more
than you or I can know,
and common sense should tell us
this glance can no more slow
the tread of time
than it can quench the sun.

But sense uncommon whispers,
into ears alive to hear -
capricious Time can stretch
this second to a year.

Grey people stand around us,
blind to a holy scene,
cadaverous and fading,
knowing not that two have been
struck by lightning on a balmy day.

chapter 27

Showdown in Sheffield

It was at atmospheric Alveston Manor, Stratford-on-Avon, where I got a taste of things to come. My father took me aside and in a voice that allowed no discussion or debate, declared:

"Son, you are not to lean on the table before, during or after meals for the duration of this tour. Do you understand?"

Yes, I understood. I understood that for the father who had missed most of my childhood, I was locked in a perpetual time-warp. I saw myself as an educated, well-travelled twenty-two year old who had demonstrated independence; he saw me as the over-protected five year old I was when he left home in early 1962. I instinctively knew that trying to reconcile this difference in perceptions would be pointless.

From Stratford, we paused outside the Cromwell-devastated Kenilworth Castle, a red blot against a grey sky, like dried blood on a dove's breast; a nod to Lichfield, birthplace of Samuel Johnson; lunch in the misty Matlocks; and then an hour wandering the stately splendour of Chatsworth, home of the Dukes of Devonshire. The day ended in Sheffield, and my relationship with my father almost did also.

After dinner in the hotel, Fred went to the room we were sharing and I stayed drinking with Steve and Brian from the tour. Fred and I had arranged that if I were to leave the hotel building, I would come up and get the room key before heading out. A few minutes after Fred had left, another chap came in and told us of the "best pub in Sheffield". Conveniently, it was still in our hotel building, although you had to go outside and in through another entrance. We had a drink there and I headed up to the room at 10.30pm to be greeted by tones of barely contained rage:

"Where have you been?"

At first, I thought he was joking, but a second look at his face confirmed he wasn't.

"I was downstairs having a drink."

"You said you would NOT leave this building without telling me."

"I didn't leave the building, I was just in another part of it."

"I went looking for you everywhere and couldn't find you."

I explained the separate entrance concept, but it made no difference. The tirade had begun.

"You know I've always been worried that you're too like your uncle Hope. You're both completely and utterly self-centred. If he hadn't been away overseas with the Navy when you were conceived, I would be convinced you are actually his child. Hope was always the spoilt one; mother and father always favoured him and you're exactly the same. I could never manage Hope and now I can't manage you. Your mother has spoilt you by letting you have your own way too much. And you care too much for people you're not actually related to. It was a mistake for me to come over here to visit you in Europe. I'm not going to interfere with your life any more." He got into his bed and turned his back on me.

Here it was: the anger, negativity and inky black moods that had led my mother to end their marriage. I had seen my father angry before, but not like this. Reason could not enter the discussion. It was pointless trying to explain the logical errors in his comments. The whole relationship was pointless. I determined to leave the tour in the morning.

The next morning, I was amazed. Father awoke and was cheerful, and there was no mention of the night before. Was it possible that he had completely forgotten the torrent he had unleashed? Was he now embarrassed by it and wanted to move on? I had no idea, but his amnesia seemed as complete as mine had been in that Swedish hospital. I decided to stay with the tour a little longer; it had been paid for after all, and it was far above my usual standard of accommodation and meals.

We passed through Windermere, crossed into Scotland at Gretna Green, and I bought a tie sporting the Elliott tartan at Ayr. Arriving in Edinburgh, I phoned Jan to arrange to meet her in York. The Edinburgh sky was a sagging grey and my spirits were in tune with it: I felt trapped between the powder keg of patriarchal fulmination and the spark of romance with an unhappily-married woman. But my spirits soon lifted, and History was once more my diversion as I became lost in the intrigues that unfolded in our guided tours of Holyrood House and Edinburgh Castle.

Jan came to York that Friday evening and again on Saturday morning. Amazingly for a Leeds native she had never been to York before, so we wandered the streets, sampling vodka in every bar, sometimes with fellow tour members, sometimes alone, always accompanied by Ricky Lee Jones singing Chuck E's in Love. We had at least sixteen vodkas each and sang along. When we finally said goodbye in front of a busload of people, I was holding the faux fur lapels of her jacket as we kissed.

"Now," she said, "I've visited York twice in twelve hours for you. Don't think this lets you off your promise of coming to Leeds."

"She seemed pretty cut up to see you go, son," my father said a few minutes later. "But your mother's not going to like the idea you're seeing a married woman." So it seemed I could expect anger from my father, but not discretion - so much for not interfering with my life any more.

The last leg of the tour took us through Lincoln and Cambridge before finally letting us off in Berkeley Square. As we staggered into the Camellia, we glimpsed two familiar faces. Derek and Dennis had just returned from Paris and regaled us with tales of French prostitutes and *beaucoup plus merde de chiens*.

Fred had two more days in London before he flew home via Hong Kong. Both days were sunny and we covered many miles together as I endeavoured to give him as much photo fodder as possible. His amnesia about Sheffield seemed to continue and he remained cheery. I caught the tube to Heathrow with him, assuming the filial duty of dragging his suitcase, and deposited him in the queue for his flight. Was that a tear in his eye as I hurried back towards the trains? My time with my father had been painful and claustrophobic, but it had certainly been educational. I had spent three weeks with him - the most time we had spent together since I was five - and I'd learnt that I never wanted to spend that long with him again.

chapter 28

Into Mexico

It snowed the next day in Selsey: Den rode into Bognor to sell his bike, while Derek and I visited Chichester where a VD test showed that he had a bad dose of gonorrhea and possible syphilis. He muttered something derogatory about the French and swallowed pills until he rattled.

A few days later, it was Christmas, and gluttony was the order of the day. Lunch was roast turkey with potatoes and beans, and pudding. Dinner was a smorgasbord: olives, cheese, pineapple, pork, sausage rolls, mince pies, pheasant, turkey, ham, and trifle. What made all this comfortable gourmandising even better was its transience; we were about to leave it all behind.

We arrived in Houston on December 28, 1978 and the U.S. customs officers were immediately suspicious of us.

"Empty your bag, please sir." I obeyed, and he ferreted through it. I took my chances that there was no law prohibiting importation of unwashed clothes.

"Where are you from?"

"Australia."

"But you've just come from England."

"That's right."

"So where were you before England?" I tried not to roll my eyes, and attempted to give him some idea.

"So are you telling me you haven't been in Australia since January? That's nearly a year ago! How have you supported yourself?"

"Savings." He looked incredulous.

"Haven't you worked anywhere in the last twelve months?"

"No." He demanded to see my traveller's cheques, and counted them. This must have convinced him I wasn't totally destitute.

"Do you know anyone in the States?"

"Yes, while I'm here I will be spending time with friends in Independence, Missouri and Binghamton in upstate New York." This finally relaxed him: clearly, if I had friends in small town USA, I must be okay.

We bussed the twenty miles from the airport into downtown Houston in warm, moist weather. Clouds perched lazily on top of the tallest buildings and after pricing hotels, we ended up in the Old Ben Milam. None of us had been to the States before, and Houston struck us as weird. The outskirts of town on the airport side consisted of ramshackle timber houses, and although the city centre was modern, it didn't seem particularly big, nor did there seem to be many people. This didn't gel with its claim to be the fifth biggest city in the U.S. Where was everybody?

We answered that question the following day on our tour to NASA. Everybody lived out in the suburbs, which were fully equipped with huge shopping centres, complete with multiple cinema complexes, restaurants and bowling alleys. As soon as work finished, everybody scampered out of the downtown area to these suburban enclaves, leaving the concrete canyons to addicts, muggers and bemused Australians. This information, and other tidbits gathered from the tour guide, proved more interesting than NASA itself. Houston was the fastest growing city in the U.S., had the world's longest main street (36 miles) and the most expensive hotel room ($2,500 per night for Astro-Village's penthouse).

The four hour bus trip from Houston to San Antonio must have crossed through three climate zones. Houston temperatures were in the mid 60s and San Antonio was literally at freezing point. We staggered across the street from the bus station and into the Nueces Hotel where we shared bathroom facilities with the neighbouring room. We walked to the Alamo, although we didn't find that much to remember, drank some Schlitz and Coors, and reactivated Derek's fear of heights by zooming to the top of the Tower of the Americas. San Antonio was more personable than Houston: a river ran through it with inviting walkways alongside, although given the surrounding temperature, it's surprising people weren't skating down it. Budweisering in another bar, we left as soon as we realised that, being neither gay nor black, we were in a distinct minority.

The next morning, $1.25 bought us scrambled eggs, hash browns, toast, jam (okay, jelly) and endless coffee at the Blue Bonnet Hotel. Now you've probably noticed that this book is not overly political, and I'm as aware as you are that America has a lot to answer for, but when you tote up the ledger, please don't forget that America invented the concept of bottomless coffee. This magnanimous humanitarian gesture alone warrants a lot of forgiveness and goodwill.

We saw coyote and deer on the way to Laredo, where we changed onto a Mexican bus for Monterrey. The countryside remained flat until about ten miles from Monterrey when we hit mountains; towns huddled in the valleys. It was 6 pm and the temperature was barely above freezing when the old Transportes del Nortes coach limped into Monterrey. This was a slight improvement on that morning in San Antonio: while we were breakfasting, it was −8 Celsius (18 Fahrenheit), which was the coldest any of us could remember being.

Despite the cold, the Hotel Villerreal was light on bed clothes and we broke out the sleeping bags for the first time since the cycling trip. The owner of the restaurant where we had dinner was also a cop. He approached us while we were eating:

"You are English, yes?"

"Yes." It was easier. Australia was often interpreted as Austria.

"I have a letter from my girlfriend in America, but my English is bad. I cannot read it. Can you tell me what it says?" Actually, his English was much worse than this and it took a lengthy "conversation", complete with gestures, to extract this information.

Between Derek's broken Spanish and our phrase book we not only managed to convey the sense of the letter for him, but also helped him write a reply. Today, they're probably married, with three fine adult sons called Derek, Dennis and Peter.

The next morning, we lingered over breakfast at our friend's restaurant for more than an hour. Two fried eggs on a fried tortilla, ham, beans and more tortillas, all washed down with café "negro". Fortified, we wandered in increasing smog east up Avenue Colon (sic!) to the House of Culture where we were turned away. After further Colonic investigation, we turned right down Zaragoza, past the Government Palace, to Zaragoza Square. On the east of the square was the Cathedral, begun in 1600, but taking 150 years to complete. The sun was out; two jumpers were no longer necessary, and in both senses, we were beginning to warm to Monterrey. Den's guidebook said that Monterrey's proximity to the U.S. meant it was relatively expensive, which augured well for the rest of the country. Street stalls offered handicrafts, cheap souvenirs, and abominable sweets. Spitting on the street appeared to be compulsory.

That evening, I had my first encounter with an avocado. I'm not sure whether avocadoes were available in Perth in the 1970s, but I'd never met one. And there they were, just in front of me in the Monterrey markets. Figuring firm was best, I bought the hardest avocado I could find. I took it back to the room and tried to dissect it with my Swiss Army knife; it was like trying to cut a block of wood. Derek and Dennis returned in the midst of my avocado-whittling, much amused.

The eight hour bus ride from Monterrey to Tampico was spectacular. After driving alongside a mountain chain for most of the morning, we climbed over a steep hill to see a valley stretching beneath us, studded with flat-topped hills like decapitated volcanoes. After Victoria, we passed through small patches of jungle and arrived in Tampico in the evening. The town was initially a puzzle: it didn't appear in Dennis's guide book and it was difficult to guess the location of the centre of town from the bus station. Our unerring cheap hotel antennae guided us to the San Antonio Motel and, bus-lagged, we crashed.

The next day we discovered the world's largest hamburgers surrounded by salad, French fries and avocado (oh, you're meant to eat it *soft*), a statue doing a Nazi salute, and Derek spotted enough exotic birds to start him mumbling about moving permanently to Mexico. The concept of permanence got my attention. For nearly a year, I'd had almost no commitments: no job, no family ties (apart from Fred's visit), no external expectations, no requirement to be anywhere at all. One day soon, the money would be exhausted, and everything would change. I would either have to go home or start earning an income somewhere, or both. I had a vision of a middle-aged version of myself, thick of waist and scant of hair, back at Social Security doing de facto interviews, clutching fading memories of my nomadic youth. I wasn't sure what alternatives were available, but I was determined to find them.

chapter 29

Psilocybinned in Palenque

The bus out of Tampico passed through riverside slums, jungle, and occasional clearings, but even in the middle of nowhere, people plodded along the roadside. It was dark by the time we got to Tuxpan, then it was on through Poza Rica to Vera Cruz, where we arrived shortly after midnight.

Next morning the harbourside was offering its wares: shark jaws, stuffed iguanas, pinball parlours and post-breakfast whores. It was an attractive town with wide streets divided by tree-lined median strips and more gringos than we'd seen anywhere else, but our sights were set further south, on the ruins of Palenque in the Yucatan Peninsula. We had one more overnight stop before getting there – Villahermosa.

On the eight hour bus ride the next day, we passed a few oil flames, indicators of Villahermosa's chief industry which had made the town both rich and expensive. The oil industry made the name Villahermosa (literally, beautiful town) sadly ironic. On the bus we met a Spanish-speaking Canadian called Barry. Arriving in Villahermosa, we went hotel searching with him, expecting his command of the language would help enormously. Thus we were sadly disappointed when we found ourselves in the worst hotel room since the Nam Wah in Penang. As soon as you got into bed, the sheets made you itch. Derek's sheet had a massive bloodstain on it: either someone had died in that bed, given birth in it, or both. The electric fan on the roof was about to fall down and the size of the cockroaches indicated they were the result of a successful cross-breeding program with lobsters. Itching and dozing, we were woken by a knock on our door in the early hours of the morning, followed by someone asking if we wanted to catch a bus to some obscure place. It was probably a standard service offered by a local entrepreneur who knew just how keen people must be to get out of those hotel rooms.

When our bus arrived in Palenque next day, we quickly booked into the Palenque Hotel, dumped our luggage, then re-boarded the bus for the ride out to the ruins. Soon, we were in another world, the centuries-old world of the Maya. Before us was a stone city, partly regurgitated by the jungle. Temples, towers, crypts, waterfalls and petrified shells all yielded to our eager explorations. Everywhere, the topography indicated there were more ruins just waiting to be scraped out of the overgrowth. The ancient city was altogether grander than the small town nearby, and far more intact than many of the Roman ruins in the Middle East. In the Temple of the Inscriptions a royal crypt had been discovered, with the occupant buried beneath a treasure of jade.

History beckoned once again: what esoteric historical formula determines that great empires must fall, usually to be replaced by something meaner and more barbaric? The mocking jungle remained insatiable, ready to swallow these bald, bold stones once more, relegating everything and everyone they represented to memory and to myth.

There were few other tourists around, and no guides, refreshment stands or postcards. In January 1979, Palenque was almost too intact to be called a ruin, too remote to be over-run with tourists, and almost too hauntingly beautiful to leave. As it turned out, we nearly didn't leave Palenque at all.

I was feeling unwell the next day, so Derek and Dennis went back to the Mayan city without me. A few hours later, they came back with big grins.

"What are you guys grinning about?"

"While we were on the way back from the ruins, we met a Mexican girl who was being followed. She joined us for safety. She spoke good English and started talking to us about magic mushrooms."

"And…?"

"The mushrooms grow on her uncle's farm and she gave us some."

They opened the bag and poured them on a bed. They didn't look magical, but I'd read Castaneda, and knew a little of the effects of the mushrooms' main chemical, psilocybin.

"Do we cook them?"

"I think you can cook them, but you don't have to. She did say to wash them though."

"How many are we supposed to eat?"

"She didn't say."

We counted them: there were thirty-six. Perfect. We ate twelve each.

It took a while to take effect. Suddenly, Dennis burst out laughing.

"What's up?"

He burst out laughing again. After more basic questioning interspersed with laughter, we got the answer:

"I'm laughing because I know what you guys are thinking! I can read your minds! Every time you say something I knew what you were going to say before you said it!"

Derek was looking at us strangely because our faces were contorting. All of us experienced some distortion of time and space. We went outside and sat in the courtyard, which suddenly became a jungle to us.

"What sort of bird was that?" I asked Derek as something flew past.

"That's a tittering flitwidget," he replied.

"I knew that tittering flitwidget when it was a white pointer."

And so it went on as we rolled with laughter in this most amusing of all possible universes.

The afternoon stretched into evening and in the mist of our unreality, we asked a few serious questions:

"How long do you think it will take us to sober up from this?"

"Do you think we should ever leave this place? Maybe we can just stay here and keep eating mushrooms forever?"

We simply didn't know the answer to the first question, but we knew the answer to the second: if we didn't make a determined choice to leave tomorrow, there was a good chance we never would. We would camp in the jungle next to the Mayan pyramids, sustained by the vitamin B12 and psychedelia of the mushrooms until we were overtaken by malnutrition, middle-age and madness. As an alternative to a lifetime in the public service though, it still had something to recommend it.

"Maybe we'll sober up if we eat something." It seemed to make sense, and we were short on alternatives, so we walked (normally, we hoped) into the hotel restaurant. I ordered a clear soup, which was a mistake. After I started eating, it occurred to me that I was taking a very long time. If I took too long eating my soup, then the waiter would notice we were high; I had to eat faster. The faster I ate, the hotter the soup got, but the more determined I was not to show I was high by eating too slowly. Then I looked down. My bowl of soup was at least ten feet deep. There was no way I'd finish it, but I had to try or the waiter would know something was up. Our panic at trying to look normal and our attempts to suppress the hysterical giggling that ensued gave us away entirely. Fortunately, the waiter couldn't have cared less.

The next morning the decision was made: we were not going to die old and wasted in Palenque, ruins amongst the ruins, but elsewhere, and in more mundane ways. We boarded the bus back to Villahermosa and drove away from one possible future towards a horizon of certain uncertainty.

chapter 30

Jungle Ruins and Ocean Terrors

After twelve hours in buses with screaming kids, we arrived in Merida and found the Alamo Hotel. Merida was cheerful: smaller and cleaner than Monterrey; less slummy and sprawling than Tampico; less modern than Vera Cruz; and dotted with colonial buildings. The streets were all numbers: from the Alamo we wandered up 69 Street to a small square with a church, then a left into 56 Street took us into the heart of town. In the evening we watched chaperoned young couples taking the air in the main square.

Merida was the jumping-off point for another set of Mayan ruins – Uxmal. Uxmal's layout was spacious and dominated by the thirty metre high Pyramid of the Magician, which had apparently been built in one night by a witch-raised dwarf. I'm not sure which was the dwarf's greater miracle – building the pyramid in one night or getting something like that approved by the local government planning department in under twenty-four hours. At any rate, it proved immensely useful for the priestly class who used to cut the hearts out of living victims with a flint knife at the top of the pyramid and throw the still-twitching bodies down the steps. Low, dense foliage surrounded the Uxmal complex, rather than the imposing jungle of Palenque. Den and I explored at our leisure while Derek disappeared for long periods, chasing birds through the bush.

Waking from a poor sleep punctuated by ants, mosquitoes and traffic noise, we left Merida for yet more Mayan and Toltec ruins – those at Chichen Itza in Piste. We arrived after a short bus trip, found a cheap hotel, and headed to the ruins. Through the market place we found the Temple of War, checked out the acoustics at the whispering wall and climbed the El Castillo pyramid. If we'd been there at the autumn or spring equinox, we could have seen a shadow image of the feathered serpent Quetzalcoatl. Across the road, we checked out the observatory where Derek developed a migraine and crashed for the rest of the day; ironically this meant he ended the day much healthier than Dennis or me.

So far, this book has contained at least two extremely helpful diet tips for travellers: do not eat deep-fried cheese balls in Kathmandu or mashed potato sandwiches anywhere. Here is another: do not eat pork in Piste. Den and I ate at the Fiesta restaurant and by the time we realised the set menu was a rip-off, we couldn't be bothered leaving. We both chose rice, boiled pork, crème caramel and coffee. The charge was 70 pesos for a meal that was only worth 30-40 pesos. Worse was to come: lurking in the overpriced meal was Monteczuma's revenge. During the night, Den and I were both struck down with diarrhea and vomiting: for me it was short, sharp and violent; unfortunately for Den, his was episodic and continued right through the night. One thing about stomachs: they know poison when they see it and they know how to get rid of it.

We spent the next day recuperating, shuddering at the thought or mention of food, and grimacing at a disgustingly healthy Derek. The following day was a bewilderment of bus trips. We caught a bus from Piste to Valladolid where a woman stopped breastfeeding her child to clean up after a hen, one of a pair she had tied together by the legs. From Valladolid, we boarded a bus to Tizimin but it had a flat battery. After several attempts to push-start it, we changed to a newer bus and arrived in Tizimin at noon where we drank coffee waiting for a connection to Rio Lagartos. When we arrived in Rio Lagartos, we didn't realise it, because there were no signs and the driver was unable to understand our query. So, thinking that Rio Lagartos was the end of the run, and the bus was clearly moving on, we stayed aboard. The end of the run turned out to be San Felipe, despite the fact the bus had Rio Lagartos on the front. Thus, we spent the night in San Felipe, a few kilometres west of Lagartos at the northernmost point of the Yucatan peninsula.

With each bus trip during the day, the locals had become more and more curious about us; at San Felipe, the curiosity was completely undisguised. Obviously, very few gringos made it here; perhaps we were the first Australians. When we asked the bus driver about hotels, he pointed us towards a shop. The shop owner seemed to know what we wanted, but he disappeared for about half an hour, leaving us as captive curiosities for his abandoned customers. When he reappeared, he led us across the road to a building which doubled as the local cinema and hotel. It was an outdoor cinema with bench seats. There was a projection room and three small hotel rooms; needless to say, the other two were unoccupied.

After a sleepless night in our mosquito-filled room above the Cinema Marrufo, we rose early and walked down to the lagoon where the fishing boats were returning with their catches of pike, garfish, Spanish flags and skippies. Felipe was a friendly and peaceful little place, but the road beckoned; we souvenired an ancient movie poster each from the floor of Cinema Marrufo, retraced our steps to Valladolid, and then to Puerto Juarez.

It was a short ferry trip across clear, choppy water to Isla Mujeres, where we uncharacteristically planned to spend about six days. According to Den's guidebook, the island featured a coral reef, two Mayan ruins, lagoons and topless sunbathers, some of whom apparently were women – it seemed an unbeatable combination.

More discussions ensued about future plans: Derek was thinking of buying a car and driving around the U.K. while I was driving around with mum and dad, who were shortly to arrive. We thought after that we'd go to Spain together. Dennis was thinking of visiting Spain while Derek and I were in the U.K., then on to Athens and the Greek islands before returning home. I wanted to go through France on the way to Spain, then down to Morocco, overland to Cairo, up through the islands to Athens, then home.

We curtailed our time on the island due to windy weather. One day, while Den and Mick from the Isle of Wight lazed on the beach, Derek and I decided to explore the island. Two thirds of the way along our map of the island was something irresistible - a skull and crossbones pinpointed Ruinas del Pirata Mundaca (Ruins of Mundaca the Pirate). Not long after we set off, Derek dived into the bushes to attend to a call of nature; he was dissuaded by nature of another sort as a metre-long snake slithered in front of him. Mundaca's ruins proved as invisible as they were irresistible, so we continued on past Garrafon Beach to the El Faro Lighthouse and the Mayan ruin at the island's tip. Due to its exposed position, this ruin was in worse shape than Dennis and I after our meal at the misnamed Fiesta Restaurant.

The next day we left the island, leaving Mick at Puerto Juarez; he caught a bus to Cancun and we went to Merida where we stayed at the Hotel Posada del Angel. The following day was nine hours on a bus to Villahermosa, the highlight of which centred on Dennis. At a small town in the middle of nowhere the usual mob of kids boarded the bus selling curried oranges, enchiladas and other *divertissements* for the coach-locked. Den fancied a bag of popcorn and, finding it cost three pesos, gave the kids a five peso coin and took the popcorn, leaving his hand outstretched waiting for his change, while talking to Derek. Unfortunately, the outstretched hand contained more money and as the kid gave Den his two pesos change, he helped himself to another five pesos, and fled.

Den was still smarting over the loss when we checked into our most expensive hotel room yet, the Hotel Maria Dolores which cost 416 pesos (about $6 each). Derek joined him in grumbling about this, but it was a great room, and we already knew Villahermosa was expensive.

After an early start towards Tuxtla Gutierrez, our bus climbed through a mountain range into cloud. The mist was so thick at one stage that the only thing visible through the front windscreen was about five metres of the white line in the middle of the road. The roadside was littered with crosses commemorating dead drivers. The mist cleared as we reached the last row of hills and the view was spectacular: a sudden drop to a flat plain with another mountain range in the background; Tuxtla was on the plain, and it had taken 7 ½ hours to get there. We changed busses in Tuxtla and drove through more mountains to San Cristobal de las Casas, which reminded us of a cleaner version of Kathmandu: altitude made the air cold and thin, and it was surrounded by mountains.

We wandered from the Hotel Capri next morning, up the hill to the cathedral and then down to a café where the freaks gathered and where we discovered sangria.

"Hey, where you guys from?"

"Australia."

"Great. Hey, don't go up near the cathedral, it's dangerous."

"We've just come from there – why is it dangerous?"

"The local Indians still attack gringos, even in daytime. Don't go there again, man."

We caught a sleepless all-night bus ride to Oaxaca to save money and arrived at 5 a.m. to find the town in the throes of preparing for a visit from the new Pope, although I didn't think he would be impressed by the local market's voodoo shop with its potions, dead hummingbirds and disemboweled toucans. I spent most of the day getting my visa renewed while Derek and Dennis headed off to Mitlan. We met up again in the evening, downed some octopus tacos and then another all-night sleepless bus ride followed to Puerto Angel, enlivened by conversation with a Canadian girl called Shiralee.

Now it may have been because we were jaded from not having slept for two nights, but Puerto Angel didn't seem to have much to offer. We lazed on the beach for a while, made friends with some horses, and then made our way to Puerto Escondido. Shiralee had told us we could stay in basic cabanas for $1 per night; we found them and headed to the beach. I had been in the same clothes without a shower for the three days and nights since Villahermosa and definitely needed some humanisation. Before we hit the water, we bumped into Mick again. He had headed to Escondido because we had told him it came highly recommended, but had taken the inland route.

The four of us plunged eagerly into the brackish water and gradually the accretions of too many miles and not enough sleep washed away. We looked back at the few basic restaurants along the shoreline and began to choose one in which to celebrate: it was 27 January 1979, and we had been on the road for exactly one year.

We left the water first and a few minutes later, Mick stormed out, seemingly irate.

"I thought I was going to die out there! I saw something huge and brown in the trough of a wave and then I realised it didn't have a dorsal fin – it was a huge turd! I know an Australian turd when I see one!" accused Mick.

"Well, it was a long bus trip," one of us muttered sheepishly.

chapter 31

A Year on the Road

Our anniversary dinner was spaghetti marinara loaded with oysters, prawns and shellfish, washed down with Negra Modelo and Cerveza Superior at a place called (echoes of Billy Joel) "the Italian restaurant". Puerto Escondido was all beach, cheap food and more beach. Whole fried red schnapper cost $2. Pancakes covered with fresh fruit and syrup cost $1 at the Blue Fly café just next to our cabanas. You could eat well and sleep in Escondido for $5 a day, and we did, as too many cerveza-fuelled rambling discussions about Uri Geller, Rasputin and U.F.O.s took place under endless stars that mocked our pontifications.

Three days later, Puerto Escondido was just another place vanishing from the rear window of a bus as we headed into our second year on the road. Twelve months away from home was significant: if I'd been trying to prove anything to anyone, I'd probably done it by now, but I knew that I wasn't traveling for anyone but myself. So why go home at all? Lack of money was one reason, although I could probably find some way of working in England; attenuated friendships was another reason. How long an absence could friendships survive? I had no idea, just a sneaking suspicion that if I stayed away more than two years, there mightn't be much left.

Other parts of the world were undergoing rapid change: according to *Time*, the Shah had left for Egypt, and Iran was now under the control of Khomeini who was described as "enigmatic", which I suppose was code for "we really don't know what the heck this guy's going to do."

Acapulco arrived and we spent our first night there just off the beach at the Hotel Sevillano, before transferring to the Hotel Coliseum which sounded much grander (if somewhat riskier), but was half the price. By night at La Quebrada, cliff divers brandishing flaming torches hurtled seawards to extinguish, sizzling, amidst the applause of the admiring timid.

We hired the cheapest game fishing boat in Acapulco; I guess no-one else wanted to head to the open ocean in an identical replica of the boat from Gilligan's Island. The marlin and sailfish gave us a big miss, but Den caught a mackerel tuna and amazingly, I jagged a yellow-bellied sea snake. Knowing it was highly poisonous, I was all for cutting the line, but the captain seemed to think it was worth risking his life to keep the hook and managed to remove it safely.

The next day, we were in an air-conditioned express bus to Taxco with only a few other passengers. We had only been on the road a short time when a noxious odour filled the bus. The three of us looked at each other. After each of us had replied negatively to the question "Was that you?", we started to look with suspicion at our fellow passengers. As we were the only gringos on the bus, they were looking at us with even greater suspicion. The smell of raw sewerage intensified and at one point the driver stopped the bus to open the roof vents. We were caught in perpetual motion between fits of stifled laughter and gagging: the more we laughed, the more we inhaled, the more we gagged. The more we laughed, the more our fellow passengers glared at us and we knew they had come to the conclusion that only gringos could smell *that* bad. Perhaps they were going to throw us off the bus in the quest for breathable air?

Eventually, a very drained-looking Mexican staggered from the toilet at the back of the bus; no-one had known it was occupied – he had taken up residence before the bus had departed. The culprit identified, the smell gradually subsided and at Iguala a SWAT team boarded the bus and hosed the toilet out with disinfectant. I found myself wondering whether the offender had any German ancestry; if only I had a Rotel business card to pass to him – he would have been welcomed by them as a true star.

Taxco, sitting prosperously on silver, seemed a blend of Italy and Spain, with small plazas, red-tiled roofs and steep cobbled roads contorting in all directions. After a brief lunch enlivened by Den pouring salt in his coffee by mistake, we went separate ways exploring the town. I found an old (and unfortunately closed) Spanish church and a great view of the town and the main cathedral.

Garlic fish and beer were demolished in the square outside St Prisca's church that night as Den developed laryngitis, then lost his voice completely. The next morning, Den was still off-colour and Mick had a dose of Monty's. A soporific bus ride later and we were in Mexico City. We got a taxi to the guidebook-recommended Hotel Cathedral, just behind the old cathedral and Constitution Plaza. Mexico City seemed nothing like the rest of the country (even Acapulco): cosmopolitan and posh, walking down its streets you could imagine yourself in London, Paris, or any large western city.

The underground was twice as modern as London's: squarish orange carriages ran on rubber wheels and there was no graffiti on the walls. We checked out the Anthropological Museum and the free zoo, and booked tickets for Tepic. After breakfast one morning, the four of us walked up into Juarez, past the Latin American tower, and caught a bus out to the main terminal where we said goodbye to Mick who was traveling home to Dallas.

During the fifteen hour bus trip to Tepic, when not reading McLuhan's *Gutenberg Galaxy*, I was hypnotised by the desolation of semi-desert: low rolling swells of hills in the foreground with looming waves of mountains in the distance. When we arrived in Tepic at 2 a.m., it was freezing, and as we staggered towards a distant hotel sign, I tripped and fell, thus occasioning much merriment. We slept late at the Hotel Nayar, breakfasted at the bus station and lounged around the main square before boarding a bus to San Blas. As the bus was leaving Tepic, there was a squeal of rubber as a young guy reversed his car in front of us to stop the bus. Was it a hijack? A robbery? No, he simply wanted to stop the bus so his mum could get on.

Between Tepic and San Blas, the scenery changed from mountains to tropical lowlands. From the Flamingo Hotel we walked to the beach, which proved to have dark sand and murky water; not nearly as attractive as Escondido, but the water was warm and the waves were good.

We spent a day on the beach, and another on a jungle cruise with Pancho. For two and a half hours we cruised in a canoe through the mangroves meeting raccoons, coati (a cross between a raccoon and a badger), rare birds, iguanas and tortoises. We were on a different planet and, as we occasionally emerged from the shade of the mangroves into a clearing, the laser beam of the sun was an epiphany.

Back in Tepic, after a *huevos con chorizo* breakfast served by a truculent waitress, we caught a bus to Mazatlan, point of departure for La Paz and our last sight of mainland Mexico after six weeks in the country. The bay at Mazatlan was much wider than Acapulco, with three sizeable islands offshore. At the Hotel San Jorge, one street from the seafront, our fourteen-sided room contained four single beds. Down at the front, the fishing trophies of the day were hanging for all to see: a sailfish, a marlin, a blue shark and a hammerhead shark. We sunned ourselves, walked along the bay, and ate vast quantities of seafood.

Our ferry was called Aztec, but "ferry" seemed a demeaning term for a ship the size of the Turkmenia which provided us with proper cabins. As mainland Mexico slipped away behind us, I had another sleepless night, because my mind was too active. What on earth was I going to do when I got back to Fremantle? I had no career planned out. Work implied making a commitment, and I had become adept at avoiding those. With my rekindled passion for history, I could possibly do a Masters degree focusing on investigation of Joseph Smith and the Mormon church. But what would I do for money? Having now lived away from home for over a year, I knew that it would be difficult moving back in with mum and dad. A place of my own would be ideal, but I would get back from this trip totally broke; that dream was surely years away. To sleep, perchance to dream of the public service – it was too risky – better to stay awake and trawl through possibilities, *invent* them if necessary; to locate an alternative that would avoid the bureaucratic vortex.

chapter 32

On Avoiding Idaho and Stingrays

While Iraq and Syria were discussing a possible merger and the Pope was attacking the influence of Marxism on liberation theology during his Latin American visit, we arrived at the very definition of nowhere – we were still 17 km from La Paz. A 10 peso bus ride through cactus desert brought us there and we discovered it was a duty-free port. The Hotel Lori was near the crystal-clear water where we spent the following day. When I gazed up periodically from working on my tan and *Gutenberg*, I saw a three-masted sailing ship, pelicans, waders, man-o-war birds and a couple assembling a large folding boat.

"We're from Idaho."

"That's nice." They'd caught me in an anti-American moment.

"It's colder than a miner's arsehole in Idaho now."

Unwanted information, unwanted images of them running around subterranean caverns with rectal thermometers. I made a mental note to give Idaho a miss and decided I definitely wasn't going to roll onto my stomach.

We caught a night bus to Loreto where we spent two days fishing, swimming and playing table tennis. Again, the water was crystal-clear and the fishing was good from the local jetty, with mountainous islands off-shore.

Once when we arrived at the jetty, someone had landed a large stingray which was lying on the planks of the jetty looking decidedly malevolent.

"*Peligroso! Peligroso!*", they cried at us.

We had a choice: this either meant "get off our jetty you ugly gringos" or "we think you look stupid enough to pick up this stingray and try to cuddle it and we advise against it". We opted for the latter, marveling at the succinctness of Spanish, and gave the ray a wide berth.

Rising early one morning we were greeted by a fairy ring around the moon and a crescent-shaped fog bank out to sea. Both mornings and evenings at Loreto were cold enough to make jumpers mandatory, the coldest we'd experienced for some time. We made friends with Manuel, tried to communicate across the language barrier, and learnt that the road between Santa Rosalia and Tijuana had been wiped out for five months, so our plans had to change. We considered catching a ferry back across the Gulf of California from Santa Rosalia to Guyamas and heading to Tucson, crossing the border at Nogales.

As the bus was full, we had to stand for the entire 135 kilometre trip to Mulege, a much more commercial town than Loreto. The first hotel we approached wouldn't let us stay, and we figured it had something to do with Den's appearance: he was wearing a Harris Tweed coat with a ceramic mouse on his lapel, his floppy Barry McKenzie vinyl hat and sunglasses at 8pm. I could hardly blame them.

Our short stay in Mulege was noteworthy for two things: a small dog snuck up behind me noiselessly and sank its teeth into my leg, much to the amusement of the others; and our meeting with Tom. Tom was a Canadian who had studied at university in Vancouver. While studying there, he had built a cabin in a huge old hollow log in the forest on the outskirts of town and lived in it for two years. During that time, only two people had stumbled across it. We were impressed, and because he had spent the previous night camped in a forest, we let him sleep on the floor of our room that night.

The four of us spent the next day on a rocky outcrop by the mission on the edge of town with man-o-war birds wheeling overhead. Tom mended his pack, played blues harmonica, and did a good job of sketching us all. We talked philosophy and worked on our tans. From the outcrop, we could see both directions along the river: west to the mountains and east to the town and a glimpse of sea beyond.

When we came back down to town we discovered that the road had just reopened and we could revert to our original plan, so we farewelled Tom and were soon at Santa Rosalia's Central Hotel. Santa Rosalia was built on a copper mine and looked like a wild West town: the buildings were mainly timber and there was no evidence of Spanish colonisation. We spent the afternoon reading, noting that *Time* had upgraded Khomeini from "enigmatic" to "stern" and in the evening joined the locals cruising around the square, to a jukebox soundtrack of Queen, the Eagles and Boney M.

As the kilometres rolled past the next morning, the cacti gradually disappeared and we rolled into Guerrero Negro, where rusty automobiles came to die. Having located a cheap room, we started out on the 12 kilometre walk to the main attraction, whale spotting. We were soon picked up by a Mexican in a Cougar with three CB aerials on the trunk and an embroidered picture of the Virgin Mary on the ceiling. A few minutes later we were at the coast and the whales were there in force, being outnumbered only by the number of Americans in Winnebagos. Eventually, we began the walk back and were soon picked up by one of the Winnebago-cocooned Americans we had met. These unsolicited lifts had reduced a potential 24 kilometre walk to almost nothing and the attractions of hitchhiking as a viable mode of transport suddenly became obvious.

The next day we left Mexico after a visit of nearly two months. After two buses failed to show, we caught one mid-morning for the thirteen hour journey to Tijuana, and had to stand for most it. The road was still in a bad condition from washouts, and littered with flooded cars (often with only their bonnets and roofs visible) until we passed San Quintin. We arrived in Tijuana at 11pm, found the Hotel San Francisco, and I had my first shower in six days.

We had no desire to stay in Tijuana as it wasn't really Mexico anymore, so early the next morning we walked the few blocks to the U.S. border and straight through both Mexican and American sections, which was just as well because there could have been some paperwork problems. When we first left the U.S. and entered Mexico, we hadn't handed in our white card to let the U.S. officials know we had left; as far as they knew, we were still somewhere in the U.S. Also, on leaving Mexico, we didn't hand in our red Mexican tourist card on the Mexican side (which saved us $5). As far as the Mexicans know, we're still there.

"Manuel, I am determined to catch these three Australian hippies!"

"But sir, it's been forty years. Is it worth it?"

"Of course it's worth it! Every administration since 1979 has been determined to catch these three renegades. I'm sure they're holed up somewhere, probably in the jungle near Palenque, out of their gourds on magic mushrooms and fathering countless illegitimate children to naïve village girls. Their continued flagrant violation of their visas is a blot on our national pride, not to mention our social security budget – they must be found!"

chapter 33

The Risks of Running

It was only a twelve mile bus ride to San Diego where we booked into the Shaw Hotel and I overindulged in second-hand bookstores. We walked up Broadway to 12th Street, then three miles to the San Diego zoo, which was located in a park with museums. The $3 entry fee was well worth it: the big stars were the only koalas in the world outside Australia. The funniest part of the zoo was the enclosure containing a herd of giant tortoises: the sight of these ancient, wrinkled armour-plated buffoons attempting to get around and even *over* each other was proof that God has a sense of humour.

Having left the zoo, it was harder to leave the park itself as we gazed at the gaggles of gorgeous bikini-clad rollerskaters shooting past, but eventually we fought our way through the morass of mobile mammaries and spent the afternoon in a triple-feature: The Gauntlet, Sudden Death and Enter the Tiger. After the movies, I began to feel slightly paranoid: after two relatively laid-back months in Mexico, we were now back in the land of shoot-first-and-ask-questions-later.

Anaheim was our next stop, with snow-clad mountains in sight, only a few miles from long beaches and 70 degree Fahrenheit temperatures. We walked the mile from our hotel to Disneyland where the $8 entry fee for a day of fantastic rides made the Perth Royal Show seem like a bush picnic. Nearby, we discovered something completely new to us: soy milk. "Look how expensive this stuff is!" I sniffed with disgust. "Of course it's expensive," retorted Derek, "can you imagine how long it takes to find the nipple on a soya bean?"

Steinbeck's Salinas Valley passed our bus window during the twelve hour journey to San Francisco where we booked into a cheap hotel in 7th Street before hitting the streets. From Chinatown to Fisherman's Wharf, past steaming crabs and streaming joggers out to the jetty for a view of the Golden Gate bridge and Alcatraz, and back via cable car. While Derek and I stayed in that night, Den found a bar full of drunks who shouted him drinks until closing time; he also found a wallet with marijuana and papers in it. He returned in an altered state at 2.30 a.m.; the wonder was that he returned at all.

Arriving in Fresno, we realised we'd made a mistake: we couldn't catch a bus from there to Sequoia National Park as planned, so we bussed back to Merced and headed to Yosemite. At Mariposa (about twenty miles from Yosemite) our bus stopped outside a café. Most of the passengers ambled inside for coffee, but we'd spotted a supermarket on a rise above the café and decided we'd buy some cheap chocolate. Den stayed back to make sure the bus didn't leave without us while Derek and I ran to the store. We bought the chocolates quickly, headed for the checkout with the shortest queue, paid, and started running back to the bus.

We were running across the carpark when suddenly a police van squealed to a halt in front of us, cutting us off from the bus. I spotted rifle racks in the back window as two gum-chewing, overweight, pistol-packing cliché-cops got out and faced us. They looked at the chocolate in our hands.

"Can I see your sales receipt for those candy bars?"

I couldn't believe it. The Clint Eastwood movies were true; Derek and I were about to be blown away in a car park outside a Wal-Mart.

"We didn't get a receipt." I tried to sound brave, realising these could be my last words on the planet.

"Get in the van." It wasn't a suggestion.

"But we're with that bus down there and it's about to leave."

"Don't worry. The other officer will detain the bus."

Derek and I got in the van and he drove us the fifty yards to the store, which contained about twenty checkouts, each of which had several customers at it.

"Which cashier?" We pointed her out.

Now it seemed to me the logical thing would have been for us all to approach this cashier and sort it out privately, but apparently not. The cop only took two steps inside the store and then bellowed in a voice that demanded full attention from every citizen within earshot.

"Did these guys pay for these candy bars?"

"Yes." It wasn't the answer he wanted, so he increased the volume.

"I said, did these guys pay for these candy bars?"

"Yes."

Disillusioned at not having intervened in the progress of a major felony, the cop returned us to the bus. I desperately wanted to make a sarcastic comment, but knew that the result would be some poor teenage employee of Wal-Mart would have to mop up my brains from the carpark.

Back in the bus, we told an incredulous Den the full story.

"You know the weird part?", I asked.

"What?"

"If we'd just been walking, it wouldn't have happened. It was all because we were running – we were arrested for running in California, the place that invented jogging! This is supposed to be the most enlightened and liberal State in America – imagine what would have happened if we'd been in Alabama!"

Our brush with the Keystone Cops stood in stark contrast to the sublime beauty of Yosemite: 2,000 feet above sea level with mountains towering another 3,500 to 5,000 feet above that; it was blanketed with thick snow. We booked into a room in Camp Curry ("Be on the alert for gay Indians," quipped Derek) for three nights and when Derek learned that 220 species of birds lived in the Park, we were lucky it wasn't three months.

During our time there, we visited the 2,000 foot drop of Yosemite Falls, walking through thick snow drifts, past crystal clear streams and rivers; caught the free bus to Badger Pass and watched skiers poncing around; illicitly hand-fed the raccoons, and drank beer in the Yosemite Lodge. It was there Derek and I met Anne and Kerry from Adelaide while Den got caught up in a card game. As the price of drinks was exorbitant, Derek and I went back to Anne and Kerry's room and talked until 1.30 a.m., making tentative plans to meet them in London.

The next morning Derek shook sugar from a container into his coffee, then realised it was actually parmesan cheese. We were still laughing as we hiked up the John Muir trail for a couple of miles towards Deer Falls and although no fresh snow had fallen since we arrived, the heavy drifts meant that we all fell over at least once.

We retraced our steps through Mariposa the next day (this time staying on the bus), through endless hick towns and walnut tree fields to Bakersfield, immortalised in the Stones' "Faraway Eyes". At the Rancho Bakersfield Motel, we found ourselves surrounded by an abundance of truckies and middle-aged whores, socialising under gigantic neon banners exhorting "LET'S EAT!" We did, but deciding the motel bar was a non-event, wandered into town and eventually found ourselves in a bar called Tex's Barrelhouse. When we sat down, the waitress asked to see our ID (Den was insulted; I was flattered) and having produced our student cards, we spent the rest of the evening drinking expensive beer and watching pot-bellied cowboys dancing to country music. It seemed ironic that this was the week *Time* magazine decided to write a feature article on The Clash.

Two bus journeys later (via Barstow), we arrived in Las Vegas at 8.30pm as the town was waking up. We booked into a luxurious triple room in the Village Motel, two streets from the downtown strip for $6 each per night, and wandered the streets in a neon daze. We soon discovered that you could live incredibly cheaply in Las Vegas: casinos offered meals for 99 cents that included steak, two eggs, potato and toast, and this became our staple diet. We found a Bloody Mary party at the Westward Ho Casino and had six free Bloody Marys each. Some casinos offered free shows and all had waitresses bringing around free drinks for slot machine players. We had a good system for this: some of the slot machines ran off 1 cent pieces, so we would each change a dollar into cents and take up residence at a machine. It took more than an hour to lose $1 at this rate, but smiling at the hovering waitresses and unleashing an Australian accent meant that we'd each had about six free Scotches in this time.

We spent our last night in Vegas watching a group called the Garfin Gathering, drinking too many free drinks and (in my case) smoking too many Lucky Strikes. The next morning we all felt like Vegas had left its lights on high, and we were a very quiet trio boarding a bus in the direction of the Grand Canyon. We passed the Hoover Dam and while waiting to change buses in Kingman, began talking with Alan, a disc jockey from St Louis, Missouri. Considering our fragile states, he must have been a great conversationalist, because it almost seemed like saying goodbye to an old friend when we hopped on the bus for Flagstaff, where we arrived late and crashed in an anonymous motel two doors from the terminal.

It was a fairly short trip to the canyon and we arrived at the Bright Angel Hotel long before our room was ready, so we left our luggage with the bellboy and explored. The canyon gaped deceptively one mile deep and twelve miles wide outside the hotel and earthquakes just weren't worth thinking about.

When our room was ready, it proved to be huge, consisting of two complete bedrooms joined by a bathroom. One bedroom contained a double bed and a single, the other had two double beds. Obviously, the former room would have sufficed (we had long ago got used to sleeping top and tail in a double bed) and I returned to reception.

"I'm sorry sir, we can't let that room out separately as it's a suite."

"Even though the adjoining bathroom is fully lockable from both sides to ensure privacy?"

"That's right sir."

I decided to sublet the room myself and looked around the lobby. The first girl I asked came and inspected the room, but she had somewhere else to stay. Shortly afterwards, she returned with another woman who wanted the room for her boyfriend and herself; they had just been turned away from reception because the hotel was full. She paid us $20 (we had paid a total of $40) so everyone was happy. I started to consider a career in property management.

As the setting sun draped dramatic shadows across the Canyon, it seemed a fitting place for our traveling trio to finally disband.

chapter 34

The Trio Disbands

It was Sunday, 11 March 1979 and we'd been on the road together for 408 days. Den was following through on his decision to be back in Perth for the Australian winter, to resume inhaling his share of the family's drycleaning fumes. We bussed back to Flagstaff together, and said succinct goodbyes at the station. I was catching a late bus east; Derek and Dennis were catching an even later one to Los Angeles. We'd travelled tens of thousands of kilometres and half a world together; Derek and Dennis had become the brothers I'd never had.

My plan from this point was to have two more major stops in the States: Independence, Missouri and Binghamton, New York. Independence was the headquarters of the RLDS Church and I was going to raid the archives for nineteenth-century material while staying with the Robinsons, an Australian family who were distant relatives. Binghamton was conveniently located near some of the early sites of Mormonism and I would be staying with the Zimmermans, whose son Dan had stayed with my parents in Perth. I braced for a marathon bus ride.

Rolling past my window: 11 pm - Winslow, Arizona (34 Fahrenheit); midnight – Holbrook; 1.15 am – Fort Courage (home of F Troop); 4.20

am – Albuquerque (Bulldog City); 7.20 am – Santa Rosa (breakfast stop); onto a fresh bus at uninspiring Amarillo; 5pm – Cordell; 7pm – Oklahoma City; changed onto a New York bus; 9.30pm – Tulsa; midnight – Joplin, Missouri.

At 2 am, I boarded the bus from Joplin to Kansas City, arriving there at 5.45am and was told that a local bus was the quickest way to Independence, where I arrived at dawn. I breakfasted on hotcakes and coffee in the centre of town, desperately trying not to count how many hours I'd been awake. A quick phone call and I was at the Robinsons', my filthy clothes contaminating their washing machine.

For the next few days, I searched the archives, photocopied relevant material and purchased books, mailed it all home, enjoyed the Robinsons' hospitality and tried to reciprocate as best I could by helping babysit their kids and cooking pavlovas.

Having survived one non-stop bus trip halfway across the continent, I signed on for the other half, feeling vaguely uneasy. As the eastern half of the United States sped past my window I felt like a voyeur locked in a perpetual peep show. I was glimpsing the lives of thousands of people who didn't know I was there. This one-way transaction made strange demands of me, but asked nothing of them; observation *was* participation. Somehow, even the existence of these other people seemed to demand some sort of commitment from me. I withdrew into a mental trench: what was outside my window was too complex and diverse to engage with; I couldn't try. I became unduly ecstatic about a wonderful, undemanding chocolate éclair in Saranton, and recognised once again the ease with which I could be seduced into a solitary existence.

The Zimmermans, devout members of the RLDS church, were scarily normal. We saw a production of My Fair Lady, a basketball game, I did some painting at their business and they even trusted me to drive their

Fiat convertible. I'm not entirely sure they enjoyed me playing Lou Reed records really loudly for their two teenagers, but they were diplomatic about it. Together we visited some of the key sites linked with the beginning of Mormonism.

Mormonism began officially in 1830 under the leadership of Joseph Smith Jr., a native of Palmyra, New York. The official story goes something like this: in his teenage years, Joseph was unsure which church to join and made this a matter of prayer. As a result, he had a vision (ca. 1820) in a grove at Palmyra in which he was told by God not to join any of the existing churches because they were all "abominations". They were so far off-track that what was needed was not just Reformation but a *Restoration*. God wanted Joseph to restore the true gospel. A couple of years later, Joseph was told by angelic visitation of the existence of golden plates, recording the history of ancient inhabitants of America; he later gained access to these plates and translated them into what has become known as the *Book of Mormon*. This was the story most of my family enthusiastically adopted.

At the end of my visit, Dale drove me into New York City and Kennedy Airport. It was an amazingly generous gesture as it was nearly 400 miles for the round trip, taking him away from his business all day. After a nine hour wait at the airport, I was above American soil, and soon, Gatwick Airport rose to meet me.

Arriving in Selsey, I discovered that Dennis had recently departed for Paris on the first leg of his journey home, leaving behind a mountain of stuff for Derek and me either to use or throw out. The next few weeks were loosely planned: my parents were about to arrive and I would spend six weeks traveling with them, after which Derek and I would borrow his dad's car and continue driving around the U.K., making the most of the spring weather.

After my unsuccessful traveling experiences with my father, I was a little hesitant about spending so long in mum and dad's company – would it work out? Would we get on each other's nerves? Underneath this was a fear that fourteen months on the road had changed me for the worse: I knew I was fiercely protective of my own space, and I suspected I was drifting towards an insularity driven by experiential overload. As it turned out, I needn't have worried.

Mum (who is two years younger than Queen Elizabeth and maintains a very similar hairstyle) and dad arrived with the news that *The West Australian* had just published an article I had written on Malta, and as we collected their luggage, I observed yet again that strange phenomenon, luggage carousel lobotomy. Why is it that 99% of human beings wedge themselves up tight against the airport luggage carousels, apparently convinced that their luggage will be the very next item through? Of course it's not, but in the meantime, they successfully obscure the view and obstruct the movement of the poor souls whose luggage has *actually* arrived. Why doesn't it occur to them that if *everyone* stayed about three metres back from the carousel until they saw their luggage, we'd *all* have a good view and easy access? That this obvious fact hasn't occurred to the overwhelming majority of air travelers after so many decades and tens of millions of flights seems a pretty convincing argument against the theory of evolution, to be honest.

Once we'd dumped our luggage at Redlands Hotel, I led my parents on a nice nine mile trot to the Tower of London, the London Dungeon and Holborn. Back at the hotel, mum collapsed with bleeding feet, and I made a mental note to scale things down a bit.

Over the next couple of days, we saw movies, checked out museums, caught up with friends and shopped. I took them to Hamley's toy shop and after wandering our separate ways, we met back at a cash register. Dad was clutching a fart cushion and mum had a set of vampire teeth (I suspected the similarity with the Queen ended at this point).

"I just want to note, for the record, that I never want to hear you two talking about me acting my age in future, okay?"

We collected our little Renault and with dad behind the wheel, headed for Canterbury at speeds of up to 85 mph, so I definitely needed the beer at the Falstaff, which dated from the early fifteenth century. The Cathedral was covered by scaffolding as they were restoring the stone and glass; inside the whole gamut of European languages swirled around the tomb of the Black Prince, but all too soon, we were on the road again and I was desperately thinking of plans to slow down dad's driving. I suggested turning off the A2 onto the A2068, vainly hoping a minor road might do the trick. Hythe and Dymchurch blurred by and we overnighted at Broadacres in New Romney.

In Selsey, we heard that Dennis was in Portugal; in Portsmouth, we clambered all over the Victory; in Winchester cathedral, a red-robed choir at evensong accompanied our visit to Jane Austen's grave. In Plymouth, we wandered the same streets I had walked with my father four months and a lifetime ago. We crossed the Tamar toll bridge to Looe, a maze of narrow, winding streets straddling both sides of a river running into the sea, and camped in the seventeenth century Osborne Hotel. That night, as I finished my lemon and garlic sole and progressed to a Tia Maria and cream pancake, I decided that there were many worse ways to spend my time than traveling with my parents. Now more than a decade into their marriage, they had branched out into several businesses, and dad had made a mid-life career change into life insurance. As a natural introvert, he had joined a public speaking club to gain confidence and, as in everything else he attempted, he succeeded.

We caught up with friends in Bath and while mum was paying the obligatory visit to the hairdresser, dad and I visited the Abbey which contained the remains of Captain Arthur Philip and Isaac Pitman as well as a father and son, both bearing the name Manley Power - if it's not broken, don't fix it. I somehow doubted that daughters of the family were christened Womanley Power.

chapter 35

Peregrination with Parents

A mini-hurricane on the Severn Bridge buffeted the Renault mercilessly on the way into Swansea, and the following day we arrived at the mecca of all booklovers, Hay-on-Wye, which we had visited on the Snowcoaster tour three years previously. I emerged with a few trophies: the autobiographies of Franklin and Cellini, Lawrence's *Seven Pillars of Wisdom*, Hawthorne's *Marble Faun*, a limited edition of de Sade's selected writings, and a reprint of a medieval treatise on the examination of witches.

Dad and I shared the driving duties, with dad still driving like he was on his own private race track. Rare sunshine accompanied us as we left Wales and drove through Herefordshire and Worcestershire, relentlessly covering the miles through Stratford to Warwick. Easter Sunday morning was for castles: the ruins of Kenilworth, and the far-from-ruined Warwick, where I searched unsuccessfully for the girl with unguarded eyes.

During the War, dad had got drunk in a pub in Leigh, near Manchester; we headed there and shared a beer in the Greyhound Inn, site of his intemperance three decades before.

"You know Peter," dad said over his pint, "I think that this trip is for you what the war was for me." I asked him to elaborate.

"The war took me overseas for a couple of years. It immersed me in different countries and different cultures and I was often uncomfortable and out of my depth. I experienced things during those years that I would never have experienced if I'd stayed in Australia. The whole experience changed me and my outlook on life. I'll never forget the experiences – good or bad – and the people I shared them with. I think this trip is doing that for you – minus being shot at, of course."

"Well, so far," I grinned, inwardly agreeing completely; however, I felt unsure whether they would like the version of me that was developing.

While we were in the midst of this cosy traveling, the Yorkshire Ripper struck for a second time. In Paisley, we searched for ancestors. Dad's surname of Hill had originally been Tannahill and Robert Tannahill, Paisley poet, was a great-uncle (with a few greats prefixed). We discovered his statue, purchased a book on his life and poetry, but were unsuccessful in our attempts to discover his grave.

During the war, dad had been billeted in Banton, a few miles north-east of Glasgow, and we drove there in search of more memories. The house he had stayed in was gone, but after a few enquiries we were directed to Sadie, in her fifties, who had been the daughter of the house at the time. Hours passed as she and dad reminisced; her dog Peppy, deaf and blind with age, pretended to pay attention. It was early evening when we left her to drive up the west side of Loch Lomond to Tarbet; while drinking in the local pub I realised it was another place I had visited a few months earlier with my father.

Snow-tipped mountains plunged into the lochs through a curtain of misty drizzle as we continued to Kyle of Lochalsh and caught the ferry to Skye. North-west from Inverness the Scottish highlands presented us with some of the most barren country I had seen. We marveled at the accent in the John O'Groats pub, penetrable only with a chainsaw, marveling even more when one of the Groattalchers turned to us and without missing a beat, spoke crystalline English with a slight Aussie accent; he'd spent time in Sydney.

This was the turning point of our trip; from now on we were on the return journey and our time together was ticking away. In Aberdeen, we strolled up Union Street to the Bell Hotel for high tea: gammon steak, egg, chips, tea, bread and cake for £1.80 each. Mum, church organist and general RLDS good girl, was so impressed with the small cupcakes, she shoved a couple in her handbag for later; mock-shocked, I recalled doing a similar thing in a Swedish smorgasbord with hard-boiled eggs and cheese. I guess it's in the genes.

In Bingley we spent two days with friends, drinking at the White Horse pub, driving through the Yorkshire dales to Skipton, and walking up to Druids' Altar, a high point overlooking Bingley where druids once sacrificed their victims. I recalled that mum's dad, Oscar, proudly displayed his membership of the Fremantle Druids' Lodge on his wall, and made a mental note to check his shed for wicker baskets, flammable fluids and body parts on my return.

We celebrated dad's fifty-fifth birthday in Grantham and dropped in on friends of friends at their farm in Wheathampstead, where we were surrounded by friendly ancient dogs, new-born foals, motherless lambs and an antiquatedly charming upper-class air, before arriving back in London, having covered 3,500 miles.

A phone call revealed that Derek had received a letter from Dennis, written in Rome, but posted in Corfu; he was inching reluctantly closer to home.

There remained one thing to do with mum and dad – a visit to the French battlefields of the first World War. With one small bag each, on the morning of May 3, we bussed to Victoria, caught a train to Folkestone, a ferry to Calais, and then found ourselves trapped in a train to Lille with 50,000 pre-pubescent kids. (I double-scratched teaching out as a future career prospect.) One more train trip saw us in Arras, where our hotel was conveniently located opposite the station.

We took a taxi around the various Somme battlefields and memorials: the twin white towers of the Canadian memorial at Vimy, Notre Dame de Lorette, the frontline trenches and the tortured earth surrounding them. We met Andre, who showed us his private war museum in his home; under his guidance, we saw more gaping craters, silent cemeteries and old trench lines. These long-dead youths had committed themselves to their cause in a way I couldn't comprehend. As I walked the blood-soaked earth with downcast eyes, I found old pieces of shrapnel and the corroded button from a uniform. For how many more years, I wondered, would French ploughs continue to disturb the relics of those doomed young men?

As Margaret Thatcher moved into No. 10 Downing Street, we retraced our journey to London, saw an unimpressive production of The Class of Miss MacMichael (despite its featuring Oliver Reed and Glenda Jackson), chortled our way through the high-camp antics of the German waiter at the Twin Brothers restaurant in Kensington Church Street, and with superhuman effort, I managed to get my parents' now obese luggage to Heathrow by tube. And then they were gone.

chapter 36

Driving with Derek

Derek was in London, staying with Yosemite acquaintances Ann and Kerry at Seven Sisters. I tubed there and we quickly exchanged news.

"So, what's the next adventure?" I asked.

"Well, I've still got dad's old car, and I've only really seen the south of England. Let's spend the next couple of weeks driving around in it and then head to Europe."

"Done."

After a night in Selsey playing cards and listening to Bob Dylan Live at the Budokan, we headed off. The weeks of up-market B & B's and high teas were over; it was back to tents and tinned tuna. Our first night was in the Longbeech campsite at Lyndhurst in the New Forest, then through Salisbury to Bath. I rang Jan from there and she was excited we were planning to visit; I was about to fulfill my Maltese promise to visit her in Leeds. It was a commitment of sorts; it made me nervous.

We crossed the Severn into Wales, diverted through Risca, and a few twists and turns took us through coal mining towns to Broadhaven. The campsite was right on the beach and we arrived at low tide to see a sandy beach fringed by rocks that rose steeply into cliffs. Cliffs meant birds, and birds on cliffs meant compulsory cliff-climbing for Derek. I tagged along, more interested in the view and the fog that clung to the beach like a child to a blanket, seemingly afraid to venture inland.

St David's, the smallest city in England and Wales, boasted a purple-grey Norman cathedral and ruined Bishop's Palace: we explored the former but avoided the Palace as entry cost the princely sum of 20p. Fog continued on minor coastal roads through Fishguard to Aberystwyth where we explored the ruined castle and bought a bottle of mead for £1.50 (hmm… 7.5 x Bishop's Palace entry fee).

Near Dolgellau, we saw a farm advertising camping facilities and our still-damp tents were soon pitched in a sheep-filled field in the Cader Idris mountain range. There was a hill/mountain in our field and we optimistically set out to climb it; near the top the gradient became almost vertical and after we staggered to the summit, much the worse for wear, we estimated we were 1,000 feet above the road. Evening descended shortly after we did, followed by more fog. We spent the evening eating ravioli and drinking mead; Derek was busy blowing a meadow pippet's egg and in high spirits because of the bird varieties he'd spotted. Industrial Wales had fallen behind us and now the towns seemed more like villages with ambition.

A couple of days later, a big loop around Wales introduced us to the vagaries of Welsh spelling: Belws-Y-Coed, Bluenau FFestiniog, north almost to Caernarvon again before riding backroads to Belws-Y-Coed, and north to walled and castled Conway. Llandudno was a Brighton lookalike with more hotels than houses, and geriatrics having wheelchair races down the main street. By the time we'd driven through Colwyn Bay, Abergele, Bylchau and Nantglyn to Cerrigydrudion we were wondering how on earth Welsh children ever learn to spell anything, let alone pronounce it. They must have the world's highest level of primary school depression due to spelling frustration.

The next day we continued through Wrexham, black-timbered Nantwich and Glossop to Leeds, and Jan and Tony's home in Meanwood. Beneath the bonhomie lay the myriad scars of marital discontent; other people and alcohol were the only anaesthetics. Entirely too much vodka was drunk in the next few hours and somehow Jan and I found ourselves in her upstairs bedroom with Derek and Tony downstairs. She was in my arms and half naked when we heard Tony's footsteps on the stairs.

"Are you guys okay?" he called out, and the footsteps continued their ascent.

Jan dived into bed and I stepped out of the room to meet Tony on the landing, closing the bedroom door behind me.

"She's had too much vodka and fallen asleep," I half lied.

We spent another boozy day and night with Jan and Tony, before driving towards Windermere, and away from one of the strangest marriages I'd encountered up to that point. Jan deserved something better than either Tony or me. Relieved I'd kept my commitment, I exhaled slowly and smiled at the road ahead.

chapter 37

The Politics of Disengagement

From Windermere through Grasmere; we settled for the evening in an elevated part of the Cumbrians just before Keswick, with a superb view over Derwent Water. We walked through the highland-like peaks above our camp for a couple of hours, discovering another meadow pippet's nest.

After changing totally bald front tyres at the polite suggestion of a passing policeman, we sped past Carlisle's square red castle, then Gretna Green, giving Glasgow as wide a berth as possible. The A81 carried us to the Loch Ard Forest, just south of Aberfoyle, where we struck an early camp. A signpost indicated the direction for a long forest walk and we followed it and, deep in conversation about women, took a wrong turn, belatedly realised it and headed in another direction, only to discover a sign indicating the end of trail markings. We had no idea where we were. We wandered around until we found a sign pointing to Aberfoyle and followed it, even though we had no idea where our campsite was in relation to Aberfoyle. Once there, we asked locals for help, described our campsite, and eventually made it back, having walked about twenty miles.

As our whistle-stop tour continued, so did our discussions about what to do when it finished. I had driven around the U.K. three times in the space of a few months: on the bus tour with my father, by car with mum and dad, and now with Derek; it was time to look further afield. Eventually, the outlines of a plan began to take shape: after returning the car to Selsey, we would head to London to investigate European rail passes, then spend June and maybe July in constant motion, exploring any countries that took our fancy. We already knew that we wouldn't be able to get Eurail passes, as these had to be purchased before arriving in the U.K., but hopefully we could get something similar.

As we headed north on the A835 we saw black-capped gulls nesting; an oyster catcher's nest with two newly-hatched chicks; a hen harrier with a captive mouse; and the elusive (so I'm told) red-throated diver. The weather deteriorated as we approached John O'Groats, but it didn't affect Derek, who had spotted birds' nests on the cliffs. We spent the night in a small campground just north of Helmsdale, and toasted the absent Den's thirtieth birthday with kippers and cheese.

We awoke to discover we were further out of Helmsdale than we thought, and very low on petrol, so we did a Dean Moriarty, turned off the engine and cruised down coastal cliffs into town. Fuelled up, we passed superb Dunrobin Castle, crossed Dornoch Firth, wandered around Inverness, and took a scenic detour which was supposed to take us alongside Loch Insh. It didn't, but the scenery was still good and Derek saw ospreys nesting at Loch Garten, so all was well.

The bleak Atholl area led down to Pitlochry to Ballinuig, where we spotted a campsite. As we drove in, we noticed a sign declaring "NO HIKERS". This seemed odd enough, but could hardly affect us as we had a car. I approached a desiccated fossil who waited for me to speak first.

"Hello. I was wondering if we could camp here tonight?"

"Who's 'we'?"

"There are two of us."

"Both males?"

"Yes."

"I'm afraid we don't take all-male parties."

Further down the road we found Erigmore House, a less discriminatory campsite in Birnam and as we settled down after dinner, I wondered whether Macbeth's Birnam woods would really move if I drank enough mead. It was worth a try. The woods *didn't* move, but the chill in the air meant *we* needed to, if we wanted to stay warm. We began kicking around a soccer ball and soon the Scottish guys in the next tent joined us; we played until 10 pm and then dived, meaded and sweating, into our sleeping bags.

After that, we were back at Jan and Tony's in Leeds, armed with Scottish beer. As we drank and played scrabble, I sensed that Jan seemed more comfortable with Tony than at any time since I'd met her – there was no more talk of divorce. Although she tried to get us to stay for a few more days until her parents' silver wedding celebration, she was not dragging me into corners and using the "L" word anymore. Perhaps she had decided that life in Leeds with Tony was not so bad after all; it certainly offered more promise than taking her chances with a hirsute Australian nomad whose affections remained undeclared.

As we left the next morning, I reflected that I had kept my promise of visiting Jan in Leeds and it seemed as if she and Tony might make it after all. I felt that she was mentally filing me in a compartment labeled "temporary holiday flirtation" and I was comfortable with that. I could see Jan flicking through old albums in future years, her smiles as she saw my photos fading in direct proportion with the photos themselves.

But as we sped directly from Leeds to Selsey, I realised that I felt a sense of fulfilment in the end of a relationship that had barely begun and I spotted a major irony: I was addicted to movement, transience and superficial relationships; my greatest commitment was to non-commitment. My grin slowly faded as I realised I was an oxymoron.

chapter 38

Morocco, Spain, Portugal

The next couple of days were spent in Selsey unwinding, washing clothes and pretending to plan the rail trip; all we knew was we were going to head south first, towards Spain and Morocco. We put our empty packs on the floor and started discussing what to pack.

"Right, so we're going to need tents and sleeping bags."

"Sure." In they went. Then we had the bright idea of re-reading Den's letters sent as he made his way home through Europe, so we shared them between us and scoured them for information. A little while later, we looked up and made the calculation:

"According to these, Den only actually camped three times; most of the time he was either in hotels or hostels."

"In which case, we hardly need to lug the tents all around Europe."

"Agreed." There was a moment's silence as the same thought hit us simultaneously.

"So why take sleeping bags?!" And instantly, our frame packs were virtually empty. A mood of hilarity struck and we began to see how many things we could leave *out* in a determination to travel as light as physically possible. In the end, the frame packs themselves became redundant and we moved down to day packs.

Here then, is the final list of what my day pack contained for (what developed into) a two month rail trip through the European summer: three pairs of underpants, a spare pair of socks, a spare shirt, a jumper, a pair of shorts, a small towel, thongs, soap, toothpaste and toothbrush, deodorant, book and small camera. That's it. The shorts doubled as bathers, the soap was used as shampoo and also for washing clothes and we figured because it was summer, things would dry quickly. Fully loaded, the packs weighed almost nothing.

Derek's granddad drove us to Chichester and our train arrived in London before noon. We headed in different directions: Derek to check out rail pass options and me to the Spanish Embassy in Sloane Square where I queued in a smoky low-roofed room for a visa. When we met later in Foyles, Derek had good news: for £97 each we could buy the Inter Rail pass which offered a month's unlimited European train travel.

On 30 May 1979 we left London for Dover, crossed the Channel to Dunkirk and a little later found ourselves in Paris's Gare du Nord. Through overcast but humid weather we walked along the Rue Faubourg St Denis (the red light district where Derek and Den dallied the year before), past Notre Dame, Shakespeare & Co., and the Seine to Austerlitz Station. A modern train sped us through flat but often heavily-wooded countryside with chateaux glimpses, to Bordeaux, where we lounged in the sun, making salami and camembert sandwiches.

Already a long way from London, the day's journey was not yet over. The big towns of Biarritz and Bayonne flew by, featuring two and three storey white houses with brown shutters (reminiscent of Austria) and after affording glimpses of a grey and windswept Bay of Biscay, the train reached its destination: Irun, Spain, and our third country in a day. After minimal immigration formalities, we changed trains again, grabbing a 2nd class cabin so we could stretch out, and drifted to sleep to a background lullaby of drunken Spaniards. We woke in Madrid: I confirmed with the Australian Embassy that I could get my soon-to-expire passport renewed there, and we booked a night train to Algeciras.

We were woken from a sound sleep at 4 am to make room for four Spanish soldiers who had seats in our carriage and we were soon tumbling into the glare of Algeciras with hundreds of uniformed bodies. The ferry crossing over calm, milky green water to Morocco took about three hours, giving us a close-up view of Gibraltar. A six-pack dolphin escort attended us, prompting numerous shouts of "Shark!".

We decided not to linger in Tangiers and caught a surprisingly modern train to Rabat, through eucalypt forests, orange and olive groves and wheat fields. On the train, the locals began pestering us to buy hashish almost immediately.

"It's not illegal to smoke it in Morocco, but it's illegal to sell it!" contributed a fellow passenger. I couldn't quite figure that out. On arriving in Rabat, we found a great room in the Grand Hotel and I peeled off the clothes I'd been wearing for six days.

The next morning we headed into the bright coolness of Rabat, initially heading west, to find only old walls harbouring swifts' nests in their crevices. Turning east, back past the train station, we found the heart of Rabat in bustling, narrow-streets full of brass, leather and food. We chatted to street vendors and a young student of the Koran before catching a meandering train to Casablanca. Old shanties were dotted by the side of the track, and old ladies balanced buckets of water on their heads.

Arriving at lunchtime, we checked into the centrally-located Perigord for 20 dirhams, and hit the streets. The friendliness of the Moroccans was overwhelming: admittedly, most of them were trying to sell us something (usually hashish or "Omega" wristwatches), but they remained steadfastly good-natured in the face of our refusals and were genuinely interested in conversation.

On the morning train to Marrakech, we were eventually chucked out of the 1ˢᵗ class carriage into *deuxieme*, near a young Moroccan who spoke fair English. His name sounded like Kandir. His eager conversation stretched his English abilities as we ranged over topics like Australia, Islam, Christianity, politics, the Middle East and, finally, sex. On this last topic his questions were absolutely fearless:

"How old were you when you first had sex?"

"How many times can you have sex in one day?"

As we fielded these and many other questions for his enlightenment and our amusement (and no doubt that of nearby passengers) we arrived in Marrakech.

We'd decided only to spend a few hours in Marrakech, and the local hotel tout, incensed that we weren't using his services, wandered off spluttering Arabic and English curses in our general direction. I responded with the ultimate American vacuity: "Have a nice day." We ended up being shepherded around town by a volunteer guide - at least I'm assuming he was a volunteer because we certainly didn't pay him anything. By the time he'd finished with us, we'd seen the market square with its snake charmers, acrobats and story-tellers, the 800 year old temple built of Egyptian stone, and miles of the low, flat, uniformly dull red buildings of Marrakech.

We realised that our money was running very low and because it was Sunday our only hope of changing money was at a big hotel. We tried a couple but their change windows were closed. Back at the station we discovered that the excess for an air-conditioned carriage back to Casablanca was 15 dirhams, so we ransacked our coin collections and made it with

45 francs to spare. Five hours later, we were back in Casablanca's Hotel Perigord, washing down a simple meal with Flag beer.

I dozed on the long train trip from Casablanca to Tangier Port, (Derek was immersed in *Even Cowgirls Get the Blues*) and arrived humming the appropriate song from Dylan's Blood on the Tracks. We swapped our remaining dirhams for a fellow passenger's pesetas and were heading through customs when a plain clothes officer raced up and did a thorough search of my bag. Finding nothing unusual, he also searched my wallet, and demanded to know if I had any hashish before leaving me alone. He ignored the Scottish girl I was talking to who was obviously completely out of it.

We had more entertainment going through customs in Algeciras. An American stormed to the front of the queue and declared to the officer:

"We're with a group. Americans!" The exclamation mark was obvious, as was the response he was anticipating – it had something to do with red carpets and profuse gratitude for gracing Spain with his presence.

"Wait a minute."

"Wait?? What for?" Both his tone of voice and facial expression conveyed the petulance of a spoilt child. And then we moved on, fervently hoping that he would be kept waiting long enough to start doubting his own deity.

In the morning we left the semi-westernised jumble of Algeciras for Granada, having bought apples and apricots for the journey (but refusing the offer of bagged snails). It was an eight hour journey in a two-carriage train with a top speed of 35 mph, with frequent lengthy stops, including more than an hour at Bobadilla. The scenery made the lengthy journey worth it: tumbling grey cliffs, golden seas of wheat, and white-washed towns occasionally punctuated by hilltop castles. A thunderstorm and torrential rain enlivened the last stage of the journey and we stepped out under menacing skies into Granada's flooded streets. Our initial impressions of Granada weren't overly favourable, so we decided to head to Madrid the following day.

In the morning, our alarm didn't work so we had to race to catch the morning train to Madrid. Once we were on board the ticket inspector said we had to pay a supplement, so we headed back into the station to discover we only had about £1 in pesetas between us. We were going to miss our train. As we looked back at the train, we started to laugh – it had "Algeciras" on it, not "Madrid" – we'd got on the wrong train by mistakenly reading the arrivals board instead of the departures!

We decided to save a night's accommodation cost by catching an evening train to Madrid, thus leaving the day free for us to explore Granada. Remembering Den had recommended the Alhambra Castle, we spent an hour or so wandering through its Moorish architecture and cool gardens before descending into the older, eastern side of the city which was much more attractive than the station area We lunched on *huevos chorizo* and sunned ourselves on the grass of the Plaza Bib-Rambla near the Cathedral until we were moved on by the shear-brandishing gardener.

The night's train journey to Madrid turned into an all-night party, fuelled by the hash and beer provided by a Spanish soldier and two Parisians. As a result, we spent most of the next day sleeping in parks while waiting to collect my new passport from the Embassy. With new passport in hand, we jumped on a late-night train to Portugal, clutching a half-completed chess game on the small magnetic board I'd bought that afternoon. Late the following morning, we arrived in Lisbon, found a room at Penason Lisboa and enthusiastically embraced the concept of siesta.

Post-siesta, we headed out into the cool of the afternoon. 1979 was a much better year to visit Lisbon than 1755, the year the city was virtually destroyed by an earthquake, tidal wave and fire in quick succession. We climbed the hill to St George's castle for the view of the River Tegg flowing through Lisbon and the 'Frisco-like' bridge that spans it. Inside the castle walls, doves, pheasants and peacocks (including white ones) roamed. At the restaurant across from our Pension, we ate grouper, omelette, vegetables, bread and olives washed down with beer for a total cost of £2.50, noting that the favourite hobby for local women seemed to be scrubbing the foot-paths on their knees. I beat Derek at chess before getting a necessary early night.

The early train to Porto consisted entirely of 1st class carriages, and we were grudgingly obliged to pay a supplement. It turned out to be worth it because the journey – about half the entire length of Portugal – took only three hours. On arrival we had the obligatory glass of Port, saw dirty, trellised buildings, and noted it lacked the old buildings and large squares of Lisbon. We planned to head back to Madrid and then through Barcelona to Andorra.

On our train out of Porto, a young soldier alerted us to the obscure stop where we needed to change for Madrid. All went well until 3 am when we reached Valencia de Alcantara and Spanish customs and immigration boarded the train. The official took one look at my two passports, saw that my Spanish visa was in the old, cancelled one, and freaked. He conferred with his colleague and they eventually found an interpreter:

"Sir, the visa allowing you to enter Spain has been cancelled with your passport. Your new passport does not contain a Spanish visa, so we cannot let you into the country."

"Look, my old passport was about to expire, so I had to get a new one. I had no choice. If I'd just let my passport expire, would you have let me into the country with an expired passport containing a non-cancelled visa?"

"No."

"So I didn't have a choice. I was already *in* Spain when the new passport was issued. The old one wasn't cancelled because I did anything illegal, and the Australian Embassy didn't say anything about me having to get another visa for the new passport." They conferred some more.

"Sir, when we arrive in Madrid, you will accompany me to the Police Commissioner where we can make arrangements for you to get a new visa in your new passport." I spent the rest of the night mentally composing rude letters to the Australian Embassy.

In the morning I was duly led to the Police Commissioner and watched three officials deliberate on the dilemma with much waving of hands. In the end, they gave both passports back to me and told me not to worry about it. Derek and I celebrated with milk and cake before walking north to the ultra-modern Chamartin station. Derek beat me at two games of chess and, after buying the world's most expensive cheese sandwich, we boarded a night train for a sleepless ride to Barcelona. After a beer and empanado breakfast, we chugged through the ugly part of the city and then past tourist beaches, overstocked with hotels and camping areas, and entered France at Cerbere.

chapter 39

Andorra to Rome

"So you guys have been travelling for ages then?" a fellow traveler asked, having heard a bit of our story. "You're like some of those characters from Kerouac's *On the Road*." I think he felt he was paying us a compliment. "Are you kidding?" I replied, "Have you actually read the book? All they do is cruise around in cars in the same country they were born in, apart from a trip down to Mexico. I know the book's regarded as a modern classic, but it certainly wasn't because of the mundane travelling they did." Judging from his facial expression, I might as well have insulted his mother.

At Cerbere we switched straight onto a train for Perpignan, where everything was shut for lunch. We met a couple of Danish hitchhikers over a beer; they had achieved the amazing feat of hitching from Copenhagen to Barcelona in two days and one night. Once again, hitching appeared as a viable traveling mode. When the shops opened, I discovered the delights of a pate and camembert sandwich and, thus fortified, we made two more train trips for the day: to Villefranche and then La Tour de Carol. The second leg of the journey on an incredible, wooden, two-carriage train took three hours wandering through the increasingly snow-capped scenery of the Pyrenees.

We caught the bus the next morning to Andorra de Vella where we booked into the Hotel Casa Joan and scouted out the prices: everything was cheaper than in the U.K., with alcohol being 1/8 the price – a bottle of Scotch was £1. Andorra was like a super duty free shop lost in the Himalayas; perhaps the isolation explained why women there weren't allowed to vote until 1970. Both Spanish and French currencies were accepted and there was a local patois that spelt chocolates as *xocolates* and *fromages* as *frotomajes*.

Overindulgence over, we retraced our steps the following day through cloud-packed valleys to Perpignan, and caught an afternoon train through Narbonne to Marseille. We met four Americans (three from New York City and one from Laguna Beach) and during the conversation one of them made the comment that he thought the image of Americans abroad was improving. Derek shook his head violently enough to cause whiplash, and after that, conversation dwindled noticeably. This was no great loss as our train ride was taking us through the wilderness of the Camargue with their famed wild flamingos.

Also on the train was a woman with the sort of face artists die for: hiding an obviously attractive body under a loose sweater, she was a visitor from another world: grey-blue eyes, long, dark kinked hair, and a girlish face. The air of sublime sadness surrounding her was so poignant it evoked a similar feeling in me. I forced myself to disengage, sensing the imminence of another Warwick Castle moment and more mediocre poetry.

After twelve hours of non-stop travel, Marseilles arrived, presenting us with a sprawling industrial port, a bewildering array of hotels, and dogs suffering from chronic diarrhea. Unimpressed, we caught an early morning train east towards the Italian border, bypassing Nice, and after the littoral eye-candy of the Riviera, disembarked at Monaco. We climbed the hill to the tower, provided a photo service for some Japanese tourists, and checked out the oceanographic museum. Then it was down through the sultriness of Monte Carlo, and we were soon on a train rumbling past myriads of topless sunbathers and through equally many tunnels in the direction of Genoa. The Liguria Pension was cheap and the scene of another chess victory for me (the score was now 7-6 in my favour).

Pisa arrived in fine but windy weather. We located the tower, paid our 1000 lire and climbed to the top. The most exciting part was the disequilibrium; my sense of balance struggled to comprehend the situation. I have no idea what it would be like to climb the tower after drinking a bottle of local wine, but there should be a sign warning against it.

After a lunch of pizza and wine, Derek levelled the chess score, and we headed to Rome. The train was packed with soldiers and we stood for the four hour journey. As we walked out of the well-appointed Rome station, the Pension Gioberti presented itself. Grabbing some food and wine, and with newly-washed jeans hanging out of our window, the chess marathon continued into the night.

In the morning we headed down Via Davour to the Coliseum and the Forum, then north across the Tiber at the S. Angelo bridge, under wheeling swifts and drizzling rain. It was only a short walk to the Vatican and the Plaza S. Pietro and as we checked out St Peter's, I couldn't help but contrast the glittering Roman Catholic trophies with the RLDS Church: a gilt-edged ancient institution, towering into Renaissance splendour here at the heart of the ancient world, compared with a small, novel, nineteenth century American-based religion, cut from the plain-hewn timbers of sectarian Protestantism. Catholicism presented obvious negatives: wealth, power, institutionalisation and arcane practices; but it appeared to have History on its side, and History still held my heart firmly in her grasp. It would all have to wait until my return to Australia and my evaluation of the material obtained in Independence. It was the only certainty in my future, my only commitment, and because it involved History, I was eager to pursue it.

Recrossing the Tiber at Vittorio Emmanuel Bridge, we headed to the Trevi Fountain but were far too cheap to throw in any coins, drooled our way through some of the surrounding delis, grabbed some pizza, and collapsed back at our Pension. We awoke to find the overcast sky had completely cleared so we headed into the streets again, walked to the Spanish Steps (where we sat with hundreds of others) and I shared with Derek an embryonic plan I had to walk from Selsey to Dublin. He seemed quite enthusiastic about it, although my original plan was to do it solo.

We wandered to the Pantheon and down to Circus Maximus, where we visualised the chariot race from Ben Hur, then up the road and around the Coliseum to the Domus Aurea where we passed Nero's house. It was a day of great historical contrast: we had glimpsed the might of ancient Rome with its smorgasbord of gods and its persecution of a new sect called Christians who stubbornly insisted on worshipping only one God. Yet the Emperors of Rome who had persecuted Christianity spasmodically for more than two centuries eventually capitulated to the demands of this one God. In one of those delicious ironies of History, the persecuted minority defeated the persecuting majority. Shortly after Christianity's spiritual victory over Rome, Rome fell physically to the barbarians and Christianity became the main cohesive force in western Europe for centuries. Today we had seen the ruined glories of the ancient Roman Empire and the current but diminished glories of the ancient Roman Church. History, I decided, was going to be an intriguingly complex mistress, one of whom I would not quickly tire.

As we drank in Roman cafes and continued our chess marathon (drawn at 9 each), La Dolce Vita swirled around us: countless male heads whiplashed as beautiful women sashayed past to consider jumping in the nearest fountain; the smell of freshly ground coffee beans, seafood and pasta initiated an olfactory fandango, and the hot night air enticed us all to remain on the streets just a *little* longer.

chapter 40

On Smuggling Stone Curlews

The train trip through Venice to Florence was accompanied by miles of cultivated fields, vineyards, rolling hills crowned with towns and castles, and Derek finally defeating me in the marathon chess championship. We found a Pension near the Duomo, wandered down to the Palais de la Seigneurie and watched wind-up plastic birds flitting around the square.

Crossing the Pontes Vecchio and Alle Grazie, and alarmed by the numbers of German tourists (Rotel alert), we found Michelangelo's gardens offered a panoramic view over the city before we respectfully nodded at Dante's statue and noted that *Time* magazine upgraded Khomeini from "stern" to "autocratic and erratic". Iran seemed a lifetime ago.

After an early morning departure from the Maggiore Sovrana Pensione with its collection of freaks (the proprietor shaking our hands as we left in deference to our apparent relative normality), we nervously breakfasted on cheese and salami rolls in the Plaza della Independencia as the air above us darkened with a flurry of pigeons. Unsplattered, we headed to the Plaza Belle Arti where our intention was to check out David's statue, but it was closed, so we crossed the Ponte Vecchio again, through a group of gypsies demonstrating great talent in smearing only half the yoghurt they were eating over their faces. The day was getting hot as I bought a couple of Dylan bootlegs and we passed through Verona (where it was completely overcast and cooler) and incredibly hilly pre-Dolomite country via Trento to Bolzano. Bolzano seemed more Austrian than Italian and the living standards were higher than the rest of Italy; we eventually scored a room in a private apartment with a great view of the mountains.

The next day, one of our stops in the Dolomites stretched on … and on… We discovered that there was a strike and that there would be a two hour delay. Exactly two hours later, the train continued on its way and a load of school kids boarded. Four German schoolgirls entered our carriage, and we could communicate a little with them. They fed us lollies and played us Bob Dylan and Barclay James Harvest tapes until we arrived in Innsbruck.

Waiting for the youth hostel to open, we drank spumante and ate 200g of chocolate each (it was cheap), wandered through the old section of town (picturesque, but touristy), crossed the river and climbed part-way up the hill for a view over the town and the ski lift. I realised that Innsbruck was virtually a new town to me; although I had visited three years before with my parents, I was bed-ridden with flu and saw little. This time, unfortunately, I would remember little.

Three other guys (American, Swedish and Welsh) shared our dormitory in the hostel. After dinner, Derek and I began drinking our 2 litre bottle of wine, which was the start of a night of overindulgence. I was told later that I spent the night running all around the hostel, from one dorm to another and down to the bar. The next thing I remember was waking up. Even before my eyes opened, I smelled something absolutely repulsive, immediately suspecting flatulence on Derek's part. Fortunately, I opened my eyes before moving my head, and realised I was smelling my own vomit. There was a trail of vomit crossing my pillow and mattress and completely covering the backpack of the unfortunate Swedish tourist sleeping in the bunk above me.

Everyone else soon woke. I discovered that during the night, someone had woken the manager who had confiscated my wallet, muttering that I'd have to pay for any damages. I was told that I would have to clean up the mess, which I did with towels, all the time feeling like throwing up again. Derek went way above the call of duty, not only placating the steaming Swede, but also washing up the vomit-drenched towels. My wallet was returned and we didn't have to pay any damages.

We discovered the Welsh guy, Roland, on the train to Feldkirch a little later; he burst out laughing when he saw me.

"Man, you drank a lot last night. No wonder you threw up."

I looked at him with feigned wide-eyed innocence.

"No, Roland, you don't understand. I blame the 200g block of chocolate I ate earlier - it must have been off."

Feldkirch saw me ecstatically inching towards recovery; Derek's ecstasy focused on stuffed birds he'd spotted in a gunshop window. I dragged him away and onto a train through Buchs to Vaduz.

After overnighting in Europe's most modern hostel in Vaduz, we arrived in Zurich to discover a hostel with more rules than a prisoner of war camp. Zurich sported a cactus zoo, a free aviary, and fishermen who got their lines tangled in overhead power lines. At the British consulate, Derek had an important question:

"Excuse me," he asked the attractive receptionist, "Can I bring stuffed birds into Britain?" The receptionist's eyes widened and she narrowly avoided spluttering.

"I beg your pardon?"

"I'm a British citizen and I have in my possession a stuffed stone curlew. Can I take it back into Britain?"

The receptionist quickly entered into the spirit of the thing:

"Last time I checked, sir, possession of a stuffed stone curlew wasn't an offence in itself, however, you will need to provide proof that it's been dead for at least two years."

"Look, it's a thoroughly ex-stone curlew, but I'm afraid it didn't come complete with a Death Certificate signed by a medical practitioner." Derek lost his temper after that and stormed out, making physically impossible suggestions about stone curlew placement.

We spent a few hours in Lucerne, crossing the fourteenth-century bridge, climbing the old towers on the wall, and gaining a lesson in Swiss rigidity. We were standing at the edge of the road near the river, halted by a red pedestrian light. Derek was standing on my left and an old man on my right. We looked both ways and there wasn't a car in sight. We were about to cross when the old man yelled "Achtung!" in my ear, gesturing frantically at the little red symbol that prohibited us crossing. As I'd virtually jumped across the street in alarm anyway, we continued crossing.

"Weird, wasn't it?" Derek mused, "I thought we invented machines to serve us, not the other way around."

"I wonder what would happen in the event of the light malfunctioning?" I pondered a few moments later. "If that light stuck on red, the old guy would stay there until he starved to death."

We trained through Geneva to Basel, where we bumped into two girls from Australia. One of them used to live in Fremantle, had attended John Curtin High School, and we had mutual friends. Amazed at the coincidence, we relived shared memories and spent the night playing cards with them and Mike, a psychiatric nurse from St Albans.

In our hostel room, there were two other Australian guys, and we entered the room to find one of them had a map of Europe unfolded on his bed.

"Hi. Been in Europe long?" we asked.

"Ages," he trilled in a high-pitched voice. "I've been away from home for 10 days and I've been through France and Austria already. How long have you been away?"

"Well over a year; we came overland from Kathmandu." It didn't register; probably it was incomprehensible.

"And I'm going to be in Europe for another two weeks before I go home, isn't it amazing?" It was.

A heavily-wooded Luxembourg passed, and I was dozing through a case of the flu as we headed to Paris. At Gare du Nord we grabbed a time-table for cross-channel ferries while a drunk waltzed around us doing a passable version of Anarchy in the U.K. After consuming bread, cheese and pilchards on a sidewalk to the amazement of Parisian pedestrians who obviously felt we should be properly seated at a cafe, we continued to Gare Austerlitz, eventually finding a room at Hotel Coypel. The ladies of the night in rue Blondel were getting an early start – they were out and about in the early afternoon. We walked from Austerlitz to Gare du Nord in just over an hour and by mid-afternoon, were at London's Victoria Station. We were soon back in the Camellia Hotel off Queensway, eating at the Grove and drinking at the Shakespeare, and the following day, 29 June 1979, we were back in Selsey.

A letter from Dennis was waiting for us. He had been back in Fremantle for a month (just after his 30th birthday), had moved into a small flat in Canning Highway near the Leopold Hotel, and was hating work. His letter was disturbing: Dennis had worked for 14 years and I had only worked full-time for a little over a year – if travelling could so unsettle someone with such established work habits, what hope did I have? I harboured grave doubts about the existence of life after travelling.

chapter 41

The Unbearable Presence of Beauty

Wondering whether the rest of my life would seem anti-climactic after this trip did not last long; such musings were best suited to inertia and we remained, as usual, in motion. For the past month, our much-used Inter Rail pass had taken us through western and southern Europe, plus Morocco; it had been £97 well invested. So we simply decided to repeat the exercise, but in different countries.

We crossed to Oostende and continued to Hamburg where on our cycling trip the year before we had camped on a works site and eaten in a cemetery bus stop during a rainstorm. Now we were swanning around in trains; we were 22 and getting soft! At Hamburg we switched trains to Copenhagen, shared chocolate with three girls from Stuttgart and decided to revisit the Copenhagen smorgasbord.

"Let's have an eating competition," suggested Derek. "Whoever can eat the most without chundering wins."

"So what's the bet?" We devised an imaginative one. Selsey's Church Norton was supposed to be haunted. On our return we would place several items around the cemetery perimeter during daylight; the loser would have to return in the middle of the night to retrieve them.

The eating competition was a draw, but there was additional entertainment. At an adjacent table were three young Americans who had obviously been on the brewery tour - perhaps several brewery tours. After a while, one of them headed to the toilet. Minutes passed, and there was no sign of him. His friends looked bemused, then concerned; one of them headed off to find him, returning a moment later, alone. They motioned a waiter over, and all three of them headed off. Our curiosity was at fever pitch, so we followed. The first guy had gone downstairs, locked himself into a cubicle, and promptly fallen into drunken unconsciousness. His friend had been unable to wake him and now they needed the waiter to help them unlock the door.

We were on the Stockholm train the next morning, sharing a carriage with two Swedish women and guys from Germany and Tunisia. Travel-related conversation intermingled with dozing until something outside caught my eye. At first, I thought a horse was running alongside the train, but then realised it was a fully-grown elk, ambitiously racing us in a loping gait.

We were keen to minimise our time in places we'd already been, so after a night in Stockholm, we continued to Goteborg, Sweden's second largest city and home to the world's most beautiful women. Derek and I walked through the town trying not to gape, struggling to cope with the unbearable presence of beauty. Derek reminded me that I had left Diane behind in Nymolla: "Why don't you see her again? She's not that far away you know. She clearly liked you, and you've had plenty of time to recover."

"Remember the note she wrote?" I replied, "Full of self-pity. Why would I go back to that? And honestly, I don't think I'm cut out for long-term relationships. You were in a relationship that lasted six years; I don't think I've been in one that lasted more than six weeks." Of course, we had to leave Goteborg quickly or go insane, and after a night in a dormitory with fifty others, the train trip to Norway consisted mainly of flattish, superbly wooded country, featuring lakes, deer and foxes.

The girls in Oslo were nearly as beautiful as in Goteborg and amazingly, we bumped into one of the three Americans from the Copenhagen smorgasbord:

"How is your friend who fell asleep in the restaurant toilet?"

"He's fine now. When he woke up he was feeling ill, and because he hadn't really eaten anything, he refused to pay his bill. They called the police and he spent the night in jail."

We caught a night train to Trondheim, and although we didn't arrive until 7am, it was so light at 3am that I woke then. We strolled across the river and up a steep hill to a castle and lazed in the grounds. Trondheim was attractive, with parks, malls, and distinctive riverside buildings: square wooden warehouses up to six storeys high squatted on stilts. A distinctly un-Nordic touch was the way the sewerage outlet emptied directly into the river, but again, the women were criminally beautiful and as the cool morning retreated into a hot day, the only downside was being shot by a sniper sparrow.

We caught an afternoon train through Hell (sic – maybe there are no beautiful women there?) to Östersund where we arrived at 9.30pm. Racing to the youth hostel, we found it full, so we sprinted back to the train station and reboarded the same train. We arrived in Ånge just after midnight, waited an hour for the next train (by which time the temperature was 2 Celsius) and it was still light enough to read. Thirteen hours later, and a total of twenty-two train hours in all, we arrived in Kiruna after passing through surprisingly flat, but densely-wooded scenery. Kiruna was humid, and the fact that we hadn't changed clothes for several days didn't help. Things took a turn for the worse when we discovered the world's biggest and least reticent mosquitoes stalking the streets; the youth hostel was full and the station hotel was exorbitant.

We hiked past a couple of guys who wanted some hash (if we'd been in Morocco, they would have been *offering* it) to tourist information where a nice girl with hairy armpits placed us in a private house for £3 each. It was difficult to find, but well worth it. Owned by a young couple, it contained not just a shower and complete kitchen, but its own sauna and gymnasium – and we were the only ones there! Just occasionally on the road, you stumble across Paradise with the gates open; this was one of those times.

The next day we headed to the northernmost point of our rail journeys (in fact, the furthest north of any rail line in the world outside of Russia): Narvik in fjordland. We chugged alongside a magnificent fjord for several miles, gazed at mackerel under the bridge, and had our photo taken under a large signpost pointing out how far we were from places like Paris and Warsaw, but we could do little else because most of the town was closed. We returned to Kiruna to find our accommodation from the previous night was booked out and the supermarket had sold out of all essentials. Oh well, you can't expect Paradise to last; we ate yoghurt and tinned fruit and stayed at no. 28 Kopmangatan.

Our train was late the next morning, which meant we arrived late in Boden and missed the train which was to take us into Finland. At Boden station, Derek held the train door back with one foot, then caught his other foot in the metal door stop, sending himself hurtling into the door of the next carriage. With only his dignity damaged, we ate icecream by a circular lake at the edge of town which Derek guessed was an ice-skating rink in winter, before heading to Lulea, then through Boden into Finland, ending up at Oulu.

There was water everywhere in Oulu and yet again, beautiful women. Was it my imagination or had Scandinavia cornered the market on beauty?

Was desperation altering perception? Or was I subconsciously preparing to marry in Europe and thus avoid ever returning home? Even the word "home" began to feel strange, with its undercurrents of familiarity, obligation and duty. Australia was beginning to feel like just another country I had once visited, "home" only because I had more family and friends there than anywhere else. I now knew there were many great places in the world where I could live and be happy. Derek, able to live and work in England indefinitely, continued to remind me of my diminishing funds and imminent departure. I knew I would have to go back, but I would be returning to a place from which the connotations of the word "home" were retreating like an ebb tide. "Home" implied more than a location – it implied an emotional commitment, and I had fierce doubts about my ability to make those. Incessant travelling had freed me from emotional and relational ties, but what had it freed me *for*? The answer remained elusive.

chapter 42

Finland to Austria

The next day was a long one through Kontiomaki to Joensuu. The trains were small, not electric, and their heating systems seemed to have no "off" switch, but it seemed mean-spirited to grumble when we were enjoying the delights of a Scandinavian summer which, as locals delighted to point out, was much warmer than its British counterpart. As we passed through the lake district, I decided that Finland would be great for cyclists: flat country, plenty of forests for free camping, lots of lakes for washing of bodies and clothes, and a good spread of youth hostels.

In Helsinki, and clutching a local map, we walked 2 km to one of the hostels. It was a community centre hostel, the kind where you didn't need to show a card, and we walked into a huge game of geriatric bingo downstairs. Our room was a cross between an army dorm (it had accommodation for 32) and a jail because it was mostly below ground with concrete walls, tiled floors, and only small squares of thick translucent glass in one corner for natural light.

Helsinki's deserted back streets looked slightly Russian, and although there were parks and grassy areas, it definitely lacked the charm of Stockholm and Copenhagen. A smorgasbord lunch followed by a litre of milk rendered us immobile, and we chatted to a young Finnish girl on her way to a jazz festival until the lead weight in our stomachs eased.

We spent the first hour on the train to Kemi shuffling around because many of the seats were actually reserved, despite not having "reserved" signs on them. Eventually we found unreserved seats, and dozed off. When I woke, it was to enter one of those demoralising discussions that make you feel your brain is the size of a peanut: the Finnish guy opposite me had just finished his fourth of six years studying Russian literature in Leningrad and was fluent in Russian, Finnish, Swedish, Polish and English.

After Goteberg, we changed at Västeras to a Stockholm train. It was noisy and crowded, with more reserved seat shuffling, and after a restless sleep we arrived at 7.30 am after 37 hours' continuous train travel. It would have been quicker by ferry, but we would have had to pay extra for that. As we walked through the familiar streets of the town we had the slightly surreal experience of meeting an American neurosurgeon who was financing his travels by selling handmade boomerangs as he went. He was doing well because of the Australian connection: Australia (and especially Western Australia) was in the news all over Europe because pieces of Skylab were falling on it.

We headed through Gamla Stan over to Skansen, where Derek spotted a baby swallow that had fallen into the river and was caught in weed. He rolled his pants up, waded in and tried to drag the bird and weed to shore with a stick. Eventually he succeeded, partly due to the bird's own efforts and (greatly admired by two Swedish women) he dried the bird and held it under his shirt. Soon it was sufficiently dry to fly away. Derek thought the bird had probably fallen into the river on its first ever flight and wouldn't have survived more than a few minutes if he hadn't intervened.

We arrived in Copenhagen to discover the hostel was full and were directed to Active University where we slept in fairly grotty conditions and awoke to take in the first Carlsberg brewery tour of the day. We met Americans from Virginia who were built like brick outhouses and a Texan PhD student who made his living back home selling boomerang-like objects to Americans. A brief stop-off at Bonn (small and attractive) and we were at Koblenz, booked into an ancient fort of a youth hostel, four kilometres from town, the walk affording an excellent view of the junction of the Rhine and Mosel rivers.

Heidelberg was coincidence time: as we were walking to the hostel, we saw an English girl we had first met on the train to Kiruna and the American guy from the Copenhagen smorgasbord whom we'd later seen in Oslo. After walking up to the castle and taking in the view over the Nekkar, we caught a train to Munich where the hostel was full, as was the next closest (Pullach), so we caught a train back to Augsburg, only to find the sign on the hostel there said "rooms for girls only". We went in anyway and they took pity on us, and a kindergarten convention kept things pretty lively that evening.

We headed back to Munich, then on to Dachau, where the Nazis' first concentration camp personified bleakness, and the weather complemented it. As we wandered around the camp for an hour, hardly speaking, contemplating evil, I shuddered - not just because 70,000 people died there, but because I shared the same humanity with the perpetrators. It was a diagnosis of shame; a diagnosis that shattered the sunny myth of inherent human goodness as effectively as the atomic bombs at the end of that same war shattered the modernist dream of perpetual positive progress. Education and science didn't make humanity "better" – they simply provided more efficient means of destruction. Education and science were remarkable facilitators, but lousy gods.

After beers in the Hoffbrauhaus, and another night in the Augsburg "girls only" hostel, we caught a train to Fussen and walked to Mad Ludwig's castle, then more steep walking to get up to the castle itself. The fairytale castle, pinup favourite of a thousand travel agents, did not disappoint. It stood in turreted romantic contrast to the sullen barrenness of Dachau, a reminder that some dreams are worth pursuing – perhaps even worth committing to.

When we returned to Fussen, two American women asked us how to get to the castle.

"It's a 5 kilometre walk in that direction," we responded.

"5 kilometres?! That's like 3 miles, man!"

We explained that it was a scenic walk, but they walked off shaking their heads, looking for motorised transport, convinced they had escaped from the presence of madmen.

Spending our last Deutschmarks on Mars bars, we boarded the train and met a Melbournian called Vicky, and Nancy from (of all places) Binghamton, New York. Much travel talk ensued until we arrived in Munich, just missing our train to Salzburg. We caught a later train and got lost trying to follow Nancy's directions to the hostel. Re-directed by a couple of wandering minstrels, we found the hostel full, and then attempted something stupid.

"Where are we going to sleep?"

"There's a concrete overhang here. Let's sleep under it. If it rains, we'll at least be dry."

"But it's going to be nearly freezing tonight; how on earth will we keep warm?", Derek asked with great common sense.

"I've got a couple of copies of *New Musical Express* in my bag; we can put those under us as insulation on the concrete. Then we can put all our clothes on and our towels over us."

Here then, is another valuable tip for travelers: don't even *think* about trying to spend the night outdoors in freezing temperatures with only ten sheets of newspaper between you and bare concrete, and just a thin towel for a blanket. Having amply demonstrated the stupidity of my idea, we headed back to the station and spent the night on a confusing succession of stationary and moving trains, traveling alternately away from and back to Salzburg until morning, when we headed purposefully for Vienna.

Our first views of the Austrian capital weren't promising: we arrived at the west station and walked six miles to the hostel through western suburbs that seemed to us to be grey, deserted and dying. A bit more life appeared further north, but our impression was still of a predominantly dirty city, populated by surly Slavs whose ambition was to be supremely unhelpful to travelers asking directions. The hostel proved to be an old chateau-type building, at the edge of both the posh suburbs and an extensive park.

The next day, our impression of Vienna changed as we walked into the centre of town, amazed by grandiose architecture and omnipresent statues. Vienna had begun as a Celtic settlement, later a Roman camp (Vindobona), before becoming a cosmopolitan mix of Magyars, Germans, Czechs and Italians. After visiting St Stephan's church and gazing into the narrow, brown Danube, I decided that Vienna was a city for the rich, and not much fun for anyone else. We ate in the garden of our semi-chateau, accompanied by nuthatches, redstarts and the headless statue of a woman covered with pro-Nazi graffiti.

During dinner, Derek made a statement that struck me as sexist. "Look," I said, "have you ever thought what would happen if you had been born a woman?" His face went completely blank for a while, and I realised I had presented him with a completely novel thought. At least fifteen seconds passed before he replied. "In that case, I'd never get anything done," he said reflectively, "because I'd spend all day playing with my tits."

chapter 43

Appendix, hey?

The next morning we walked for two and a half hours through light drizzle to the south station, caught a train to Klagenfurt, then through Villach to Tarvisio. The train from Tarvisio to Udine stopped 40 kilometres short of its destination; the mountainous region had just been devastated by earthquake and all trains were being used to convey building materials. A bus took us directly through the devastation. In one town a 10 storey building had been split in two length-wise, with one half peeling off and crashing to the ground. This revealed a surgical glimpse into the remaining half, like peering into a doll's house.

It hadn't been our intention to spend the night in Udine, but as trains were virtually non-existent, we headed to the Al Fari Pensione. It was set in an extended private home, and I offered the prim proprietress my best choirboy smile as she looked us over. It worked, we settled in, drank wine and played chess.

The next day dawned on another milestone: we had been on the road for 18 months. In a self-congratulatory mood, we headed to the station to find that the trains, which were supposed to be running, weren't. We decided to catch a bus to Venice and discovered we'd just missed the direct one, so we opted for Latisana, and continuing to Venice from there. We boarded the bus, and a little later, I almost achieved losing Derek.

The bus made a quick refreshment stop at S. Dona Di Piave-Jesolo and Derek shot off in the direction of the nearest toilet. Minutes later, the bus began to drive off with Derek nowhere in sight. For a few seconds, I wondered if Derek would see the funny side of being stranded for a few hours with no possessions, but deciding I wanted to live to my twenty-third birthday, I got the driver to stop the bus at the end of the street and walked back. I walked into a scene of high comedy. Derek had re-emerged, realised that the bus had gone, and by the time I got there had apparently succeeded fairly well in explaining with broken English, two words of Italian and lots of gestures that his belongings, money, passport and ticket were all on the just-departed bus. He yelled out "Amigo!' on seeing me and we laughed all the way into Latisana, where we caught a train to Venice.

After locating a pensione, we adopted local custom and crashed until late afternoon, then strolled in the early evening heat to the Rialto and St Mark's Square. Venice presented an intriguing duality: one minute you were in a famous location surrounded by a million tourists, the next alone in a cool, quiet alley, untouched by time.

We continued through Rimini to San Marino, a castled city surrounded by precipitous drops, returning to Rimini that evening. Breakfasting in a park, we prepared for the final train trip of the Inter Rail epic. While waiting for the train to Brindisi, we got into an argument about (of all things) whether Greenland should be considered geographically part of Europe. I was arguing it should be seen as part of America on the grounds of proximity; Derek argued it was in Europe. As the argument heated up, I noticed Derek develop a twitch near his eye.

"Your eye is twitching."

"Yes, I know, I can feel it, but I didn't think it would be visible."

"So now I know when I've pushed you too far."

"You're right. If you'd been anyone else, I would have flattened you by now.[3]

The discussion about the twitch cooled off the argument, but not the heat of the day and we spent ten hours reading, standing up on the train, because there was no possibility of sitting down. I was pushed so tightly into the woman next to me, I thought she might think we were engaged by the end of the journey.

We booked into a cheap but luxurious room at the Hotel Regina and spent the next day lounging around the square in Brindisi with Christy from Boone, North Carolina, waiting for our evening ferry to Corfu.

We boarded the Ionis at 8pm, slept underneath some steps, and woke to find Corfu on our right and Albania on our left. It was a day of decision for Derek: he had been suffering from increasing stomach pains, and was concerned it was appendicitis.

"Look, appendicitis is supposed to be some sort of shooting pain isn't it? Your pain isn't a shooting pain."

"Yes, but this pain has been increasing – it might be a prelude to appendicitis."

"I'm sure it's not appendicitis."

"You're not a doctor. Besides, what am I supposed to do if we get out to some remote Greek island and it *is* appendicitis? They don't have any real medical facilities out there."

"Well, they do have ouzo and I've got my Swiss Army pocket knife. We could make do."

Derek had made his decision: he wasn't going to risk the islands. We walked to the airport together and he bought a ticket to London. While

---

[3] Later, I ended up agreeing with Derek's viewpoint, based on the relative depth of the water. It's much shallower between Greenland and Europe.

Derek was changing money, I heard a loud squeal in my ear. Turning, I saw "what's-her-name?": without ever exchanging names, we had met first on a Swedish train, next in the Heidelberg youth hostel, and now in another of those amazing coincidences of the road, on the streets of Corfu.

I booked into a shared room in the Hotel Acropolis on the waterfront, and Derek and I spent the time before he had to go drinking.

"Look after that appendix."

"Give my regards to the Greek islands."

I hit the beach for my first swim since Mexico, reveling once again in the luxury of solitude and unlimited options.

Later that afternoon, I was having a quiet drink when John and Julie introduced themselves. Based in Bristol, they were working their way around Europe and as we talked, drank, and ate into the night, I realised the ease of meeting others was one of the great benefits of traveling alone. When I got back to the hotel room, the two other guys sharing it were already asleep.

After spending the next day at the beach, I returned to the room and met one of the guys. He was impossibly good-looking, reminiscent of a young Paul McCartney. I asked what he did for a living.

"I'm a roadie. I work for Pink Floyd."

"You're kidding."

"No. Really." But I still wasn't convinced.

"So what are you doing in Corfu?"

"I'm trying to get off drugs. The drugs have really stuffed up my system and I'm trying to diagnose what's wrong with me through Chinese medicine."

I decided to test him about Pink Floyd.

"So you're going to go back to work with the band?"

"As long as I can get clean and stay that way."

"So what is the band up to now?"

"They're working on a new album called The Wall. When it's finished, they'll take it on tour. They're going to perform the entire concert behind a fake wall, which will only be demolished right at the end of the concert."

I looked at him dubiously, mentally wishing him well in getting off the drugs, but of course, a little later, it all happened just as he'd described.

chapter 44

Ios: ode on a Grecian sojourn

I woke just in time to catch the Ionis to Patras. The trip took all day and as we glided past rugged islands, I chatted to Tony and Ruth from Melbourne and lay in a lifeboat improving my tan. The three hour bus trip from Patras to Athens soured in the presence of noisy Americans and I eventually jumped off the bus into the Athenian night with glee.

Athens was a completely new city to me and with a frisson of delight, I realised my situation. It was ten o'clock at night; I was in a strange city and the bus had dropped us in an obscure industrial area. I had absolutely no idea where I was, no map, no concept of the location of the centre of town or hostels, and there were no spires or tall buildings visible. I was completely alone. I was thrilled. If Derek had been there, I would have automatically deferred to his intuitive navigational skills and followed his lead. Now, it was up to me.

I listened for noises that might indicate activity and tried to discern which parts of the sky seemed more brightly lit above the tops of the buildings. After a few twists and turns, I stumbled across the Semiramis Hotel, but managed only a fitful sleep in an overly hot room. The next morning was August 3, and after some calculations about how long to spend on the islands, I booked my passage to Ios the following day, and a seat on the Magic Bus back to London for the 14th. I bumped into Christy, who had spent three days in Athens doing absolutely nothing, and we ended up drinking for a while in Panepistimiou Street. She decided to come to Ios with me, but by the time we tried to book her ticket, the boat was full, so she booked to Crete instead. I changed accommodation to the Funny Trumpets hostel which Dennis had recommended, and found myself sharing a room with three French guys, two Israelis, a Canadian, and two English girls I didn't discover until I woke.

Next morning, I walked through Omonia Square to Monastiraki Square, pausing for a shishkebab and a beer and a glance at the distant Acropolis. Six tube stops later, I was in Piraeus, hanging around the docks. The ferry left shortly after 4 pm, calling at Tinos (where most of the passengers disembarked) and Mykonos, finally arriving at Ios at 2 am. A small boat transferred us to shore and deposited us on a beach where most of us spent the rest of the night. I found a beached zodiac and slept in its lee, waking at 6 am and walking to the village on the other side of the bay. Although Ios was supposed to be "the island of women", first impression was that men definitely seemed to be in the majority. Homer was said to be buried somewhere on the island.

I paid to sleep on the roof of Domatia guest lodge and spent the day on the nude beach and drinking with two Australians, Louise and Jenny. After they headed to bed, I sat down in the main square with Sue and Sandra from Herefordshire, who were staying at the same lodge, and drinking with George, whose family owned the Domatia.

"So what do you do when you're not bumming around the Greek islands?", I asked.

"I sing in a band," replied Sue, "It's called Cluster." She produced a small black and white promotional flyer with a picture of herself and a group of hairy guys in white flared suits. It turned out she knew Chrissie Hynde of The Pretenders. I was impressed. The fact that I knew Pink Floyd's roadie and that Deborah Harry once sweated on me seemed paltry by comparison.

After another night on the Domatia roof, in a sleeping bag borrowed from Louise, I noted two Scandinavian women had booked in, and elected to stay on the closer, non-nude beach, to minimise sunburn. That night, Sue, Sandra, George and myself went out to dinner and George insisted on paying the bill amidst much protest. His goal was obvious: he was hoping the girls would be so overwhelmed with gratitude they would be compelled to throw off their clothes and repay him with sexual favours. George was outvoted on where to go next, and we headed through labyrinthine alleys to the Galaxy club, which was closed. George's mood deteriorated, even when we ended up in his choice of disco; he forced Scotch on us and was becoming boorish at his lack of progress with the girls, thereby guaranteeing failure. From the next disco, I took the girls home via a café, leaving George staring morosely into his drink.

After a very late start to the day (I was now sleeping on the floor in Sue and Sandra's room) we headed to separate beaches. When we met later, Sandra was feeling unwell, so Sue and I walked to the Galaxy, and, unimpressed by the band, left at 11pm. Despite having spent lots of time together, I found it hard reading Sue; she was certainly not flirtatious, and I had detected no encouraging signals.

Then, suddenly, we were caught in one of "those" moments. It was late at night and we were alone on a high hill on one of the most romantic Greek islands. Hundreds of feet below, the warm Mediterranean caressed the beaches and a full moon sent a platinum pathway across the water towards us. In front of me was a sensitive, talented woman whose wide eyes indicated that she, too, had recognised a perfect Mills and Boon moment. She even knew Chrissie Hynde. We both knew what we were supposed to do, but with an inward chuckle, I felt set up; somehow, I felt I had wandered into someone else's soap opera script. Rebelliously, we let the moment pass with a chaste kiss.

There was one more beach day, and then the girls left. Sue gave me her address, took my photo surreptitiously, and they were gone. I found another roof to sleep on, complete with mattress and blankets and a stunning view over the harbour. I was having a late afternoon beer with two Irishmen and a Welshman, when the two Swedish girls I'd seen previously, said "hi" to me and sat at an adjacent table. When a drunken Welshman spilt beer over me, it became my excuse to move to Lena and Christine's table, which soon became a party of nine, including Dutch, Germans, a Belgian and an Israeli. We progressed to the Galaxy, then Farinari's, and I put my arm around Lena as we walked. Later, we walked down towards the coast together, embracing, until she withdrew.

"I like you very much," she explained, "but I don't want to make love to you yet. People think that Swedish girls are too easy." Pondering her "yet", I complied with her wishes and we said goodnight on her doorstep at 3 am.

Christine, Lena and I spent the next day sunbathing topless on Milopotas Beach. As I lay between them, I thought of Derek back in the chill of Selsey, undergoing tests for possible appendicitis, and grinned until the corners of my mouth cracked. That night, Lena and I slept together on the beach, huddled under a sleeping bag, and watched dawn creep over the bay, gradually illuminating an island of cacti, white buildings and ruined windmills.

On the ferry that night, I watched the lights of Ios fade into the background, and woke as we were pulling into Piraeus the next morning. Catching the train into Athens, I headed straight for the Acropolis, waiting with thousands of others for it to open. As soon as it did they swarmed over it like ants over sugar cubes and my enthusiasm dimmed. I took a few photos, headed to Syntagma to find Funny Trumpets full, and ended up with a spot on the roof of Joseph's House near the Stadium. The evening was spent eating and drinking with Matt from Brisbane, and the next morning I discovered a letter from Derek at the Poste Restante. He *didn't* have appendicitis after all; the doctor thought the pain had been caused by jogging on bare feet with a full bladder. I responded the only way possible – by composing a rhapsodic reply about Ios.

The following day, I boarded the Magic Bus to London: straight through, three days, minimal stops. It was clearly not the place to acquire diarrhea, so I adopted a constipation-inducing diet of bread, cheese and hard-boiled eggs, and on 17 August 1979 arrived in London unsullied.

chapter 45

Ireland

It turned out that Derek's "appendicitis" had also been fuelled by varied diets mixed with alcohol. After a couple of days' R & R in Selsey we headed to London, booked into the Camellia again, and checked out Virgin's Christmas (sic) party where the three bands playing were Local Operator, Fingerprintz, and Cowboys International. *Time* magazine was unable to get Yasser Arafat to give a clear answer on whether he acknowledged Israel's right to exist, but if Yasser was being vague, I had made two definite decisions: to spend some time hitchhiking around Ireland, and to fly home in early October.

I booked a return fare to Rosslare (£38) and my flight home for October 2 (£270), and we caught Crystal Palace's first home game in first division. Derek returned to Selsey and a casual job in the local bakery; I caught a night train from Paddington to Rosslare, arriving at 6.30 am.

I found myself walking along the road with an Irish guy hitching home from Greece. In another incredible coincidence of the road, we discovered we had been on Ios at the same time. We got a ride to Wexford, where we headed separate ways, then I caught another into New Ross. At the tourist office I failed to get a Ramones ticket, but successfully made an AUS sign for my pack from borrowed materials.

A commercial traveler took me to Waterford, but then I waited an hour for a ride to Cork. Eventually, a truckie called Liam obliged, his cab aswim with Coke, Mars bars and pornographic magazines, and although riding in his rig was akin to riding a horse, we shared an amiable 80 miles together.

Arriving in Cork, I reflected on the joys of hitching: on my first day, four rides had taken me half-way across the widest part of Ireland. However, the hostel was full, and I had a three mile walk to the campsite, which charged an exorbitant £1.60. Nevertheless, it was great to have the tent up again.

The next morning, a young chef from Cork took me to Kinsale, where I wandered a drizzling mile out of town to the castle at Summercove, which offered free camping. Two more lifts, the second with an old farming couple, took me to Timoleague, a small town with a thirteenth-century ruined church and mudflats with roaming waders. A Cork doctor and his wife came into the Mill House pub where I was having dinner, and I discovered they were graced with nomadic sons. They bought me a pint and then drove me through the rain to the campsite a mile out of town.

The campsite proved to be a farmhouse, run by a couple with five kids. I was hit by a gale of hospitality: they insisted that I have a room in the house rather than pitch a tent in the rain and they gave me freedom of the kitchen. Their children were delightful and Elaine was the most mature eight year old I'd ever seen. I'd also been invited by some fellow campers to visit their barrel-shaped, horse-drawn gypsy caravan. It was only my second day and I'd only covered 36 miles, but I was already falling passionately in love with Ireland (years later, I would discover that I had Irish ancestors on both sides of my family).

After spending far too long in the caravan that night, eating smoked salmon and drinking poteen moonshine whisky with three crazy Dutch women, I got off to a late start the next day. I met a young Italian hitch-hiker called Madeleina and we got a lift fairly quickly to Clunakilty, then a young plumber took us to just east of Roscarberry. After a long wait, we walked into Roscarberry, where I suggested it might be easier if we tried separately. Madeleina walked on through town to try her luck and I headed in to explore it. I found the square full of ponies and horses, all led or being ridden by children, with dozens of people standing around watching. The second car after lunch took me to Skibbereen, picking up two more hitchers, Linda and Mary, on the way. As they were also heading to Cape Clear, we started walking together from Skibbereen and were picked up by a fisherman who drove us the nine miles to Baltimore, the departure point for the ferry. We had a few drinks before catching the 7 pm ferry across to the rugged, Scottish-looking island, then a few more in one of the island's pubs before blindly wending our way around the coast to the hostel where we discovered Madeleina.

The next morning Mary, Linda, Madeleina and I walked to the lake on the island, caught the noon ferry back to Baltimore, where we met Lyn and Sally in the pub, two friends of Linda's who had been driving around looking for her. They took us back to Skibbereen where we dropped off Linda and Mary (they were heading back to Cork) and I found myself continuing with Lyn and Sally around the Ring of Kerry. I was amazed at the social aspect of supposedly "solo" hitching and the implicit trust that was automatically extended to fellow road warriors. I decided "solo travelling" was an oxymoron.

In Kenmare, we drank in the bars and took a six-pack back to a B & B that was built in 1798. We fixed the trailing exhaust on the Renault, drove through some of Kerry's coastal delights, washed lunch down with Guinness and Bushmills in Cahirciveen, and wasted an hour sunning ourselves on the south side of Dingle Bay. We were fortunately undercharged in Dingle for a posh dinner of smoked mackerel pate and poached salmon.

"So, what did you study back in Australia?", Sally inquired.

"Literature. I initially wanted to be a journalist, but I couldn't drink enough."

"You could've fooled us. If that's the measuring stick, I think you've got a chance of winning a Pulitzer."

"I think you have to be American to get one of those."

"So, what's your favourite poem, then?"

I had to think about this, as I'd never been asked the question.

"I've got two favourites: a poem by Keats about a Grecian urn, and one by Marvell about his girlfriend."

"But they're old poets aren't they? Both long dead."

"True, but I don't think we should hold that against them."

"What's so special about these poems then?"

"Keats's poem equates truth with beauty and therefore makes truth subjective. Romantics like him argued for the legitimacy of subjectivism; our century has made subjectivism compulsory. So Keats was something of a pioneer."

She thought about this.

"Keats died young, didn't he?"

"Yep, it was pretty much part of the Romantic profile to die of tuberculosis. If you also happened to be starving in a garret, it just added to the image."

"What about the other poem, why do you like that?"

"I like that he's honest about lust, and he has a unique way of convincing his girlfriend to go to bed with him: essentially, 'We're getting old, we're going to die very soon, and corpses don't have sex, so let's not wait.'"

She laughed, "Did it work?"

"I've no idea, I just read his poetry, not his biography, but he sounds desperate. Perhaps she found desperation attractive."

Mountbatten's murder dominated the headlines on August 28. After pausing to take photographs at the top of Conair Pass, we drove into Tralee and made our farewells over a drink at the Brogue Inn, exchanging addresses. During our three days together, I had grown to love the bizarre black humour of these Belfast nurses and I marveled at and mourned these gratuitous, satisfying, but fleeting intimacies of the road, which seemed like metaphors of my life.

After a three hour wait, a truckie dropped me at the hostel in Limerick where I met an Australian who worked in the Australian Embassy in Amman. The next morning, he and his son dropped me in Ennis, then a young girl drove me to Lahinch. At the campsite, I talked late into the night with a young German couple from Dachau, and the next day a guy from Leeds took me the short distance from Lahinch to Liscannor.

Grabbing a tin of pears for breakfast, I walked the four miles to the Cliffs of Moher, checking out an abandoned farm house on the way. The cliffs were spectacular: semicircular gouges plunging hundreds of feet into the ocean and pockmarked with thousands of crevices housing birds. If Derek had been with me, he would have insisted on abseiling down them. Walking away from the cliffs, I hitched the first car leaving the parking lot, a mother and daughter from Buckinghamshire, now resident in Dublin. We drove from Moher to Doolin where they paid for tea and scones, through Lisdoonvarna, down Corkscrew Hill and the rocky hills nearby, through Ballyvaghan to Galway.

I was in a pub, minding my own business, when I was asked an abrupt question: "So do you believe in God, then?" Clearly, my interrogator didn't believe in conversational foreplay.

"Yes, I do."

"Well, I don't – I'm an atheist. Won't catch me believing in something I can't see."

"Okay, so you don't believe in love either?"

He looked momentarily startled, then laughed, "Well, based on my 'love life', no, I don't!"

I tried again: "So, as an atheist, you believe that all life on earth happened through some accident, and then evolved through survival of the fittest?"

"Absolutely. I don't have any time for all that faith stuff."

"Interesting, because I don't believe I've got enough faith to be an atheist."

"Ha! It doesn't take faith to be an atheist, we just believe in what makes sense."

"Really? Okay, so, I've got a question for you – do you own a car?"

"Yep, a clapped-out old Ford."

"Let's say you parked your old Ford in the middle of a field and left it there. And for the sake of the argument, let's say you had a time machine and leapt 50,000 years into the future to look at your car that had been parked there all that time. Would it have evolved into a Lamborghini?"

He looked at me as if I was insane.

"Of course it wouldn't – it would just be a pile of rust."

"So, everything we know about the natural world tells us that if things are left to themselves, without any outside influence, they don't improve – they decay. Just as we know it's impossible for your Ford to evolve into a Lamborghini no matter how much time you allow, or how much radiation you hit it with, it's even more impossible for your Ford to evolve into Marilyn Monroe. Yet without God, that's basically what we have to believe – that somehow life came from minerals, and everything gradually became more complex by itself. I don't have enough faith for that; it's easier to believe in God."

"I don't need faith to be an atheist."

"Oh, I think you do, but you don't want to acknowledge it. One last question: how long do you think evolution has taken?"

"Millions of years."

"Okay," I replied, "so think of any life form you like – how long does it have to evolve a fully functioning reproductive system? Exactly one generation, no more: if you don't evolve a fully functioning reproductive system in *one* generation, there is no second generation, and your options are over."

"So are you a Christian then?"

"No. I'm just convinced it makes more sense to believe in God than to be an atheist."

"Well, one thing I believe in is Guinness."

"I think we're singing from the same hymn sheet on that one."

chapter 46

The Return

Lamenting the cancellation of the Ramones gig, I met Fiona and Paul, a couple of young literature graduates from Stirling University, in a Salthill backyard. Despite their obvious cleverness, they had managed to lose all their tent pegs, so I lent them my spare one and the children of the house gleefully bent spoons into makeshift pegs for the remainder.

"What are you going to do when you return to Perth?" Paul asked.

"I have no idea. I don't know how to make a living at the things I'm passionate about, so it will probably be a case of taking the first job that comes up."

"So what are you passionate about?"

"Writing. History. Travel. Oh, and avoiding commitment! Know how to make a living at those?"

"Well, the first and last sound like a few journalists I know!"

"Ha! I think we must know the same people. Unfortunately all the journalists I know are alcoholics and I am a bit too fond of the drink myself, so I'm determined to avoid that career."

"Teaching?"

"I'd have to do more study, plus I don't think people respect teachers. Ultimately, we all have to choose between passion and prostitution, right? I think it will be prostitution for me for a bit longer."

"You're a prostitute?" Paul looked astonished.

"A metaphor. Look, the way I see it, people either get to work at something they're passionate about, or they sell their time and their bodies to something they're not passionate about – prostitution. I suppose there's an intermediate phase – preparation – as well. But about 90% of the people I know are prostitutes. What we all want to do is spend more time on our passions and less time prostituting ourselves, but most people never get there." It was a recently worked-out theory, but I was quite pleased with it.

The next day, although there seemed to be some chemistry happening with a barmaid in Oughterard, I headed into the rain and was picked up by an English ex-Army officer who owned a farm in Tipperary and was trout fishing in the area; he dropped me at the Carna turnoff and I walked four drizzly miles to the Ben Lockery hostel.

After spending the evening talking to a chap from New York and a cyclist I'd met previously on Cape Clear Island, I was on the road early in the morning walking seven of the nine miles to Clifden on a deserted road before getting a lift for the last two miles with fellow hostelers. After a big brunch in Clifden, a maniacal breakdown driver on the way to an accident dropped me by the roadside, and I was soon collected by a young German couple who drove me the twenty-six miles to Westport. A lift to Castlebar was followed by one to Swinford with a driver who could have spent the rest of his life typecast as Magwitch. The final lift of the day was with two staunch Roman Catholics and I endured twenty-nine miles of dodgy religious conversation as we drove into Sligo.

At the tourist office, a couple of young Aussie girls told me the Sligo campsites were all a fair way out, so I joined them at their B & B. They had been away from Australia for six months and had also come overland from Kathmandu. An emotional cocktail of nostalgia, envy and uncertainty swept over me: these girls were in the same position I'd been in thirteen months before, when it was all new; their road was stretching ahead of them, but my road was coming to an end and I would be home in a month. News that Soviet troops stationed in Cuba were causing concern and that the Yorkshire Ripper had claimed his twelfth victim only added to the gloom.

The following day was the longest in terms of miles covered. The first lift took me to Cliffony, where I photographed Mountbatten's mansion from a distance; the next to Bundoran where I waited for an hour before getting a short ride into Ballyshannon. A young guy on his way to see his girlfriend drove me to Donegal where I waited for nearly another hour before a liquor wholesaler in a Volvo drove me through Barnesmore Gap to Ballybofey, passing a famous pub and a car in a ditch. I walked across the river to Stranorlar, caught a ride to Castlefinn, then a kid with a supernaturally large blackhead on his nose drove me to Lifford.

At Lifford, I crossed the border into Northern Ireland. The border was what I expected: a tower, corrugated iron, barbed wire and soldiers. While walking through Strabane to Omagh, I turned a corner and unexpectedly blundered into a control point where a dozen armed soldiers eyed me suspiciously. In their jungle greens and berets these guys meant business, and the machine guns slung at their hips followed me as I walked around them. I breathed deeply, tried to assume an air of total harmlessness, and walked past. Suddenly, an elderly couple stopped (I didn't even have my thumb out) and gave me a lift to Newtownstewart. I had hardly walked through the town when a Mini stopped and the driver offered to take me through to Dublin. By the end of the day I'd covered about 213 miles, and collapsed at Mountjoy Hostel.

In the studious gloom of Trinity College, the Book of Kells glowed with the inspired industry of an earlier time, spoilt only by the presence of a group of "I-must-utter-absolutely-everything-that-crosses-my-mind-no-matter-how-vacuous" Americans, and I wondered yet again why so many avoided the silence and solitude I found so attractive. Dublin Castle was less impressive, but at least there was no background chatter. The highlight of the day was the vaults of St Michan's church in which the dry atmosphere mummified the bodies. Apparently it was here that Bram Stoker conceived the idea for Dracula. I did the obligatory Guinness tour, checked out every bookshop in Dublin, and for reasons not clear even to me, decided not to call Mary and ask to sleep at her place. After a second night in the Mountjoy, I transferred to Isaac's in Frenchman's Lane.

From Wicklow to Arklow, then a drunken magazine journalist (confirming my stereotype) from New York took me to Wexford. A couple more lifts and I was back in Rosslare, having covered a 900 mile circle in 14 days. As I boarded the ferry I realised from that point, everything headed in the direction of home – was I ready? Did I even know what "ready" or "home" meant?

The next week or two was spent shuffling between Selsey and London. The travel agent initially insisted they had posted my ticket, and by the time they discovered it had fallen behind a desk in their office, I was in London and collected it personally, only to discover they had dated it for September 2 instead of October 2.

"According to this, I've already missed my flight," I lamented. They flustered around, repairing the mistake. I also discovered that in pursuit of the cheapest flight home, I would be returning to Perth via Moscow, Bangkok and Kuala Lumpur.

My father was passing through London to join a three week European coach tour. I met him at Heathrow, got his luggage into his luxurious

Grosvenor Hotel room and we met Derek for drinks at the Shakespeare and dinner at the Apollo. Then Derek and I headed back to Selsey. The 8.30 pm train didn't arrive, so we caught the 9.10, and changed at Barnham. More connections failed to materialise and we finally arrived at Chichester at 1 am. We walked to Selsey in 110 minutes, jogging in from Norton.

After a few days in Selsey and fond farewells, I left 2 Holford Green for the final time, Derek's granddad driving me to Chichester. Back in London, I dumped my stuff at the hostel near St Paul's, and in the next few days saw Woody Allen's Manhattan, Alien, and a performance of Love's Labours Lost at the Aldwych. One night I headed to Dingwall's to see Destroy All Monsters and Viva - both bands were abysmal and I fluked the last tube, arriving back after 1 am. Of course, the hostel was completely locked. As I pondered the options of trying to break in or sleeping in the gutter, a light came on in a ground floor window and through a small gap, I asked to be let in, thanking God for insomnia.

On October 2, I fronted at Heathrow to read that in Iran, Khomeini was demanding people obey the Islamic republic or be annihilated; unsurprisingly, *Time* was no longer describing him as "enigmatic". Having discovered with some trepidation that the first two legs of the flight home were with Aeroflot, I arrived in Moscow for an ostensible stop of two hours. Then there was a problem: as we queued to board the flight to Kuala Lumpur, it became obvious we weren't all going to get on.

"Our apologies, but we have overbooked the flight to Kuala Lumpur. Some of you will have to remain in Moscow for the night." I could see that they were deciding who was going to remain, and of course, they focused on the single males. About a dozen of us were shepherded to one side.

"I am sorry, but all of you will have to remain in Moscow for 24 hours, until tomorrow night's flight."

"What's going to happen to our luggage?"

"Your luggage has already been loaded on board. You can collect it tomorrow when you arrive in KL." I wasn't overly encouraged.

"So what happens to us now?"

"We will provide you with accommodation this evening and food at the airport. I am sorry for the inconvenience."

None of us had visas for Russia, so our movements were closely guarded. Hopes of a reasonable hotel vanished as armed soldiers escorted us to what looked like army barracks. We had a room each, and as I shut the door, I became completely paranoid. I was stranded in a country for which I had no visa; most of my belongings (including irreplaceable slides and photos) were supposedly flying to Kuala Lumpur, (but judging by Aeroflot's efficiency to date, were probably in Greenland); and I had in my possession items worth a small fortune on the Russian black market – jeans and dozens of records. It occurred to me that a covetous soldier could slit my throat in the middle of the night, dispose of my body, and gain a nice supplement for his meagre salary.

I took what measures I could, including the standard movie fare of jamming a chair under the door handle, and balancing something on top that would make a noise if it fell. I awoke with my throat unventilated, but still in the middle of a bad dream.

Our military minders shunted us to the airport where we spent the day shuffling in and out of the cafeteria, eating free but stodgy food. Eventually, we eagerly lined up for the next flight, but once again, it became obvious that Aeroflot had overbooked, and some of us weren't going to make it. This time though, I was lucky, but sorry for the few guys still left behind, and praying that my luggage would be waiting for me in KL.

Fortunately, it was, and as I transferred onto the luxury of a Malaysian Airlines flight to Perth, I vowed never again to fly Aeroflot. Perth arrived, I taxied home in the early hours of the morning, and snuck into the downstairs room of 36 Burt Street. On the flight home, I'd done some calculations: I had been away for 20 months without working a day, traveled nonstop through 37 countries, and spent a total (including numerous book and record purchases) of $8,500 Australian dollars. It was the adventure of a lifetime, and a bargain, but now decisions of a different sort awaited me.

chapter 47

Reasons for Disbelief

During the next few weeks, I caught up with family and friends, showed Den the slides, and discovered that Perth had finally acquired a 24-hour restaurant. I did a circuit of Perth pubs - the Dianella, the Raffles, the Balga, the Shents, the Albion and Clancy's – in pursuit of gigs by Warner, The Dugites and The Elks. In the midst of frantic socialising, I signed on the dole, applied for jobs, worked at the Church campsite in Serpentine, and helped clean out my grandparents' shed, which showed a reassuring lack of sinister Druidic implements.

Temporary Government jobs came and went in early 1980 and in March, I started a permanent job with the Commonwealth Employment Service; Derek returned to Perth the same month. I worked at the CES office in Phoenix Shopping Centre, Spearwood, and although the Public Service trap had closed on me again, I was grateful for the salary and the job was not without its lighter moments.

"Mr Savage?" I called out to a roomful of people waiting to be interviewed, "Mr *Randy* Savage?" I've got no idea why he was looking for work; he could have sued his parents for psychological and emotional abuse and retired on the proceeds.

Apart from a regular stream of attractive young women looking for work, there was also Cathy, a colleague. Cathy with her platinum blonde hair and ice-blue Celtic eyes was not averse to a drink or three and we spent hours together in the Phoenix Hotel sharing lager and locking lips.

So life arrived at a certain stability, and it was novel enough not to be oppressive. I now had the opportunity to begin poring through the materials I had gathered and investigate the claims of the RLDS Church; this became my evening job. However, I needed to spread out all the papers and make a mess; my room at mum and dad's was too small, and it would have been unfair of me to impose so much clutter on their neat lifestyle. I felt confined, and needed a way out, so I prayed a simple but demanding prayer that went something like this: "God, I want to do this research, but I can't do it here. I need somewhere to spread out. What I'd really like is a place of my own, but I don't want to share with anyone else, I don't want to pay rent, and I don't want to have a mortgage over my head." Having asked for the impossible from a God who had no reason to listen to me, I wisely forgot about it, and would not have remembered it, except for subsequent events.

About six weeks later, mum started a conversation:

"Pete, your father rang me the other day with a strange question."

"Was it the one about whether I'm really Hope's son and not his?" She laughed.

"No, completely different. He asked me, 'Do you think Peter would mind if I bought him a town house?'" I was stunned; my father had spent all his life in the public service and wasn't wealthy.

"Let me explain his train of thought," she continued. "As you know, your father's fifty-five and it's been fifteen years since our divorce was finalised. He would really like to re-marry and is actively looking around. However, it occurred to him that any woman he marries at his stage of life

– even though he would like to marry someone younger than he is - will probably have been married before and may still have dependent children, and he would have to assume some financial responsibility for them. And of course, if he pre-deceased his new wife, she would inherit a large part of his estate. As you're his only child, he doesn't want you to miss out. He wants to give you something significant now, so he can feel that he's done the right thing by you, no matter what happens later."

"I can see the logic, but why now? It doesn't make sense. He's not actually going out with anyone at the moment so he's not about to get married; he never mentioned this idea at other times when he *was* going out with someone."

Nevertheless, I wasn't going to argue, and within a very short time I had gratefully taken up residence at Unit 5, Quay Gardens, Stirling Street, Fremantle, which was a two-storey town house a literal stone's throw from Fremantle Prison. And then I remembered the prayer, which I hadn't mentioned to anyone. It was impossible for me not to regard what had happened as an answer to prayer, and I was dumbfounded. I had asked God to do something, burdened the request with unreasonable conditions, and a few weeks later it had all happened. My father had paid cash for the unit and my name was on the title. No-one had ever taught me to pray or to expect answers like that; was there a whole dimension to God that I was missing? At any rate, I had my end of the bargain to live up to: I had asked for my own place so that I could investigate the RLDS Church; it would be churlish not to throw myself into the project now.

And so I did. My social life dwindled as I worked until the early hours of the morning and on weekends, reading and taking notes. About two weeks into the process, it happened: for a whole complex of reasons, I realised that I simply couldn't believe the claims of the RLDS Church any more. Generations of my mother's family had stood by a set of beliefs and now I couldn't maintain them. I had believed that my investigations would actually *confirm* those beliefs and that I would eventually become an active participant in the RLDS priesthood, having outgrown the wild and willful ways of youth. Now that certainty was gone. I had sought a testimony of the truth of the RLDS Church, and now had a testimony of its falsity. I leaned back in my chair in my study, amazed at my new-found disbelief. What now? Obviously, I would have to leave the Church, but then it occurred to me that I needed to do something more; I needed to write down everything I had found for the benefit of other RLDS members who had no access to what I had seen. Anything less would be selfish.

Taking my existing notes as a base, I worked on and for the next month only slept a couple of hours a night. By the end of that time, I had typed 80 foolscap pages titled *Reasons for Disbelief: A Survey of the Historical and Theological Beliefs of the Reorganized Church of Jesus Christ of Latter-day Saints*. Now, I hasten to add that much of the material in this book was not original and many of my key objections had been discovered by others. Others had noted anomalies in the *Book of Mormon* such as horses being mentioned in the Americas prior to the fifth century AD when they were only introduced by Europeans a millennium later; and why would Jesus, in an alleged American ministry after his resurrection in Palestine, speak in a "reformed Egyptian" that, when translated by Joseph Smith in nineteenth-century New York, would turn out to be word-perfect with the seventeenth-century English of the King James Bible?

These and many other objections affected the RLDS and mainstream Mormonism equally. What was even more pertinent for me was the material that undermined the RLDS distinctives – points on which they disagreed with the Utah Mormons. For example, the RLDS Church had traditionally maintained that Joseph Smith had nothing to do with the introduction of polygamy, but that it was an invention of Brigham Young's, who claimed

Joseph had preached it before his death. The RLDS Church also believed that Joseph Smith had nothing to do with the introduction of the doctrine of plurality of gods, a doctrine that was encapsulated in the saying "As man is, God once was; as God is, man may become."

The documents I had seen forced me to conclude that the RLDS position was wrong and that Joseph Smith *had* taught polygamy to his inner circle and had married other women before his death, and that he had also taught plurality of gods. Now while these conclusions superficially moved me closer to the position of Utah Mormonism, I refused to support either doctrine. I was no expert on the New Testament, but I knew enough to be sure that Jesus Christ was not polytheistic.

In October 1980, my mother and I ran off two dozen copies of the book on a Gestetner machine at Fremantle Technical College, and I began to distribute them to RLDS people. Some expressed disgust with what I had done; others couldn't read more than the first few pages; still others just stopped talking to me altogether. My hope was that some would be interested enough to challenge me and ask to see my evidence; few did, even though I kept attending church regularly for months to make myself available.

Shortly, there was another shock.

"By the way," mum said, "I've sent a copy of your book to the First Presidency."

"You've *what?!*"

I had only ever seen the book as having a limited, local readership; now it was winging its way to Independence, Missouri and onto the desks of the senior leaders of the RLDS Church, complete with a "please explain" letter from my mother. I felt like the canary-weight contender, pushed against his will into the ring against the sumo champ. "In one corner we have the twenty-three year old Fremantle boy with a hastily written pamphlet; in the other we have the seasoned leadership of a denomination with post-graduate degrees." It was an uneven contest.

The First Presidency referred my book to Richard Howard, then the Church Historian, and for several months, Richard and I exchanged letters. Richard criticised some of my methodologies (and with hindsight, I would have done some things differently) but he also complimented my reasoning and writing abilities and invited me to join the RLDS Historical Society. But as issues of ego faded into the background, I noticed something fascinating – Richard actually agreed with a lot of my findings. "So why don't you just publish all this stuff in the *Herald* [the RLDS magazine]?," I wrote. I found the answer chilling: they had a "long-term" plan to change the thinking of the people in the Church. It was clear that they knew they would lose too many members if they published all the material at once.

At the beginning of *Reasons for Disbelief*, I had discussed the complementary roles of faith and reason and how the resources of reason should be fully employed before making a "leap of faith". At the end of the book, I concluded that, having applied reason to the history and doctrine of the Reorganized Church of Jesus Christ of Latter-Day Saints, the results firmly discouraged me from making a leap of faith in that direction. "Truth is under no obligation to be palatable", I wrote in the final lines.[4] History, that passionate coquette to whom I had long ago lost my heart, had come to my rescue, and the result was a break with my own past and the avoidance of the one commitment I *had* expected to make.

---

4   *Reasons for Disbelief* was properly published in America in 2010, in an extended version which included our correspondence with RLDS church authorities.

chapter 48

Days of Gold and Madness

With Derek, Dennis and myself all back in Perth, certain things were inevitable. We had all been drawn back into our previous employment: Derek to cartography; Dennis to drycleaning; me to the public service. We all wanted to travel again and work was the necessary evil to finance the next trip. Where would we go next?

As 1981 dawned, discussion became more intense. One day, we decided to go gold prospecting. Of course, it was Derek's idea; in his job he could access unlimited free maps and identify old goldfields with ease. And it all happened with great alacrity: we purchased a second-hand Land Rover and a new metal detector, quit our jobs and headed north to the goldfields around Leonora and Laverton. Once again, I had left the security of the Public Service (this time after working exactly 12 months) and on what was obviously a fool's errand. Whether or not we found any gold, my plan was to travel again immediately after we finished prospecting. Appropriately enough, we drove out of Perth on April Fool's Day, 1981.

Leonora, with its two pubs and caravan park, became our weekend base. Most of the week we camped out in the bush in promising goldfields and gradually became expert at finding old nails using the White's Metal

Detector. A week went by, and another, without finding gold, and it didn't matter. We knew we didn't deserve to discover anything: we were novices and we'd done minimal planning. Mainly, we had escaped our jobs, were away from home and immersed in the bush. Once again, I was in a flight from commitment and while I was aware of this, I had no idea what I was running *towards*. We discovered spiders the size of new-born kittens; snakes slithered through our campsites; and we washed by climbing ladders at the side of corrugated iron rain water tanks, and pouring the ice-cold water over us as we tried not to fall the four metres to the ground.

For hour after hour we scoured the most promising quartz and black rock ground around the old workings. When the detector set off a promising signal, one of us would dig, move the ground into two piles, and isolate the signal. If the source of the signal was not obviously rubbish, one of us would pop it in his mouth to clean it with saliva. One day after we'd been prospecting about three weeks, I popped a sand-covered rock in my mouth and out came a small gold nugget. We couldn't believe it, and after that, couldn't stop. During the next three weeks we found another fifteen or sixteen pieces of gold: most were small nuggets; some were "specimens" – rocks shot through with layers of gold.

Despite this success, it wasn't worth much – about $1,000 at 1981 prices. Dreams of the three of us pictured on the front page of *The West Australian* holding a nugget the size of a chubby toddler were shattered, along with the sybaritic lifestyle it would have supported. So, as we sat under a stunning starscape in the very definition of the middle of nowhere, with a campfire bravely thrusting orange into the velvet blackness all around, we talked of travel. None of us wanted simply to slip back into our old jobs after being on the goldfields for only six weeks.

"These John Hillaby books are great. Can you believe such an old guy can walk so far?" We'd taken reading material in which we were all interested and we'd read of Hillaby's mammoth pedestrian journeys through Africa and around England, often of more than 1,000 miles a time. Secretly, I coveted the solitude of these long, solo walks.

"Yeah, most old people I know are battling to walk around a supermarket."

"I think I'll do something like this after we finish prospecting." Derek and Den looked at me with interest.

"So where will you walk?"

I thought furiously: "I'll walk from Athens to London!"

"You're insane!" Derek spluttered, making a rapier-fast calculation, "That's 3,000 miles!"

"Alright then, I'll walk around Ireland!"

And that was it: I'd said it; I had to do it.

After we returned to Perth, I calculated it would take me up to three months to walk around Ireland. I wasn't going to follow the coast slavishly, but head to places of greatest interest and minimise my time in Northern Ireland to ease my mother's fears. I decided to take advantage of the recent Camp David accords to visit both Israel and Egypt, traveling between them by land. Mum was horrified: to her I had deliberately chosen to visit three of the most troubled places on earth alone. In her mind, it was virtual suicide.

It was 24 June 1981, and a small group of people were at Perth Airport to say goodbye, mum dressed in funereal black. The mohawk haircut Derek had given me on the goldfields was gradually turning respectable. Cathy took me to one side, fastened her smiling, ice-blue eyes on me and instead of the goodbye I was expecting, said:

"If I asked you to marry me, would you stay?"

My mind went into overdrive at this request for a commitment. When I'd left work to go prospecting, the card she'd given me said she'd see me at our wedding after I found a large nugget. Naturally, I'd taken it as a joke, but now this. She had to be bluffing. Why the drama of a marriage proposal in an airport departure lounge? Why not earlier? And was hours of snogging in the Phoenix Hotel and a drunken coupling on the floor of a South Perth flat sufficient justification for marriage? I thought not. Then I noticed her conditional phrasing; it wasn't an unqualified proposal after all.

I smiled back: "No," kissed her, and got on the plane.

As Singapore became Bahrain, fillet steak Madeira became roast duckling with lychees, and on a flight that was 75% empty, I drank far too much wine, celebrating leaving it all behind once more. With each passing minute, jobs, family, and friendships all lay further behind the jetstream of the 747, and with barely controlled exhilaration, I entered the meditative state known as deep shiraz.

This time, all the travel decisions would be mine: in Ireland, I would get up whenever I wanted, walk as far as I wanted, and stop wherever I wanted; I wouldn't have to take anyone else's opinions into consideration; I would not even be dependent on passing drivers for lifts. My euphoria moderated as we arrived in London and reality set in. I had done no training and little planning for this trip which had begun in a moment of madness on the Leonora goldfields. Ostensibly, I was there because of the bet; in reality, I was there because I had to be somewhere and I didn't want it to be the public service. The future was a vacuum, and I had to fill it somehow. On the previous trip, I believed that part of that future would lie within the RLDS Church; now, that was all behind me and the future was even cloudier than before. I loved reading, writing, and history, but I had never met anyone in Perth who managed to make a living in any of those three areas; for a Fremantle boy from a fiscally responsible family to attempt it seemed beyond bohemian – it felt like arrogant presumption.

I took my pack off the luggage conveyer at Heathrow, slipped it on and headed for the tube. It was standing-room only and I decided to keep wearing my pack for the 45 minute ride to see what it felt like. By the time we arrived in central London, I knew I had made a serious mistake: my shoulders were aching from the backpack already. I pondered whether I could drop the whole idea of walking around Ireland, and decided I couldn't. I had a pint in a pub opposite the Praed Street clinic where Fleming discovered penicillin, but I was going need something stronger than penicillin to help me walk around Ireland.

I arrived in Fishguard, Wales shortly before 3 am, and calculated that I had been awake for 51 hours straight. When the ferry deposited me in Rosslare, I shrugged the pack onto my back and walked ashore under lowering skies to be greeted by a statue of the Virgin Mary with open arms, overlooking the harbour. I felt like passing her my pack.

It didn't start to rain until I got fairly close to Wexford, then it poured. It was the middle of the Irish summer – *now* I was beginning to understand why I hadn't heard of anyone walking around Ireland before. On the south side of Wexford were rocky ledges, planted pine rows and a pile of abandoned cars, every one of which seemed an attractive place to sleep. I made it into Tim's Bar and ordered a pint of Guinness for morning tea. As I slipped the pack off, my chest and shoulders felt like they were wrapped in barrel-hoops.

Fuelled by Guinness and exhaustion, I was in an altered state on the N25 out of Wexford. I passed Forth Mountain where they were cutting a scarp, and looked over a bridge to see a large rat taking swimming lessons. Having covered 16 miles on my first day, and having been awake for more than 65 hours, I put my tent up in an obscure place and fell asleep before I could really begin feeling sorry for myself.

chapter 49

A Confluence of Self-pity and Stupidity

On the second day, my shoulders felt pain first, and when hills appeared, I had to stop several times during the first eight miles. My right knee felt like someone had driven a nail through it. At this weak point, temptation arrived: several drivers stopped and offered me lifts, which I refused. Self-pity came to an end when I passed a small cemetery which contained the graves of about thirty children: the silence of those stilled lives stopped my grumbling; I was suffering by choice.

I lunched at Dunphy's pub in Campile where the friendly barman deliberately undercharged me, continued on a circuitous route to Dunbrody Abbey where I spent a pleasant twenty minutes clambering over the ruins, then plodded on to Arthurstown. I had covered a total of twenty miles for the day and was in a state of near collapse, hardly able to walk.

I felt better the next morning, but my legs were still sending subtle messages they weren't going to take any nonsense. I decided to listen, and after catching a necessary ferry across Waterford Bay, only walked as far as Waterford itself, a distance of seven miles.

Waterford was a town of contrast: in the outlying suburbs to the south-east, beautiful Georgian mansions and rich people returning from church; near the centre, it was plainer and harder, with a liberal sprinkling of skinheads. Houses rose straight from the footpaths, sporting brightly painted front doors and gleaming door knockers. I booked into Lonergan's B & B and had my first bath since Australia.

Despite the ever-present risk of rain, the Irish summer days never seemed to end: it was light at 9.30pm when I went to bed and already light whenever I woke. I realised this meant I could walk for as long as I wanted each day, and take more frequent breaks.

It took forever to walk out of Waterford, through bleak industrial zones, past putrid little streams and, as I approached the Arco factory, the overpowering smell of glue. My right knee began to ache, and about six miles out of Waterford, I stopped on a small stone bridge for a rest. Further on, an old man with graying hair and pure white eyebrows looked like God in a tweed jacket, except the fork he was pitching hay with slightly spoilt the image.

I paused on the bridge at Kilmacthomas to look up at the Comeragh and Monavullagh mountains, and eventually asked a woman who was gardening if I could camp in her field.

"I'll have to ask my husband, but he won't be home for an hour."

So I continued on, obstinately passing one B&B, then deciding to take the next one I saw. A pine forest arrived before the next B&B, so I pitched my tent on a carpet of pine needles, having walked another twenty miles.

Mist was rolling down the mountains the next morning as I made an early start. It was low tide as Dungarvan harbour came into view; yachts stood erect, their keels held firm in the mud. I dived into Casey's, one of the more disreputable-looking pubs fronting the main square, for a pint of Smithwick's. The barman was a short, fat, florid chap called Frank who wanted to know all about Australia; a couple adopted me and enthusiastically suggested possible routes of travel.

Although I had intended to stay in Dungarvan, I had already walked past my intended lodgings. I was also fascinated by a nearby monastery at Cappoquin where I was told the monks simultaneously observed a vow of silence and made guests welcome; presumably, the welcome was somewhat subdued.

After camping near Clashmore, I arrived at Melleray Abbey near Cappoquin in mid-afternoon to be greeted by one of the monks.

"Good afternoon, Father," I offered, uncertain how to address monks. "I understand that you have some accommodation here for travelers?"

"Well actually," he said, in one of those lilting Irish accents that sounds like a piano scale, "we prefer only to have people stay on week-long retreats." Was it my imagination, or was he less than taken with my manner of dress and regenerating Mohawk?

"I tell you what though, there is a new youth hostel in Lismore just eight miles away, and if you stay around another half-hour, I'll be back and give you a cup of tea."

He'd obviously made the assumption I was hitching, but the cup of tea sounded good. I spent the next half-hour and longer, poring over my map looking for short-cuts to Lismore; after my wrong exit and long detour I needed one. The monk didn't show again and I headed off, peeved at the lack of promised tea, walking quickly back to Cappoquin and on to Lismore. The last mile into Lismore really dragged, made slightly more bearable by glimpses of the magnificent castle and the river flowing beneath it.

One person told me the youth hostel was 1 ½ miles out of town, and I thought I could just make it, until a garage attendant told me it was actually 3 miles, and it was also in the wrong direction. I trudged back into Lismore, found a delightful B&B for £5 and luxuriated in the bath as the aches and road grime washed away; at 25 miles covered, it was my longest day so far. I weighed myself, found that I had lost 6kg in six days of walking, and accepted the fact that at trip's end, I would look like a cross between Superman and Quasimodo – Superman's legs and Quasimodo's back.

Despite my stupidity in heading off to walk around Ireland at the rate of about 20 miles per day with a 17kg pack and no preparation, I was starting to believe I could actually do it – provided I wasn't wiped out by a truck on the often verge-less roads. My mind turned to other things, and I began reading the New Testament on a daily basis. I had rejected the RLDS Church, but the RLDS Church had made the sectarian claim of being the "one true church"; maybe some of the other churches had it right? Then I realised I didn't know what "having it right" meant. Maybe Christianity was wrong and another religion was closer to the truth, or perhaps they were all wrong? The RLDS Church had focused on the person of Joseph Smith; Christianity focused on the person of Jesus Christ. All churches ultimately claimed to be based on the teachings of Christ, so it seemed only sensible to try to discover who Jesus was and what he taught. If my investigation led me to reject Jesus, I could always look elsewhere – even embrace fashionable agnostic existentialism. But that seemed too cavalier a move when there were other options to investigate: History – my one remaining and tantalising commitment - required me to go back to original sources, so as I trudged the green fields of Ireland, I read in the New Testament of someone who had walked in distant, dustier fields two thousand years before.

chapter 50

The Ultimate Irish Joke

The following day's steep descent into Tallow put pressure on my knee, but the sight of the town by the rushing river Bride soon made me forget the pain. At the entrance to Conna, I clambered over a fort that had been destroyed by Cromwell, then headed into the Fisherman's Rest pub. One Harp and two Murphys later, I was best friends with a guy called Mick, a Conna local who worked as a panelbeater in Cork and had the day off "sick".

We talked of walking and drink (Bushmill's was "Paisley's brew"), taxes and maps (he'd been in the Army), and writing.

"Let me tell you a story about this woman I know in Clare," he said. "She lived a long way from any town, and only recently had electricity connected to her farmhouse. You know what the problem was?" I shook my head. "Well, no-one had told her how to switch the lights off, so the only way she could figure out how to do it was to smash the globe with a broomstick."

"You're not serious?"

"I'm completely serious. I know the woman."

And so I was introduced to the ultimate Irish joke: the Irish delighted in telling jokes and stories (true or otherwise) in which the Irish themselves looked foolish. Usually however, they picked on another part of the country, and the poor folks of Kerry fared worst of all.

"You're a journalist, aren't you?" Mick asked later.

"Why do you say that?"

"Because of the attention you're paying to everything I say."

"I once pretended to be a journalist, but I couldn't drink enough."

He talked of the Troubles and my knowledge of things Irish increased exponentially in the two hours we spent together.

I had barely walked out of Conna when it started to rain, but after sheltering under a tree for a few minutes, I kept walking, on past a pub called the Big Tree (with a medium-sized tree in front of it) through farming country to a couple of deserted buildings at a cross road. I considered camping in these, but they were dusty and smelly (a bit like me, actually) so I ended up in a farmer's field, about 17 miles from Cork.

The next day, I refused two lifts, one from a Cork dentist recently returned from eight months in Australia and New Zealand. I arrived in Cork mid-afternoon and ravenous, having walked 18 miles on a bottle of Lucozade and a small chocolate. Burgers, fries, sandwiches and coffee were soon demolished in the Queens Old Castle Centre and I wandered out into old, dirty and unashamedly working-class Cork. Cork was a gloriously grubby little city. Poverty was rife and beggars were in the streets. There seemed to be no conscience about littering, but strangely, it bothered me less than elsewhere because as garbage bins overflowed into moss-lined alleyways, and street market debris gathered in gutters, it created an oddly nineteenth-century atmosphere – I could imagine myself in the streets of Dickens's London.

Den's old army trousers had finally worn through at the knees and had a three-inch rip in the back; I replaced them at a shop in Corn Market Street and walked to the youth hostel in sartorial splendour. For the second time in two years, the hostel was full, and I stayed in the same campground as 1979.

I awoke to a day of typical Irish meteorological caprice. The most cloud-free morning so far nearly persuaded me to leave my jacket behind; an hour later in the centre of Cork, it was completely overcast and remained so, drizzling, for the rest of the day. It was easy to lose yourself in Cork, as the main city is on an island, and the view down most streets ended with the river Lee. Signs proclaimed "End British Terror" with an English flag and skull and crossbones dripping blood, next to the faces of the hunger strikers.

I lounged in the Picnic Area in Queens Old Castle, drank lots of black coffee (which I didn't drink on walking days), tried not to enter too many bookshops, and enjoyed the simple pleasure of walking around a city with no pack on my back.

"Why do you drink your coffee black?" asked someone in a café. "I couldn't drink coffee without milk and sugar."

"You know," I replied, "I used to be the same: white and two sugars. Then I travelled overland from Kathmandu to London. I had a few too many coffees in which the milk had gone bad, so I decided to drink it black. Then I discovered a few too many sugar bowls that had things moving in them. So I got the message: black and nothing."

"D'ya like your women the same way?" he quipped.

Macroom revealed itself as larger than I expected, and I was intrigued to see about half a dozen workers, at different places, all trying to hitch a ride to work in Cork. I'd always seen hitching as a form of recreational travel, not a form of commuting. Although its range of cafes and B&Bs made Macroom inviting, it was too early in the day to stop, so I continued through countryside that became dramatically more rocky and gorsy with correspondingly less farmland. Numerous roadside monuments celebrated IRA bravery in the 1920s.

In the foothills of the Derrynasagart Mountains, the road climbed abruptly to the highest pub in Ireland, which contained an unsmiling, Smithwick's-wielding landlady. A feral little girl was playing with the front wheel of a long-dead tricycle which was covered in cowpats, and insisted on running it up and down my pack. I downed my pint, made a quick exit, and camped half a mile further on.

I woke to find all the road signs were in Gaelic, and managed to interpret An Niedin correctly as Kenmare, purely because it seemed the right distance away. Fortunately, it was downhill, because blisters on my left foot caused me to stop frequently. I booked into Shelburne Guest House where I had stayed before with the girls and walked into the tourist-filled town. 240 miles down the road, I had arrived at the Ring of Kerry.

Having walked across Ireland, I paused to review the exercise: I had no doubt now that I could complete the walk, as I was about 25% of the way through, so there was a subdued sense of impending accomplishment. But there was also the nagging awareness that what I was really doing was avoiding commitment, stability, and significant decisions. I was determined to avoid the claustrophobic expectations of others, which I figured was easier as a moving target. Yet, ironically, I was immersed in one of the most passionate, committed and polemical nations on earth; every Irish person I met was prepared to argue their opinion, with various degrees of volume and violence.

A short distance out of Kenmare the next morning, I applied methylated spirits to my blisters and they improved. After sandwiches and lager in the cosy bar of a Tahilla guesthouse, I walked on past Parknasilla, haunt of George Bernard Shaw, and into Sneem. I booked into the Church View B&B and explored the picture-postcard, multi-coloured little town. On an honourboard headed "Personalities of Sneem" I was amazed to see that the first name was Charles de Gaulle, who had holidayed in Sneem in 1969.

I started the night in the smallest and dingiest pub in Sneem, where I met Roger and Lucy, who lived in Gronningen. Lucy was Dutch, and spoke English with Roger's Midlands accent. We soon moved on to another pub and drank with a group of locals; comparisons between Dutch and Irish characteristics ensued, until one of the locals who had been to Amsterdam summed it up:

"If the Dutch had Ireland, they'd feed a fifth of the world's population; if the Irish had Holland, they'd all be drunk." After that, there wasn't much more to say, especially when the pub closed shortly after midnight and we were asked to leave.

chapter 51

Suicide by Travelling?

It was a slightly later start the next day as I nursed my Guinness head slowly down the road, and Roger and Lucy waved as they roared past on their 1000cc motorbike. I trudged on through bleak but impressive scenery and the hamlets of Castlecove and West Cove. On the edge of Caherdaniel, I met an old man in a tweed coat with albino fairy floss for hair.

"So, yer hitchin' then?"

"No. Just walking."

"Sure. But I mean ter say, yer stick yer t'um out and take lifts, dontcha?"

"No. I refuse lifts even if they're offered. I'm walking the whole way."

"Christ, I don't know how you do it! Is there any money in it?"

"If there is I haven't found it."

"Yer bent on self-destruction, you are, just like dem hunger strikers."

If there *had* been money in it, would he still have thought I was bent on self-destruction, or would financial reward have sanctified the whole enterprise in his eyes? On the other hand, was there a kernel of truth in his final statement? I *had* chosen three troubled places to visit and in an earlier lifetime, I had tried to jump off a tenth-floor balcony. My mother was convinced I wouldn't return alive from this trip. I had also abandoned my family's long-held belief system, not found a replacement, and seemed congenitally incapable of committing to anything. Was I subconsciously suicidal? Or at least masochistic? Or was it simply self-discipline? And when does one of these categories end and the next begin?

While the boundaries between these categories may have been ill-defined, I quickly decided I wasn't suicidal; there were easier ways of killing myself than walking around Ireland. A few minutes later, I decided I wasn't masochistic: several times each day I would find myself literally suffused with joy. These joy-filled moments might come at the sight of the spires of the next town, or at the sound of a stream, or as I took off my pack in a pub, sat down with a pint of Guinness and rolled myself an Old Holborn. At moments like these I was immensely grateful for the journey I was on, despite any physical discomfort, and the joy did not come *from* the discomfort, but from somewhere else altogether. No, I wasn't a masochist. And while what I was doing took some self-discipline, that was a means to an end, not an end in itself. So what *was* I doing? Partly, avoiding commitment of all kinds, and trying to determine who I was at a distance from the confines of family, friends and employment. I was also pursuing a quest for meaning and my underlying (and possibly flawed) assumption was that meaning is more often found through action than inaction, through movement rather than inertia, through dislocation and exposure to the unfamiliar, rather than the comforts of home. (I had clearly adopted at least some of the existentialism so dominant in my Arts Degree.) Freud, of course, would say that the search for meaning is itself a sign of mental problems; my response is – have you ever seen a photo of Freud smiling?

The next morning dawned miserably and I walked westward through a heavy mist and continual drizzle. A few miles from Caherdaniel, I staggered into the Scariff Inn, the wettest I had been so far on the trip. I sat by the fire and gradually dried out, trying to figure out what to do next. I was determined to visit the Skellig Islands, but the waitress informed me that boats for the Skellings only left from Portmagee, not from Waterville. The weather remained dire. A couple from Cork encouraged me to stay the night at the Scariff: "It's a bit expensive, but the food's fantastic." But I was running low on money and no banks were open the following day.

After nearly three hours loitering in the Scariff, I headed for the door. As I did, a young guy approached me:

"Did I hear you say you're walking to Waterville?"

"Yes."

"I'd advise against it. The mist is obviously still really thick and beyond here the road narrows alarmingly. You've got a very good chance of being run down by a truck in these conditions."

His concern was touching, but I thanked him and ignored it. As I walked on, I could see his point: the mist got even thicker, the road narrowed, and tourist buses and trucks thundered past on a road with no verge. The mist played tricks with the sounds and it took a lot of concentration to determine from which direction a vehicle was coming. I missed out on what was supposed to be a great view from this road, but the experience of walking through a dense blanket of mist as huge crops of granite descended to stop abruptly at the edge of the road made up for it.

Waterville was on an unimposing bay, its main street a clutter of hotels, B&Bs and restaurants. On arrival, I called the Roddys, who ran the boats out to the Skellings.

"Sure the boat actually leaves from Portmagee, not Waterville," she said, "but you don't have to walk all the way down here. My husband Joe will pick you up from your campsite and drop you back there at the end of the day."

Joe arrived punctually the next morning and turned out to be a professional diver.

"So have you caught much of the news?" he asked.

"No," I admitted.

"Ach, there's riots on over in Britain now and they've declared a state of emergency. It's all about the hunger strikers."

"Last night in Waterville, I saw a car driving through town and a guy with a megaphone was announcing a march in honour of the latest hunger striker to die," I commented.

"That's right. The I.R.A. has massive popular support. You know the people of Portmagee remember the Royal Ulster Constabulary being down here. One of the locals was working on the bogs for one of them and was later fined by him for using a cart without a light! You know Whitelaw lets the R.U.C. fire rubber bullets at rioters in Northern Ireland, but they don't let them do that in England – they're just not consistent – there's one rule for England and another for over here."

Swedes, Germans, French, Dutch, Irish and Australians all got onto Joe's boat for the nine mile trip. The three Swedes were all divers and were dressed in dry suits. We were dropped on the island at noon, to be collected three hours later. Seabirds were everywhere; it was especially amusing watching water-logged puffins trying to take off. Disembarking, I headed straight to the top of the mountain-like island and ate my lunch watching the spectacular 700 foot rock face plunge to the sea, undisturbed except for the endless circling of seabirds. Far below, a BBC crew was filming the puffins, and toy boats toiled on a grey sea under a grey sky.

On the road to Cahersiveen, a car stopped and the driver hailed me. Inside was a farming couple in their seventies, on their way to Mass. The husband's nose was holding a blackhead convention and, from the way his purple tie was arranged, he apparently suffered occasional bouts of epilepsy. His scarfed wife leant over and offered me a lift, which of course I declined. After some R&R in Cahersiveen's Scellig Rocks Bar (where I'd lunched with Sally and Lyn two years before), I pushed on to Kells, pursued by rain. Eventually, I sheltered in an abandoned farmhouse which was an utter mess, although it had an intact roof, and even a bed. I ate there, and considered spending the night, but the presence of fresh cowpats was an omen, and I was soon invaded by curious bovines.

I hit the road again, foolishly walking past several B&Bs, as the road skirted mountains. A pine forest approached, but the trees were planted too close together to allow for good camping. Another B&B proved full, then I was caught in a rain storm. I dived into a partly completed building, stretching out my sleeping bag under a roof that was held up by a million struts. It had been another 25 mile day and I was happy to regard any dry place as home for the night.

chapter 52

It's a Long Way to Tipperary

Glenbeigh crept past the next morning, with an offshore island preternaturally lit by a sunbeam laser cutting through the clouds. As I paused on the outskirts of Killorglin to lance a blister on the back of my heel, gypsy kids took advantage of my immobility to pester me and I gave them a few coins.

Killorglin was in chaos: donkeys were "parked" in the streets, cows wandered through the centre of town, a market was in progress in the square, and tourist buses circumnavigated road works. I dived into a pub for a break and, having slept poorly, nearly nodded off over my Guinness. Deciding not to walk further that day, I found the campsite. Later, a car with a loudspeaker announced a meeting that night in town; Martin, another hunger striker, had died.

I rose early, passed through Aghadoe with a great view over the lake, and down into Killarney. The locals were complaining that it was their worst tourist season for twelve years, but the place was pumping. All the B&Bs were full and the town was in the middle of race fever. I found a new B&B on the edge of town, and the following morning, strolled the three miles or so to Muckross and explored its green fields by the lakeside. On the way back, I passed Ross Castle accompanied by the smell of jaunting car horses, ate fish and chips near the black-shrouded statue on the west of town, heading out on an obscure byway that eventually took me to the main road to Limerick.

After picking up some provisions and a pint of Harp at Farranfore's "half way house", I headed in the direction of Ballydesmond. A mile down the road I found a farmhouse and an old lady answered the door.

"Excuse me, I was wondering if you would allow me to camp in your fields overnight?"

"Well now, it would have to be my son making that decision. He's over there in the cowshed."

I dutifully waded in, faking indifference about stepping in cowpats, and Pat gave me permission.

Pat and I talked a lot that evening and he got more information from me than I from him. For an Irishman, he already knew a lot about Australia, and talked knowledgeably about snakes, sharks and the Darwin cyclone. I discovered that he had twenty-three cows and didn't know much about the hunger strikes. After a glass of hot milk, I retired to my tent in a field, surrounded by haystacks and an insect swarm of Biblical proportions. Moving through Ballydesmond the next day, I crossed back from Kerry into Cork, and calculated I had walked 342 miles so far.

Kilmallock proved larger than the map indicated, and filled with ruins. The town had once been walled in: two of the old gates remained standing and there were two ruined cathedrals, which I discovered by taking the wrong road out of town. There were no signposts in the centre of town at all, so it was appealingly not geared for tourists. A cobbler was busy at his trade, and I had to refuse two more offers of lifts. The Ballyhoura and Galty mountains formed on my right as I continued into a tiny town called Elton, unmarked on my map, and drank in a pub called the Kozy Kitchen, which ironically didn't serve food.

The Magnet pub in Knocklong *did* serve food, and two middle-aged ladies burst spontaneously into a series of Irish folk songs, finishing with "Daisy a Day". I left just as they were starting up again, and had nearly arrived in Emly when a huge honking of horns startled me out of my reverie. A wedding party of about twenty cars full of people drove by; unsurprisingly, Emly was virtually a ghost town when I arrived. I pitched my tent behind a school lunch shed in Lattin.

Pushing on through Tipperary towards Cashel, I realised something was wrong at Kilfeacle: all my strength was gone. I thought I was dehydrated, and I hadn't been eating well for the past few days. I sat on a bench to recuperate, but forced myself onwards because rain was coming. Across a field, History beckoned as a distant ivy-covered ruin invited investigation; a passer-by told me it was Thomastown Castle. But it meant cutting across fields and I was still feeling weak. For once, I resisted History's siren call, knowing I was poorer for it. I suspected that she would not take my rejection lightly.

The town of Golden arrived with a wrecked Norman tower and an IRA memorial on the bridge. I mentally switched my mode to "automaton": my shoulders were sore, my armpits stank, and there was a fetid aroma coming from my feet. I told myself that all my feet had to do was keep moving, and then, suddenly, I glimpsed the rock of Cashel through the trees, and was soon booked into (appropriately named) The Haven. I showered, surreptitiously washed my clothes, and dragged myself to the nearest café for my first proper meal in several days. My last meal had been in Killarney, so I'd walked virtually halfway across Ireland on snacks and Guinness. I realised I had missed a golden opportunity to seek the Dublin brewer's sponsorship for my round-Ireland walk, which probably meant that I lacked the DNA to be successful in business.

The rock of Cashel, seat of the Kings of Munster for 700 years and the location of St Patrick's shamrock demonstration of the Trinity, was impressive; it was also an accident waiting to happen. The stairs were worn and clammy; the battlements windswept and unfenced. Kids were climbing fearlessly in all directions while I tried to act cool with whitened knuckles.

The following morning I was once again doing a passable impersonation of a human being. Cashel was the centre of Ireland's dairy industry, which was attested to by the green, green hills and roads covered with cowpats. These made walking an art, as you had to ensure you were not level with a fresh one when a car drove past.

Dodging flying faeces, I walked through the villages of Knockavilla and Dundrum. Annacarty village contained a ruined barracks and I stopped for a pint in the one pub. In the gloom I spotted a middle-aged man with a cap and a slightly younger man with a beanie, and we started chatting. They discovered I was walking, and they both hefted my pack:

"That's quite a weight to carry," said the older man.

"Whereabouts are you from?" asked the younger man.

"Fremantle, Western Australia," I replied, thinking he'd probably spotted my accent and might have wanted a specific answer.

He looked amazed: "You speak really good English."

"Thanks, yes, I've been practising for a while; I knew it would come in handy."

chapter 53

Camp Cowpat

After camping in a field west of Doon, I refused three lifts on my way into Limerick. One of these cars returned after a few moments; the driver stopped and began a conversation through the window. He was about forty, smoking, and only in possession of one tooth, which was blackening from the base, about to die of loneliness.

"Yer know yer've just passed a monastery a little ways back. You could get lunch dere and stay the night."

I thought about it, but didn't want to double-back.

"When I was a lad," he continued, "I had to walk from Tipperary to Limerick with a herd of cattle to sell at market. They don't do that now — sell 'em by auction." And with that, he was gone.

In a Limerick pub, "Murder on the Orient Express" was on TV, and a drunk insisted on discussing the literary merits of Agatha Christie at great length while regularly prodding me in the arm. Escaping, I booked into the hostel, even though I disliked the curfews, possibilities for being ripped off, and too many people per square inch. Noting my recurrent solitary streak, and my potential for turning into a grumpy old man at a surprisingly young age, I spent the next couple of days exploring Limerick. At St

Mary's Cathedral, the tower was closed, you couldn't take photos inside without getting permission from the Dean, and King John's castle wasn't overly inspiring, so I drifted aimlessly, exploring backstreets and cracked faces, poverty and wealth. I realised uneasily that conscious observation resulted in engagement; engagement resulted in vulnerability; and vulnerability opened the door to… commitment.

The main road between Limerick and Galway went past concrete works that wore a halo of dust and poured hundreds of yards of mud into the gutter, into which I was constantly being herded by the dozens of flatulent trucks roaring by. Bunratty Castle had been the highlight of the morning with its "restored" old village, but I was not going to be lingering for one of their medieval banquets. Ennis arrived as a refreshing change, with streets so narrow it was difficult to negotiate them with a pack. A young guy from Cork extolled the beauty of his home town and his fluency in Gaelic; in a pub a young girl told me she collected coins and I was able to give her a nearly complete set of Australian ones. As I headed towards Lahinch on a minor road edged with brambles, I clocked up twenty-five miles for the day and camped near a crumbling tower - a broken, nicotine-stained fingernail, pointing at smoky clouds.

Ennistimon proved to be a bustling town in a hollow where two classic characters were holding forth in a pub. One, with a mouthful of stumps instead of teeth (what is it about the Irish and dentistry?) spat as he spoke a barely-decipherable variant of English. Eventually, I was able to understand what he was trying to tell me: he had traveled all around Ireland, but hadn't had enough money to see America. I was unable to tell if he wanted sympathy or congratulations.

At Lahinch, people were albino limpets on the rocks, the fish and chips were overpriced, and Hogan's pub had a notice saying they wouldn't serve anyone under 25. This mattered little as the main event was the Cliffs of

Moher and I was there early the next morning in the mist and drizzle. All the tourists there were complaining:

"Well Martha, we paid good money for this, and I can hardly see the ocean!"

"What is it with this country? Don't they know this is supposed to be summer? In California, we know how to do summer! They should send the whole Irish tourist board Stateside for some lessons."

And so on…

They were right – you couldn't see far out to sea – but I couldn't believe they were complaining. The mist was rolling in from the sea, hitting the cliffs and roiling its way up hundreds of feet to pour over the top like steam from a cauldron. It might have been a difficult photo opportunity, but it made for great poetry.

At the Moher Inn, I calculated that I'd covered 500 miles so far, and the barmaid told me there was a campsite between Lisdoonvarna and Ballyvaughan, so I headed off. Lisdoonvarna had a couple of large hotels near the spa, an overabundance of B&Bs, and very little else. As I pursued the barmaid's campsite, which proved to be invisible, I entered the strange world of the Burren. Squarish, wave-worn rocks were scattered everywhere and seemed to be in a battle with the moss and lichen for domination; Stone Age burial chambers were rumoured to abound. The mist was even thicker here, severely limiting visibility, making the scene sub-aquatic. The road corkscrewed and then I was in Ballyvaughan.

"Are you looking for a place to camp then?" a lady asked.

"Yes thanks – is there anywhere nearby?"

"How about there?" She pointed to some vacant land in the middle of town. I gave her a blank look.

"I'm serious," she continued, "that land has been set aside for a future Gardai station. In the meantime, quite a few campers use it. All you have to do is ask permission from Mr Collins in the pub."

It seemed a great idea, but the pub was shut. As I stood outside it, I caught a glimpse of Collins at an upper window. All it took was a gesture from me towards the vacant land, a nod from Collins, and we had an arrangement.

There were cows in the field, but that was not a problem, surely? I set up my tent and instantly became the object of bovine curiosity, surrounded by cows chewing madly all around my tent. In between eating, they amused themselves by holding an excreta contest for my benefit and the area was soon besieged by cowpat landmines. Going into town for a drink suddenly seemed a great idea, but what if they wanted to eat the grass *under* my tent while I was gone? There wouldn't be much left on my return. I had to stay. But what if one of the cows tripped over a tent peg in the middle of the night and fell on top of the tent? I had a mental image of screaming myself awake as I was crushed under a several hundred pound milk factory. What would the headlines back home say? "Irish cow mistakes Perth boy for sofa"? "Fremantle lad meets udderly awful fate"? Derek and Dennis would be hospitalised with hysterics.

chapter 54

Castlebar Rocks

I survived the night intact, and the next morning, the scenery was all coves, inlets and tumbling castle ruins, some of the nine hundred castles in County Clare. I lunched in Kinvara with my back aching to a soundtrack provided by a faux-furred tart from Brighton whose jewellery was as loud as her voice.

Gogarty's Dun Guaire castle drifted by, and in Clarinbridge I had a pint at Paddy Burke's, winner of Guinness's best-kept pub award in 1979. It was crowded with well-dressed people, and I drank under the watchful eyes of monochromed Burl Ives and JFK before taking the barmaid's advice and camping across the road in some long grass with not a cow in sight.

The following day, I decided I had done Galway an injustice on my previous visit. It had a superb, European square with narrow streets radiating from it and several canals with remarkably clear water, containing trout. Galway seemed to be as big as Limerick, but the map showed it as smaller. No wonder Yeats chose to live on Galway Bay: great grey stone hills streaked with green, like beached whales garlanded with seaweed; coves, inlets, crumbling castles, thatched cottages. Having covered about 550 miles, I was probably past the halfway point of the walk.

At the Silver Teal in Moycullen the next day, screaming kids were breaking glasses and overturning stools, so I was soon off into an increasingly Connemaran landscape of grey hills, thatched cottages, stone fences, and ponies, to camp on the edge of a football field in Oughterard. I woke to 29 July 1981, the day of the wedding of Charles and Diana. As they were walking down an aisle before a watching world, I was hobbling unnoticed down a road surrounded by hills, peat bogs and mercury lakes. Just before Maam Cross a friendly puppy raced across the road to greet me and was killed by a passing truck. Devastated that something so new and full of life had died through showing me affection, I slumped into the Maam Cross pub/deli/garage/souvenir complex and forced myself to watch the end of the Royal Wedding as penance.

A few miles further on, I came to Maam itself at the junction of the Leenaun-Cong road. A poster advertised the Castlebar Festival in a few days' time and I scheduled my pace accordingly. At Cornamona, I spotted a priest:

"Excuse me Father, would it be possible if I camped in the grounds of the school here for a night?" (Another traveler had told me he had done this before.)

The priest took his time answering: "Well, son, it's being used for Irish classes tonight."

Although I assumed the Irish classes would take place *inside* the building and therefore I would hardly be in their way, I interpreted this as a "no".

"Is there anywhere else I could camp nearby?"

The priest directed me across the road to a rocky and marshy area being reclaimed from Lough Corrib. After some effort, I located a spot that was marginally better than woefully inadequate, set out clothes to dry on gorse bushes, tented myself ahead of a descending insect horde, and entertained more uncharitable thoughts about Catholicism.

The banter in the Cornamona pub focused on the weather, getting the hay in, and a chap who had broken his fingers and written off his new, uninsured car when he swerved to avoid some donkeys. Eavesdropping, I sat back, inhaling Guinness and Old Holborn, wondering about the Catholics and Mary. Repeatedly on the walk I had seen statues of the Virgin Mary by the roadside, but I'd finished the New Testament now and I couldn't understand the fixation with someone who was not a major character. Why did Mary seem to get equal billing with Jesus? Was it some sort of pagan leftover or a perverse fixation arising from clerical celibacy? When I had the opportunity, I asked someone who looked like they might have an answer and got an interesting reply:

"Well, now here's my theory. Mary is Jesus' mother, so she's got influence with him, right? Look at how he did that water into wine thing when she asked him to, even though he didn't think the timing was right. All good boys listen to their mums. But Jesus is pretty busy running the universe, so how has he got time to handle all these prayers, and he must have to prioritise them anyway. So what hope does Patricia Peatbog have that Jesus will listen to and answer her prayers? None. But she knows that Jesus will listen to his mother, so the sensible and political thing is to approach Mary to speak to Jesus on your behalf. Then he has to listen."

"Doesn't that seem like trying to manipulate God? Can you successfully use political lobbying on someone who knows everything anyway?"

"This is Ireland, you know; we're nothing if not hopeful."

I'd noticed the Irish were committed and passionate about almost everything, especially religion and politics; the opposite of many Australians who avoided those subjects to minimise confrontation. The Irish knew what they believed, and were vocal about it; by comparison, many Australians seemed like hollow shells. The Irish passion and vibrancy was magnetic, but I realised that the cost was commitment, and I still had an allergy to those… but what if the alternative was a vacuous life?

The next day I walked into County Mayo and Cong simultaneously, then on to Partry where I had a drink in the smallest pub I'd ever seen. It had sitting room for six close friends, provided they could drink without bending their elbows. I had no option but to become friends with the others in there. After the obligatory cost of living comparisons between Ireland and Australia, I picked up some local knowledge. There seemed to be a general north-east movement within the country: Mayo farmers traveled down to Kerry, bought calves, took them back to Mayo for about two years, then sold them to Offaly farmers who fattened them up on their bigger farms. Paddy bought me a drink and sang a song, then left. I continued to Ballintober where I found a much bigger bar and Paddy again. He was still singing, in between playing frantic harmonica. "You know," he slurred, "if my place wasn't crawling with the wife, kids and in-laws, you could camp in my front yard furrrevver."

As it turned out, one of the other drinkers, John Jo, insisted I camp in his field. It was late, I'd drunk too much, and it was too dark to see properly as I erected the tent. I dropped and lost the vital piece of A-shaped metal that held the top of the tent together. I made do by lashing the tops of the poles together, and in the absence of wind, it held. When I somehow dragged myself out of bed the next morning, the missing part was revealed. I passed Ballintubber Abbey, survivor of Henry VIII and Cromwell, and the oldest continually used church in the British Isles, and arrived in Castlebar for the festival.

People were everywhere. I bought a ticket, walked to the concert site, and pitched my tent with about forty others. As this event was new, I was hoping there wouldn't be the 40,000 punters who normally turned up for Lisdoonvarna.

The main acts were the Undertones, Ian Dury and the Blockheads, and the Pretenders, with Otway and Barrett, Moving Hearts, and Clannad as support. Chrissie Hynde took the stage in black leather, Honeyman-Scott was in red and it was all jangling guitars and attitude. Ian Dury, resplendent in white sunglasses, polka-dotted scarf and bowler hat, tore through a set that climaxed in a firestorm of lighting. The Undertones unleashed Teenage Kicks and Feargal Sharkey's trademark tremolo made him sound like Bryan Ferry's love child attached to a defibrillator.

This was the soundtrack for the next forty-eight hours, as thousands of us danced, sang, drank, and slept in the fields. As drizzle turned into rain, fields turned to mud, but no-one cared. Theft was rife, but although my tent was ransacked, nothing was stolen; I was surprised they hadn't made a donation. After two days of rock and roll idleness, I was eager to move on through Bohola, with its church out of all proportion to the size of the village, to Swinford where I indulged myself by booking into the hotel and had my first shower in a week.

At about this time on the other side of the world, Derek and Dennis were boarding the Trans-Siberian express, having sloughed off jobs and succumbed once more to travel's siren call. They were heading in the direction of Europe: somewhere soon, we would meet again.

chapter 55

Into the North

The next morning I felt like the Looney Tunes coyote on a bad day: two days of standing, shouting, loud music and little sleep had taken their toll. Despite sleeping an impressive eleven hours, it felt like five minutes. I dragged myself towards Charlestown in overpowering weariness, punctuated by occasional nausea. I stopped for a while to watch boys throwing rocks into a stream, and a little further on, having entered the county of Sligo, I collapsed in a field. At glacial speed, I began to feel better and was actually able to appreciate Tubbercurry, where I camped on a football ground.

The next morning was drizzling and miserable, but at least I felt better as I walked through Achonry and Ballinacarrow. At Collooney, I met a young guy from Mayo who had also been at the Castlebar festival and we talked for an hour about rock and roll, the IRA in Sligo, Gaeltacht, and Swedish women.

It was late afternoon when I arrived in a busy Sligo on the verge of race day. Most of the B&Bs were full, but a lady with a slightly wonky eye offered me a room, then threw me out after discovering I usually slept in farmers' fields. I ended up at St Joseph's and strolled out the next morning to inspect Loch Gill, lingering in the friary until I was overwhelmed by tourists.

Next day, I passed a horrible, hatcheted housing development at the edge of town and kept walking non-stop the five miles to Drumcliff, with the grey/green tidal wave of Ben Bulben threatening to break. After visiting Yeats's grave, and passing through attractive coastal scenery, I saw Mountbatten's castle again, seemingly much closer to the road than I remembered from two years before.

On a day that didn't stop drizzling, Bundoran grabbed me by the scruff of the eyeballs. On the outskirts, a large royal blue sign announced your arrival in county Donegal, followed by a two mile strand of amusement parlours and B&Bs. It was Blackpool, moved slightly to the west, and might have been garishly attractive in sunshine, but there wasn't any. However Bundoran instantly redeemed itself by presenting me with a delightful bakery and real coffee. I wanted to linger, but the road beckoned and I hiked in full rain gear through Ballyshannon and Ballintra to Laghy. The owner of the pub let me camp in his field, which was obviously also where he kept his platoon of pet slugs. I shunned the slugs and spent the evening drinking in The Seven Arches with Donegal farmers who wanted British troops removed and United Nations troops placed on the border.

The next day was clearer and church bells welcomed me to thickly-greened Donegal with its tidal river. Campers had set up river-side tents and seabirds wheeled. After a quick wander around the town and the fort, I took the Derry road which climbed, and climbed for miles. The road rose steeply to the bald, windswept and beautiful Donegal hills with their peat bogs and isolated farms.

Pettigo was right on the border, with no soldiers, just a customs post that was closing as I arrived. The immediate change as I walked into Northern Ireland was that the road signs were British, all modern and designed to reflect at night. That night, I camped in a haystack field next to an abandoned house, one mile inside Northern Ireland. The farmer said the old house still had fresh water and a working toilet, so I was perfectly set up for the night.

Kesh arrived next morning, and I noticed more differences from Eire: cheaper prices, luxurious cruisers on the river, and my first sign of the "troubles" – a R.U.C. building with twenty-foot high cyclone mesh fencing, spotlights facing out, and a camera at the gate. Kesh seemed quiet enough, but I was there before the banks opened, so decided to push through to Killadeas. After detouring into pine trees at Castle Achdale National Forest, I rejoined the main road to discover Killadeas was a virtual ghost town with one post office and no bank. I had to scrape by on the small amount of cash I had, and continued to Enniskillen under an intimidating sky.

Enniskillen arrived with an ominous warning that the centre of town was a control area and that cars were not to be left unattended. The built-up northern suburbs showed this was my first sizeable Northern Ireland town. The tourist office conveyed the cheery news that the town contained neither youth hostel nor campsite, and as I didn't have enough money for a B&B, I started walking out on the south road. Before long, I spotted a chap standing in his yard, which contained a beautifully manicured lawn. I took my chances, asked if I could camp there, and he agreed. He stuttered badly and his dog was a snarling boxer/black panther cross with luminous eyes. I had a vision of the beast ripping me to shreds in the night and the Enniskillen constabulary posting my mother a small box containing a few blood-stained ribbons of flesh.

"Knock if you need anything," he said, and his wife came down to greet me as well. After I'd pitched my tent he came down again to ask if everything was okay, and the panther seemed friendlier this time around, although I noticed it was sniffing snottily, and I wondered if it had a cold or whether this was its normal, non-snarling breathing mode.

"Do you want to come for a drive to our boat?" he stammered.

"Sure." And as we drove to the boat and did a bit of maintenance on it, I learned that his wife was originally from Essex, they had three sons about my age, and they'd had tourists camp in their yard before. Clearly, I wasn't the only one with the effrontery to ask.

The next day I lazed around Enniskillen, more amazed that it contained no record shops than I was at the concrete-filled drums blocking off side streets to prohibit car-bombs. Ingesting caffeine, I realised something about the relationship between traveling and time. When you spend time in one place, you are constantly amazed at how quickly time passes: "Was that *really* five years ago?" I found traveling had exactly the reverse effect: "Was that *only* two weeks ago?" Clearly, the effect was directly proportional to the amount and variety of experience crammed into the time period; once again, I wondered if I would be able to handle "normal" life; it seemed like swapping a crystal clear, fast-flowing mountain stream for a muddy pond.

My host, whose name was Fearis (pronounced Ferris) came down the driveway and invited me in for a cup of tea. The cup of tea never materialised because we went straight to whiskey and our conversation revolved around travel and the troubles. Fearis was Protestant.

"If the majority decides in a democratic way to stay part of Britain, why should a minority try to force them out of it?"

He wanted to see a united Ireland as part of a British commonwealth and had lost friends to the violence.

"You know, I think unity was possible under de Valera, if only it'd been made more attractive to the north. And I bet you don't know that it was the *Catholics* from Derry and Belfast who first invited the British troops over!"

I shared with him about the sacking of the Whitlam government in Australia.

"So what happened afterwards?" he asked. I told him, and he looked incredulous:

"If that had happened in Ireland, the streets would've run with blood."

As I snuggled into my sleeping bag that night, warmed by Fearis's whiskey and polite political conversation, I suddenly felt profoundly grateful for a town called Fremantle in a country where blood is mainly shed at football matches. Clearly, passion and commitment had their downsides.

chapter 56

From Lisnaskea to Dublin

I had learned that after a lazy day or two, it was folly to try to cover too much ground the next walking day. Lisnaskea arrived via the incredibly quiet B514, close to the east shore of Upper Lough Erne, where the only traffic was tractors. Castlebalfour was partially reconstructed, but not terribly impressive, so I headed into O'Casey's Bar and Folk Museum for a pint. I didn't see the Folk Museum, but stayed in the pub all afternoon, eavesdropping on a conversation about building site accidents. One chap had survived 13,000 volts after putting a jack hammer through a power cable. When they left, the barman and I were the only ones there. He poured me a free pint and we (mainly he) talked.

He was born in Ireland, grew up in England, walked the Pennine Way when he was thirteen, married a Lisnaskea girl and was living in the town against his will.

"D'ye know there are Catholic pubs and Protestant pubs, even in a small town like Lisnaskea? And there's more violence per head of population in this town than in Belfast."

His grandfather had bought a farm in the district in the 1930s. One night a gang of Protestants threw him in a pit; when he tried to climb out, they broke his fingers. They told him to sell his farm (which was very profitable) and leave the district. He put his farm up for auction and there was only one bidder; it sold for a pittance, and the family moved back to Cork.

"Nah, I'm not really bitter about it," he replied to the obvious question. "It all happened too long ago, and I grew up in England remember – I wasn't immersed in all this. But if you ask an IRA man about history, he'll know some – his side of it – but he probably won't know about the Jacobites and Catholics stabbing pregnant Protestant women in the stomach. An Irishman will fight to the death for something, and not really know what he's fighting about. The only time this country's come close to unity was during the famine. And here in Lisnaskea, they do the job properly – it's either a severe beating or a murder – none of this namby-pamby stuff like knee-capping."

Clearly, anywhere was safer than Lisnaskea, and the next day I walked through drizzly but humid weather to Newtownbutler, which was control zone-free. I got into a brief conversation with a couple of U.D.R. soldiers:

"Hey, you should pop into Barney's pub," they suggested.

"Why?"

"Yvonne. She's a stunner."

They were right: Yvonne was gorgeous, intelligent and well-travelled. It was two hours and three pints well-spent, but it left me with a muzzy Guinness head as I negotiated the long, uneventful stretch from Newtownbutler to Butler's Bridge. The Derragarra Inn had been recommended by two people and was delightfully eccentric: a life-size model of a woman and donkey cart was perched on the roof; an entire wall was covered with matches, and inside was an eclectic collection including old cameras and turtle shells. Before leaving the next morning, I visited the town's folk museum, and left most impressed with the ingenuity of the local cockroach-catching device, which involved spinning stones.

The next night, camped between Cavan and Virginia, I calculated I had covered 800 miles. Kells featured a topless round tower and a worn high cross; my camp for the night was a school yard. It was a Sunday morning as I left Kells with half the town flocking to Mass. I passed a posh golf course and estates and a father and son fishing.

"Is there a fish on?" the father asked.

"Yes dad!" his excited son replied, holding the bending rod.

"Aagh, I think he's just playing with it," the father told me.

But a moment later, the son was brandishing a 3 pound bream.

"Look Paddy, I've caught a whale!" the father exulted to an unimpressed passing motorist.

After a pint at an obscure village surrounded by post-Mass revelers, I walked into Slane during its concert. Hazel O'Connor piped me in through the skinheads and punks as I sought out the quietest pub in town – The Poet's Rest. For the quietest pub in town, it was still remarkably busy, and I was soon drinking with a crowd from Monaghan who were obsessed with arm-wrestling. Their arm-wrestling champ made himself £5 or £6 per night.

"I've never arm-wrestled an Australian before – how about it?"

I knew I had no chance unless it was left-handed.

"Only if we do it left-handed."

He agreed and, amazingly, I beat him.

"You should come to the pubs of Monaghan – you'll make a fortune," he offered generously. Before he could think to challenge me right-handed, I retired undefeated to a nearby field.

The next day anglers were hugging streams like remora on a shark's belly as I passed the site of the Battle of the Boyne to lunch in Drogheda in a pub in the shadow of Lawrence's Gate. Drogheda had a good feel to it: stacks of cafes and pubs with a waterfront reminiscent of Cork's with worn bricks and arches, bricked-up windows, and ivy growing out of weathered buildings.

After a couple of hours chatting with the staff of Mildred's Restaurant in the Abbey Centre, I plodded out of town at 5 pm. Looking back on the dark mass of Drogheda, I noticed its ancient churches and forts were still the tallest buildings in town. An old man gave me incorrect directions and I ended up on the main road to Dublin so I cut back onto the amazingly quiet L6 at Julianstown, with its gaudy orange El Molino Hotel desperately trying to look Spanish. I crested the end of a long uphill climb just past the turnoff to Bellewstown and knew I'd shortly have to find a campsite. Then I spotted a farmer, a man in his sixties with a vertical wedge of white hair and paint-speckled glasses. As I got closer, I realised he was sporting eyebrows of sufficient magnitude to receive FM radio signals.

"Hello. Would it be possible to camp somewhere here for the night?"

"Are you British?"

"I'm Australian." And I was welcomed with open arms; apparently a local lad had just returned from Melbourne. I spent the night camped near an amphibious vehicle.

The next day was miles of nothing until I approached Dublin airport where descending planes blowdried my hair. Dublin from the north showed its ugly side: the high rise ghettos of Ballymun with their stark truncated tree stumps encircled by wire gave way to the older decay of terraced houses and cottages with collapsed roofs, boarded-up shop windows covered with posters, and further in, the dust of new development, decaying vegetables from yesterday's markets, kegs of beer rolling into the maw of pub basements that resembled prehistoric tombs. Ah, Dublin.

I collected some welcome mail from home and collapsed in Isaac's after a 22 mile day. Next morning, I wandered around O'Connell, Henry, Moore and Grafton streets and bought Elvis Costello and Springsteen bootlegs.

O'Connell's statue stared down glumly, but whether this was due to his disapproval of the Japanese invasion in the form of SONY and FUJI signs, or the fact he was garlanded with guano, was impossible to determine. Brian Boru had kicked the Vikings out of Dublin a millennium ago; the subtler Japanese invasion appeared more successful.

Dublin was a city in which the elderly were determined to work until the grave swallowed them: septuagenarians pushed vegetable-laden trolleys to the market; a grandmother stood in the middle of O'Connell Street and preached in front of "Food for Poland" placards. I discovered the Sistine Arts shop, which would have been perfect if I'd been in the market for a wood carving of the Pope looking as if someone had karate-chopped the bridge of his nose. I lingered in the main library's reading room, with its sixty-foot high domed ceiling and Wedgewood-like white cherubs pointing their collective genitals down at the readers, which was a trifle disconcerting.

As I wandered the streets of Dublin, I contemplated the approaching end of my Irish journey. Clearly, I was going to succeed in walking around Ireland, but my time here had achieved much more than just fulfilling a foolish boast made on the goldfields. I had fallen even further in love with this green, violent, poetic, passionate, paradoxical, Guinness-drenched land. At that stage, I had no idea Irish blood ran through my veins from both sides of my family. I simply knew that I had invested more time and effort in Ireland than in any country outside Australia, and I had been amply repaid. I had made a commitment of sorts to this Irish ramble, and was richer because of it. It dawned on me that not all commitments were to be shunned or feared; commitment was not always a loss to be avoided; occasionally it was a wise investment to be pursued. And the corollary gradually also appeared: avoidance of the investment of commitment could result in loss of the spiritual and emotional benefits such an investment returned to the wise investor: the ramifications of this lesson for relationships were obvious, if a trifle unsettling.

chapter 57

Dublin and Kilkenny

I scoured the second-hand bookshops, noting a poor selection of science fiction everywhere, and an excellent selection of colourful and eccentric Crowley at the Alchemist's Head. In the basement of Bewley's in Grafton Street, where a dozen pipes serpentined their way around the ceiling in a room that looked like it had once been a sleazy Victorian bar, two young women were proof-reading a novel between them. At St Stephen's Green, the gardener was singing badly while clever children hunted miniature aquatic things with small nets on sticks. Outside the Guinness factory, boys struggled with a hooked seagull by the side of the grey, slimy, but fish-filled Liffey.

As I left Dublin, there was a sense of freedom at once more leaving a city and striding down an open road on a hazy day. This was soon mitigated when I took a wrong turn on my road to Enniskerry (I'd like to blame the maps), found myself having coffee in Stillorgan and only made it as far as Shankill campsite. The local pub was dirt cheap: soup, two rounds of sandwiches and a pint of Smithwick's for £1.94 and, surrounded by sea-mist, I slipped into unconsciousness with a full stomach and a smiling wallet.

The mist remained the next morning on what would be the hottest day of the Ireland trip. After coffee in bustling Bray, I hit the N11 for about a mile until Kilmacanoge, where I turned west and then south on the T61. Copper-patinaed rocks jutted from hillocks and I visualised snipers behind each one of them. The road was uphill and I was soon sweating profusely. I overnighted at Roundwood, which boasted two really attractive pubs and a trout farm, continuing next day to Laragh, where I left my pack with a moustachioed old lady and wandered into the green magic of Glendalough valley.

In this valley of the two lakes, a monastic centre was established in the sixth century by St Kevin. Women who wandered into the vicinity were viewed as potential chastity bandits and treated accordingly: Kevin threw nettles in the face of one and threw another into the lake, thereby assuring his celibacy, but destroying his chances of becoming the patron saint of hospitality. Later visitors to Glendalough included the Vikings, who, not being known for their appreciation of things monastic, promptly trashed the place. Willful women and Vikings aside, Glendalough saw more than its share of pilgrims over the years, drawn by its isolation and tranquility.

After retrieving my pack in Laragh (where every house was a B&B), I plunged through pine forest striped with streams, through hilly country and good views to a rough camp near sleepy Rathdrum. Through a misty mountain morning, Aughrim arrived with a timber mill and left with Lawless's Hotel and tame mallards under the bridge, followed by picturesque Annacurra; then it was all pine trees, fields and bookend horses until Coolboy. A drink at the Little Moon pub was followed by more hills until Carnew, which boasted a very wide main street, with all the houses freshly plastered and painted as if auditioning for a movie set. I camped in a football field and calculated I had covered 932 miles. As the light was fading, I ate opposite the castle, which is surrounded by a wall where 28 men were shot in 1798. A lady in a café told me the castle had just been bought by a Polish countess, who was yet to move in. The day diminished in the colours of a dove as grey, mist-filled valleys were topped with a smudge of soiled pink. The next day I managed the feat of walking through three counties (Wicklow, Wexford and Carlow) with the trout river of Kildavin featuring.

Bagenalstown initially made a good impression, but on the far side was a foul-smelling meatworks. I joined the main Carlow-Kilkenny road at the ambitiously-named obscurity of Royal Oak, and arrived in Paulstown. A neat school seemed a good camping possibility, so I asked the lady in the shop.

"Well, now, I'd be thinking you'd have to ask the priest permission if you wanted to camp in the school ground," she replied.

Based on past experience with clergy, I was inclined to give it a miss, but as I was stuffing my food purchases into my pack, another lady came up to me.

"The lady in the shop told me you're looking for a place to camp. You can camp at my place if you want."

It turned out her place was two miles away, so I limped off in that direction.

She had two adopted sons, and I got into a conversation with Eddy. Eddy was a first year engineering student who was spending his Uni holidays working in a quarry with a jackhammer.

"You know, I love Ireland," he said, "but I can't stand the Irish."

"Are you Irish?" I asked.

"Yes."

"Then I just think you've told the ultimate Irish joke." He grinned.

"Yah, I know we tell jokes about ourselves all the time; maybe it's because we're so good natured we can't be bothered to pick on any other nationality."

"So why don't you like the Irish?"

"Where do I start? Okay, too many Irish people talk but don't act – it's all wind. They're so full of their plans and what they're going to do, but most of them never do it. So you get sick of hearing them talk, talk, talk, when you know it's never going to happen. Secondly, they're too conservative. Thirdly, they always take things personally when you win an argument against them. And this comes out with the whole Catholic versus Protestant thing: there's so much propaganda, that people are never allowed to just move on and relegate something to the past."

While I was pondering all this, he asked, "So would you ever fight for Australia?"

"At some point, yes," I replied.

"That's a nice vague answer," he countered.

"Okay, I'll try to clarify it. Yes I would fight for *Australia*. The whole point would be to determine whether I would really be fighting for *Australia*, or just fighting because the Prime Minister asked me to, to bolster someone else's economic or political agenda. I wouldn't want to fight that sort of war. And it seems to me that in hindsight, we often think that the wars we fought weren't worth it; that if we knew then what we know now, we would have avoided involvement."

In Kilkenny, I booked into a B&B for two nights. It would be my final B&B of the trip, and I worked out that of my 67 nights in Ireland so far, 12 had been spent in B&Bs, 11 in youth hostels, and 44 under canvas. After a gargantuan breakfast, I staggered to St Canice's Cathedral, photographed a tomb and climbed the round tower. The Black Abbey was a tasteless amalgam of old and new. The only other occupant was a man who bowed before a Christ in an "aquarium", touched the rosary of the life-sized statue of St Martin, and on his way out, knelt untidily at the statue of Christ. On the kneeling board there were three prayers to St Martin and one to the infant

Jesus of Prague. I was upset; I thought someone would have told me there was a new Jesus around, and I wondered why he was considered an upgrade on the previous model. The L-shaped church featured a psychedelic main window and five offering boxes: two for restoration of the building, one for Our Lady's Shrine, one for St Martin, and one unmarked. Considering the restoration they had done so far was horrible, St Martin was dead, and the last thing Ireland needed was another shrine to Mary, they had no chance getting any money from me. On my way back to the castle, I mused that the initials of Immaculate Virgin Mary – I.V.M. – sounded like a cross between a computer company and test tube fertilisation procedures.

Dragging myself away from the dynamite coffee at the Roma café, I trudged onwards. Just before Bennettsbridge, the Quigley Magnesite stenchpot stretched across the road, assaulting all five senses simultaneously. I sped up and before long was in Thomastown where blood was flowing straight from a butcher's yard through a pipe into the river. The town was quiet, and in the pub a snooty British lady with teenage daughter in tow was boasting:

"And my friend, my friend you know had lunch with Xaviera!"

"Who's Xaviera?"

"Oh dear, of course you know – Xaviera Hollander. The good-looking prostitute who wrote that book *The Happy Hooker*."

I decided not to hang around in case she asked me to camp on her front lawn and continued to Inistioge where I found a quiet campsite in a field in the middle of town with a horse and nineteen cows.

chapter 58

The End of Ireland

The next day did not have a promising start. I packed a wet tent in light drizzle and the first three miles out of Inistioge were almost vertical. For a short time after leaving New Ross, I felt sad: the walking trip was nearly over and from now on, there were no new roads; I would be walking down roads I had seen before. This feeling was quickly replaced by joy as I realised that my quixotic goal would soon be achieved. With a smile locked on my face, I increased my speed; more passersby looked at me, and I understood how rare an unprovoked smile is – you wonder what the sod's been up to.

After camping near Ballynabola, I walked into Wexford the next day to be greeted by good news. A letter from home informed me that the Landrover had now been sold and that my share - $1,000 – was on its way to me. I now definitely had the funds to continue to Israel and Egypt. The town of Wexford was also celebrating; I'd arrived in the middle of a three day mussel festival. I spent a rainy day eating mussels and watching the cobalt blue and dull copper of oil slicks on water.

I woke on Tuesday, 8 September, 1981 expecting another wet day, but the sunlight on the tent and birdsong accompaniment indicated the day would be fine. After a light breakfast at Fortuna's, I walked past the Banville pub where I had my last drink on my previous visit, past Talbot's, and Wexford was gone. There was the occasional beckoning pub, but I didn't succumb until Killinick, where I downed my last Smithwick's at The Merry Elf. My last offer of a lift was a novel one: an ancient woman on a tractor, towing a wolf in a packing case on a trailer. I had more reasons to decline than usual, and I arrived in Kilrane and ultimately, Rosslare, as I'd always hoped – on foot and not in need of urgent medical attention. The modernistic church, the Great Southern Hotel, and finally, the harbour, and it was the end of this particular road. I had walked 1033 miles in 58 actual walking days, an average of just under 18 miles per day. No world record, certainly, but much more than my cavalier approach to the whole thing deserved. A few days previously there had been an article in the papers about some soldiers who had walked 50 miles in 2 days to raise money for charity (without packs, I bet!) and they'd raised £5,000 – at that rate, I was worth £100,000. Once again, I cursed my lack of initiative in not seeking sponsorship from Guinness.

After a final touch of B&B luxury, it was an early morning ferry crossing, followed by the discovery there were no buses at Fishguard. Now free to hitch, I was in Swansea three rides later, caught a train to Plymouth where I arrived (after three changes of train) just past midnight. Some friendly cops encouraged me to sleep in the wedding cake under Drake and the next day I caught up with friends, slept in the youth hostel, and bussed to Portsmouth, where it was a long walk to the YMCA near the pier. The following day I arrived in Selsey and finally took the pack off my back.

The next few days were spent shuffling between Selsey and London as I booked my final plane fare home through Hong Kong (Magic Plane £395) and on the Magic Bus to Athens (£38), and catching up with the newly-arrived Derek and Dennis. We shared tales of Siberia and Sligo and became mini-celebrities at the local pub.

Derek wasn't sure what to do next, and Den was cooling on his original intention to stay on a kibbutz: "I don't fancy being bossed around for three months." But our reunion was short-lived because my departure to Athens was imminent.

The bus left King's Cross at 9 pm on Saturday and arrived in Athens at 3 am on Tuesday. Our rather ratty courier informed us that this had been the fastest ever London-Athens journey for the Magic Bus, shaving five hours off the previous record. Most of us collapsed in Hotel California, a smelly, overcrowded little youth hostel near the bus terminus. After a few hours' sleep, I strolled to Joseph's house, where the price to sleep on the roof was 130 drachs, including continental breakfast. The weather was amazing, almost like summer in Perth. Somewhere in Yugoslavia, you cross over an invisible weather barrier and then it's Grecian light and warmth all the way. For the first time in months, I felt completely relaxed. The three month walk around Ireland had a goal (and I was unsure whether or not I was actually going to make it); the gold prospecting before I left Perth had been more relaxed, but decisions still had to be made in conjunction with Derek and Dennis. Now I was alone, and under no pressure to do anything or be anywhere at all.

I spent my last few drachs on a bottle of duty-free red demestica at the airport, met an Aussie on his way to a kibbutz, and shortly before we took off, a boy jumped up to say his prayers in front of a rabbi: Israel was going to be interesting. The view from the plane was dramatic: half the sky was on fire and half in night as rugged islands peaked from the sea like mountaintops through mist.

Arriving in Tel Aviv, I met "Bruce" who'd been a crowd extra in the film Gallipoli, and together we found the Hotel Josef. It was there we met the Fijians.

"So what's a bunch of guys from Fiji doing here in Tel Aviv?" Bruce asked.

"We're part of the UN peacekeeping force in Lebanon. Our battalion is in the worst area."

"Suffered many casualties?"

"Too many. Because we're in the worst area, our losses are higher than any other battalion. We've lost twelve men so far. The last of our friends to be captured by the PLO were burnt alive."

At this point I uncorked my bottle of demestica and it rapidly disappeared. Bruce, fascinated with things military, became enmeshed in detailed discussions about armaments. My attention drifted, and I wandered over to talk to Chibby, the proprietor.

Chibby's father had had ten siblings, all of whom had been killed by the Nazis. I tried to grasp the impact of this on the family, but failed utterly.

"You've done some hitching, right?" Chibby asked. I nodded.

"Well, this anti-Semitic thing is still so strong, that if I went hitching in the States, a lot of people would throw me out of their car the second they discovered I'm Jewish."

It was 1 am when we finally stopped talking and drinking. As I got into bed, I reflected that my first day in Israel had been a hard-core introduction to the damage caused by racism and the politics of hatred. I'd aged more than 24 hours that day.

I spent the next day wandering slowly around hot, humid and grimy Tel Aviv, and made my usual disastrous choice when shopping for sandals: after they removed the top layer of skin from both of my big toes, I made a vicious alteration to them with my pocket knife. In the middle of my perambulations, I met an elderly lady who, quite unprompted, told me her life story. She had been a teacher of Hebrew and a preparer of Bar Mitzvah boys in New York State for about twenty years, where she had a very successful, married son. I listened, nodded, and congratulated in the appropriate places.

The next day, I successfully caught a train to Haifa, despite the best efforts of several people to the contrary. I first had to catch a bus to the train station: the tourist information person said I needed a no. 20 bus; the no. 20 bus driver said I needed a no. 21 bus; then a friendly fat fellow shepherded me to a no. 23. Just when I'd decided I was probably going to end up on the front line with the Fijian UN peacekeepers, we headed in the right direction, although the bus driver unsuccessfully attempted to extort some more shekels from me.

In Haifa, I saw stalls selling green olives and greener bananas, negotiated the subway/funicular to the top of Mt Carmel, and found my way to the exorbitantly expensive hospice of the St Charles sisters. Having spent 17 consecutive nights in rooms with other people, the privacy was worth the price.

The next day was Sabbath, so I had to walk down and back up Mt Carmel, past the glittering Bahai dome, and after some hours in the town and museum, met another new friend. He spoke German, French, English, Russian, Hebrew, Yiddish and Arabic and we sat overlooking Haifa and talked for an hour. He had traveled widely and worked in a bonded warehouse at the end of the war. He pointed out the various features in the view: the old Technion, the jetty which the Brits had built and the Israelis extended, the concrete-covered oil tanks, the high-rise medical facility.

"All of this," he said with a sweep of the hand and a sense of pride, "has arrived in the fifty years I have known this town."

Next morning, I caught the funicular back downtown, being searched as usual on entering the subway by the inevitably delicious Israeli female soldiers. An hour's bus ride later, I was in Acre, wandering in search of a cheap hotel. The old city was completely walled (and moated) off from the new, and I eventually found the youth hostel in the old section. Apparently, Acre had only one hotel: it was huge, expensive, and a mile down the coast.

Acre, built on a reef and rising directly from the ocean, was a photographer's paradise; there was absolutely no point putting the lens cap back on your camera. Acre was a museum of the Middle Ages that genially allowed people to take up residence. Formerly Ptolemais, it had changed hands frequently during the Crusades, and withstood a later siege from Napoleon. Underground crusader cities and museums, narrow alleyways and hessian-shaded street stalls, mobs of Arab kids wanting shekels. The Museum of Heroes and the gallows were almost overwhelming. History was a complex mistress: she could be pure delight, providing pathways to salvation, but in certain times and places she made unexpected demands on your soul. I began to see History as a sequence of dialogue and diatribe between value systems. People fight for what they value and believe in, and I felt a nagging sense that my own values and beliefs remained unclarified. To believe nothing, to value nothing above comfort and self, was surely to live a spectral, disengaged half-life. The currently fashionable hybrid of hedonism and existentialism had lost its appeal. Having finished reading the New Testament, I understood its central claim that Jesus was risen and that was the core value for his disciples: but could I accept that?

chapter 59

Felony and Faith

The next morning I unwittingly walked between a tearful German girl and several Arab guys who were hunting her through the streets. They evaporated as soon as they realised another European was on the scene.

Forgetting it was the Jewish New Year, I walked to the Nahariya road and unsuccessfully tried to hitch. In the end, I caught a taxi into the clean, tree-lined town and as evening fell, I watched everyone sashaying down the streets in their new clothes for New Year.

On the first day of the new year (1st October, 1981) I traveled via Zefat to Capernaum and strolled the ruins, trying to absorb their biblical influence by osmosis. Although I'd read the New Testament as I'd walked around Ireland, I regretted not being more biblically literate, so I perfected the art of lingering a certain distance behind the frequent tour groups, listening to what the guide was saying. Then I was alone in the ruins, and I noticed a black camera bag sitting by itself on a rock. I went over to it and discovered it didn't contain a camera, but did contain quite a lot of money in US$1 notes. I looked around: no-one was close by and certainly no-one seemed to be looking for it. Planning to drop it off at the U.S. Embassy, I shoved it inside my canvas satchel (it was a tight fit) and moved on.

Later, I came across a Bible study group. They were trying to put a skit together about Peter's vision of the unclean things, and wanted me to join them. I stood back, watching how things were developing, and when they included cheeseburgers, I decided I needed to be somewhere else. It was much more pleasant drinking Maccabees with Renata and Heidi from Karlsruhr. The next day I woke feeling dazed; Renata and Heidi joined a tour to the Golan Heights and I hitched to Tiberias.

Like many youth hostels, the one in Tiberias was closed during the day, so I had to hang around the streets for six hours. While I was sitting in a park, three guys came up to me and started a conversation. They seemed very helpful and were interested in my travels. They suggested unfolding my map of Israel and pointing out certain things. All told, the conversation continued for about twenty minutes. It was only after they left that I realised they'd been trying to rob me.

The unfolded map had been sitting on top of my canvas satchel, and one of the guys had undone the satchel straps, attempting to find valuables inside. Fortunately the leather camera bag I'd found was wedged inside tightly, and he hadn't been able to find his way into that. My passport and cash, as usual, were in a money belt.

The attempted robbery highlighted that what I liked most about Israel was also the thing I liked least: the approachability of the people. It was great when you wanted to meet people, but bad when you wanted privacy (or didn't feel like being robbed). The Western concept of "personal space" seemed absent here, and in trying to flex with the local ways, you often let your guard down inappropriately, as I had done in the park.

After a restful bus ride to Qiryat Shemona, I hiked 3 km north to the Tel Hay hostel and, having dumped my stuff, hitched to Tel Dan. After an hour wandering through luxuriant foliage, I walked back to the main road and foolishly tried to hitch to Baniass. Although it was only 4 km away, I walked half of it before giving up. I got as far as seeing a Crusader castle on a hill in the distance before my sandals wore through my ankles and I hitched back to Shemona. I eased my wounded ankles with beer (taken orally) and noted that the place was suddenly crawling with soldiers.

The next day I headed back through Tiberias to Nazareth, dumped my stuff at the Sisters of Nazareth hospice, and walked around the crowded, ramshackle town. It was at the rather overdone Church of the Annunciation that I met Paul from California.

"Do you believe in God?" he asked. At least I was in a church this time, so I wasn't caught completely off-guard by the question.

"Yes, I do. I guess from your accent that you're Californian – do you believe you *are* God?" I felt his abrupt question permitted my rudeness. He was somewhere between puzzled and shocked.

"Of course I don't, man! I'm just a born again ex-drug addict saved by Jesus."

"Sorry. I didn't quite catch that… did you say you're an ex-born again drug addict, or a born again ex-drug addict?"

"A born again ex-drug addict."

"Great," I replied, "now I know what you're about to offer me."

"Do you know Jesus?" he asked warily.

"Yes, I used to live next door to him on Calvary. Sadly, he drove his car into the harbour and didn't rise again." By this time, he knew he was talking to a madman. I decided to ease up on him, and explained.

"Okay, so you know your next door neighbor wasn't the real Jesus, but do you know the real Jesus?"

"Well, I know of him, of course. But he's been dead for 2,000 years, so I can't actually know him."

"Ah, everyone knows *of* Jesus, but the important thing is do you have a personal relationship with him?"

"Not that I'm aware of. It's not like I've ever received a birthday card or anything, and I've certainly tried to do my bit. I've sung the carols each Christmas and I grew up in church. I spent so much time on hard wooden pews that I got hemorrhoids."

"Spending time in church isn't the same thing as having a relationship with God. Spending time in church doesn't make you a Christian. You could live for years in a garage but you'd never become a car. All you have to do is invite Jesus into your heart."

"That's it? And then what?"

"God lives inside you forever."

"Sounds crowded."

"And your life will begin to change for the better. And your sins will be forgiven and you'll live with God after you die."

"So this is a fairly comprehensive insurance policy you're offering here. A better life in this world and the next? Seems too good to be true. So what's the downside?" I should have known he'd have an answer for this one.

"The downside is the premium: it costs everything you've got. God wants all of you."

I walked away with something to think about. I hadn't met anyone who talked so confidently about having a relationship with God. Most people I knew had a relationship with a church. I'd read the New Testament; I knew Jesus was supposed to be alive, somewhere, elsewhere, but a *relationship* with him? Maybe this was just the ex-drug addict, reformed hippie, I'm-at-one-with-the-universe spin on Jesus?

Ironically, my next stop after meeting Paul was Armageddon, well, Megiddo at least. The ruins were not terribly exciting (except for the water tunnel) but the view across that wide plain easily summoned the biblical vision of hundreds of thousands of soldiers storming through there. So this is where the world as we know it is coming to an end? That same day, Anwar Sadat was killed, and I decided it was a good time to be somewhere else.

I bussed to Jerusalem, where I made the serious mistake of checking into the Jerusalem Student House. After inspecting the bazaar and the areas around the Damascus and Jaffa Gates, I retired to a room where the resident colony of bed bugs and mosquitoes violently objected to my presence. I managed about 4 hours' sleep, and read and slapped for the rest.

Grabbing a falafel for breakfast, I visited Mary's tomb opposite Golden Gate, climbed to Gethsemane, and then to the top of the Mount of Olives where I spent ages admiring the view. When I eventually descended, it was to drift through the old city, along the Via Dolorosa, to the Christchurch hostel where I had decided to spend the next few nights. I shared my room with two amusing French guys:

"Pierre, can I ask you a question?"

"Of course. Would you like to know why we Australians are so excited about Vegemite?"

"Vege – what?"

"Never mind. Ask away."

"What is your zodiac sign?"

"Sagittarius." He exploded with laughter and slapped his friend on the back.

"See Philippe! I told you!" They carried on laughing and slapping for a few minutes and then noticed my questioning expression.

"Aah, sorry Pierre. Let me explain. I have been doing a little bit of research while we've been travelling. I ask every traveller I can about their zodiac sign. So far every one I've asked has been one of the Fire signs, and you're no exception."

If he'd asked Derek and Dennis, his theory would have been blown: they were Taurus and Gemini.

I checked out the citadel of David and headed to the Israeli Museum and the Shrine of the Book. Both were impressive, but painful, in more ways than one. My right ankle had still not healed from my disastrous sandal episode at Qiryat Shemona and I determined to see a chemist. Also I only had two hours at the museum before it closed, and the richness and depth of human heritage it displayed deserved more; I had to go back.

The following day I hunted down some of Jerusalem's major sites: the Dome of the Rock (magnificent); the Church of the Holy Sepulchre (disappointing); Mt Zion, the Jewish Quarter, and failed utterly in my search for Bethesda pool. Christchurch hostel was certainly an improvement on the Jerusalem Student House: it had hot water, sheets, and a common room. I was also pleasantly surprised that although it was a Christian hostel, not everyone was as assertive with their faith as Paul had been. But there was Howard.

Howard was a Jew who had converted to Christianity about nine months previously. One afternoon, a few of us were in the dormitory and someone asked Howard a few questions about his faith journey. It was clear that he had been thoroughly immersed in Judaism prior to his conversion. Then, in mid-conversation, something amazing happened. Howard stopped simply responding to questions, and quietly began preaching. Soon, he was mobile, moving between the bunks, and the rest of us had changed from questioners to congregation. There was no script, it hadn't been rehearsed, it just flowed out of him. I had the definite sense of him being moved by something other than himself, and I quietly marvelled: I had seen nothing like this before – was this the result of the "personal relationship with Christ" Paul had talked about?

chapter 60

High Noon in the Garden

Ironically, despite ever-present violence in the city, I found Jerusalem very restful. Partly, it was because I was easing up slightly for the sake of my foot; partly, because I discovered that in Jerusalem, you could "dial-a-mood". If you wanted things hectic, you could go to the Moslem quarter; the Jewish and Armenian quarters offered a more placid pace; and if you wanted modern, you headed to Yafo and King George Streets.

Over the next few days, I visited the Holocaust museum, revisited the Israel museum, saw the Passion Play staged at St Peter in Gallicantu (the traditional site where Peter denied Christ), and enjoyed the convivial breakfasts at Christchurch. I soon realised that I had spent eight consecutive nights in Jerusalem, something I didn't think I'd done anywhere else, even in London. I took a trip to Bethlehem, if just to prove I could actually leave Jerusalem, and stayed at a Franciscan convent. Bethlehem was high and cool, but the Church of the Nativity with its hot, smoky vault was barely interesting.

Back in Jerusalem, I had to spend a night at Jerusalem Student House again, because Christchurch was full. Jeff (Bristol), John (Belfast) and I decided to bus out to Hebron, where Abraham, Isaac, Jacob and their wives are buried. We escaped a hand grenade attack on the Western Wall, but did not escape the massive crowd at the Central Bus Station.

Then it was down to Masada, via Ein Gedi and the Dead Sea. Masada was a nice challenge for the reasonably physically fit.

"It takes ages to climb up it," was the universal warning, "and the earlier you start the better, otherwise it's too hot."

We heeded the advice and headed up at first light. An hour or so later, I was standing on the top of the massive site where the Jews made an heroic last stand against the Romans. Nine hundred Jews (five hundred males) versus eight thousand Roman soldiers and the siege took three years. Looking down, the rubble of the ancient Roman fortifications was still visible. I spent six hours on Masada, marvelling at the water cisterns and the scale of the tragedy.

On the way to Masada, I sat with Dave, one of the guys from Christchurch. I asked him what brought him to Israel. He grimaced.

"It's a long story."

"I bet this bus trip outlasts it."

"Okay. I was raised in the States in a Christian family, but eventually I became a professional gambler."

I looked at him and wanted to laugh. I had never seen a professional gambler before, but I was sure I wasn't looking at one now: no waistcoat, no cigar, no cover-up, comb-over hairstyle. Dave was in his mid-twenties and looked like he belonged on a beach, not in a casino. I think he read my mind.

"No. Really. I got in with a group and we were professional card counters. We were good at it, and made a lot of money. We'd travel from one casino to the next – Vegas, Reno, Hawaii."

"Not too many casinos in Israel."

"Exactly. One day I was lounging in the hotel room in Hawaii. I had thousands and thousands of dollars around me, and I asked myself why I was doing it. I realised I could keep going on that circuit, travelling around the world and making good money just by turning up and playing card games. But what was the point? It suddenly seemed a completely empty existence to me. I decided to get away from the whole lifestyle and try to rediscover some sense of the spirituality I'd had as a child. I took just enough money to get to Israel, and then back to the States, and left the rest there."

"Must've been a great tip for room service." I still didn't believe him, but a little later, I asked him to demonstrate some of his card-counting ability, and was convinced. Here was someone else whose faith had caused a complete recalibration of his life.

After Masada, Dave and I headed to Eilat, sitting in the aisle of a full bus. We were greeted at the bus station by Asher, who took us to his impromptu youth hostel in his flat in Los Angeles Street. We unsuccessfully tried to get him to locate some scuba gear for us, then took two Israeli girls to Caesar's Hotel for expensive drinks and a free movie (Little Big Man).

Next day, Dave and I lazed on Eilat's beach before teaming up with Andrew, a recently-arrived South African theology student, to catch a bus to Sharm El Sheikh. As the desert scenery bussed by, I wondered where else in the world would I have such travelling companions: a South African theology student and a reformed professional gambler on his way back to God? Surely, only in Israel.

We arrived in Sharm and, as the hostel was expensive, only spent one night there. The next day was snorkelling amongst amazing corals; we slept on the beach, only to be woken at dawn by dogs. We hitched to Naama for more psychedelic snorkelling and another night on the beach, this time under spiky shelters with about 100 others. In the afternoon, we were lazing on some rocks, dimly aware of the proximity of a group of modern ascetics. Suddenly, a completely naked young woman arose from the ocean like Botticelli's Venus, and walked, dripping, towards us.

"Would any of you have a cigarette?" she asked.

We all shook our heads, suddenly struck mute. She smiled, and was gone. I wasn't entirely sure if I was awake or sober, so I checked with the others. It was official: for a few minutes we had been graced by the presence of a gravity-defying goddess.

Andrew and I returned to Jerusalem - where I nursed my gangrenous toe and got caught in a bomb scare in Jaffa Street – before heading to Tel Aviv where we met up with Dave again. We met Jeff Watson, an Episcopalian priest from Winchester, and another guy from Seattle, and spent the night eating and drinking together.

"So you guys all believe that Jesus rose from the dead?" I asked, realising I was surrounded by committed Christians.

It was a unanimous "yes".

"This means that you base your lives on an alleged miracle that happened centuries ago. How does that make sense?"

"It only makes sense if it's true."

"And why do you believe it's true?"

"Lots of reasons. One is the accounts left by eyewitnesses or people who knew eyewitnesses. You said you'd read the New Testament, right?"

I agreed I had.

"So you've read the accounts. Those people believed Jesus rose from the dead because they'd seen him. They ran away at his death because they thought it was all over but three days later when he arose, they believed. Most of them also gave their lives for this message – they weren't lying. You said you're into history, so evaluate their testimonies with an open mind."

"So you believe Jesus is alive today?"

"Absolutely. Alive and changing lives."

I remained unsure how to evaluate a miracle, but none of them tried to convert me as Paul had done. Their lives made an indelible impression: these were guys whose faith was at the centre of their lives, and informed all their decisions. I saw an integration between belief and action in them that I had rarely seen before. These guys knew what they believed and were unostentatiously living out those beliefs.

Andrew flew out to Athens the following morning on his way back to South Africa. Then, to my dismay, I discovered that the Egyptian embassy was closed for the next three days. Getting my Egyptian visa had been my main reason for heading to Tel Aviv; unwilling to linger in its humidity, I returned to Jerusalem.

One of my favourite places in Jerusalem was the Garden Tomb, otherwise known as Gordon's Calvary. I liked it because it was peaceful and entry was free; I'd been there a few times. It's a well-known tourist spot, with a tomb that dates from the first century as its centrepiece. Some believe that the rock tomb in the garden could actually have been the tomb of Christ; certainly, it's more attractive than the traditional site. Was it the tomb of Christ? No-one really knew, but on my first visit I was amazed to see a huge natural skull impression on the adjacent rock face – surely this had to be Golgotha, the place of the skull? Either that or I'd somehow been transported to the Bay of Bengal, and needed to be on the lookout for a masked man in purple leotards.

Now, on the verge of leaving Jerusalem for the last time, I thought I'd pay a final visit. Tourists filed in and out of the tomb, taking flash photos of blank rock walls, or, as one woman did, motioning her friend into the photograph to "make it interesting." It all seemed incredibly crass – surely the only appropriate reaction was to sit, stare and ponder – was this really the place where the God who became man rose from the dead? The Event that, if true, had to be the most significant in the history of humanity: was this stark rock tomb the fertile soil from which a Faith had grown and spread around the world? Had the death of one really resulted in new life and faith for so many? My friends and acquaintances of the last few weeks seemed evidence that, somehow, it had. But this would surely mean that God was somehow in control of all events, able to work in and through our choices, shaping the future....

I was sitting in the middle of the Garden, facing the open tomb. Gradually, I became aware of movement and noise around me, and one by one, three worship services started up. On one side of me was a group of Germans, on the other, a group of black Americans, and behind me a group of Japanese, all worshipping God simultaneously in their own languages.

At that moment, I realised God has a sense of humour. I was twenty-four years old, and I'd spent most of the previous four years travelling through about forty countries. I had looked for meaning in various places in my life, dabbling in drugs, casual relationships, and investigating everything from astral projection to the I Ching. Now I was in Jerusalem, where it all began, and the Day of Pentecost was being re-enacted for my benefit. It had been a long and very winding road to this point, but I sensed that I was now immersed in a crucial scene, a scene in which the stage management was ridiculously obvious. A number of images ran through my mind like a spinning merry-go-round. I'd been set up, and the only one who could stage-manage all this was God. I nearly laughed out loud: this was a God who valued me enough to work through the detritus of my life to bring me to this moment in a garden, and then, with a flourish of soap-opera over-kill, confront me with flashbulbs in an empty tomb and surround me with no less than three international gospel choirs, so I wouldn't miss the point.

The syntax of my life had been subverted: I realised I had always been the subject of the sentence, tending to treat everyone and everything else as objects, or even prepositions. I saw my avoidance of commitment in this context. Now, I was the object and God was the subject, and it felt strangely liberating. So it was there, alone, yet surrounded, as three gospel choirs blended their voices in the background and camera flashes crudely bounced off tomb walls in front of me, that I recognised my role as object in a Divine meta-sentence, bowed my head and uttered the most danger-ous words anyone can say: "I surrender. I'm yours." To have done any less would have been an act of cosmic ingratitude.

chapter 61

Near Death on the Nile

Conscious of having made a major commitment and therefore a little uneasy, I left Jerusalem for Tel Aviv and while waiting for the Egyptian Embassy to process my visa, visited the Diaspora Museum and chatted with an Israeli spiritualist woman. Early the next morning, I was on a bus to Cairo with only four other people, both English couples. More people boarded at Ashkelon, and then we settled in for the long haul: the Israeli border (Neot Sinai), crossing no-man's land, the Egyptian border (El Arish) where we spent two hours, an Egyptian bus to Kantara, and a crowded ferry across the Suez. We arrived in Cairo in the evening.

One of the English couples, Jim and Linda, booked into the Anglo-Swiss Pension; I booked into the Golden Hotel and spent most of the next few days drinking and talking with them. At thirty-one, they were seven years older than me, and because they were both involved with writing and publishing, I was fascinated with them.

"Yes, but I've only done a few books," Linda said, "and they've just been 'gift books'. Nothing serious."

"Self-deprecation? I thought us Aussies were supposed to have cornered the market on that."

"No. What you've cornered the market on is ending your sentences in a higher tone of voice, which makes everything you say sound like a question! Every Australian I've met does the same thing. Have you noticed? It sounds hilarious."

I hadn't noticed, but then I concentrated on how I spoke and understood what she meant. I made a determined effort to do the opposite.

"Yes, well I suppose you wouldn't notice", she added, "because you've grown up with it. I'm sure a goldfish doesn't feel wet, either."

We were at the Felfela restaurant eating stuffed vine leaves, quails, and pigeons stuffed with wheat when the subject of the Royal Wedding came up.

"Do you know Prince Charles has got someone else on the side?" Linda asked, looking intently through huge pink-rimmed glasses.

"You're kidding. Diana's gorgeous – he'd be crazy to do that."

"Seriously. A couple of weeks before the wedding, Charles was travelling by train and a friend of mine saw a woman get onto Charles's sleeping carriage late one night. It certainly wasn't Diana."

"Perhaps she was delivering pizza?"

"She was no teenager, and I suspect she was delivering something of a different nature."

As our conversations progressed, I noticed that the relationship between Jim and Linda seemed a bit shaky, and he seemed more eager to hold on than she was.

"I've got to tell you something," Linda said when Jim had gone to the toilet. "Jim and I are actually married."

"Oh? I thought you were just shacked up together."

"You Australians have such cute expressions. Well, we're married, but it was my idea to pretend we weren't married while we were travelling. We have an open marriage."

"Isn't that an oxymoron? Do you mean you've just made a lifetime commitment not to commit to each other?"

"Did you just call me a foxy moron?" she faux sparred, "Look, I'd really like the opportunity to talk to you in private, but it probably won't be possible. I need to tell you I love you."

"You've had too much to drink."

"Absolutely. But it's still true." And Jim reappeared.

Our wide-ranging conversations forged a firm friendship in a few days, and about the only things I saw in Cairo during that time were the pyramids and the Sphinx, with its nose shot off by high-spirited Frenchies in Napoleon's time. When it came time to leave, there was a promise:

"If we don't bump into you again in Egypt, we're going to fly down to Fremantle to find you, you know. I'll probably come down first and stay with you, and Jim will come a little later. You did say you've got a place of your own, didn't you?"

After a sleepless night on a train to Luxor, I checked into a hotel, and found a bar with a view over the Nile. Part of the ancient city described by Homer as hundred-gated Thebes, the ruins at Karnak, built to honour 13th century BC Rameses II, were more impressive than Luxor's. Karnak's Great Hall carried an overwhelming sense of timelessness, fostered by the rigid stylisation in Egyptian art that confirmed their view of eternity. Giant buildings, created for a time when the world seemed bigger, heroes abounded, and local councils didn't have building regulations. Then it was sacked by the Mesopotamians.

I ate at the New Karnak restaurant and took an expensive Valley of the Kings donkey ride which covered a bewildering variety of tombs, before heading to Aswan and the Saffa Hotel. For financial reasons, I didn't continue to Philae – suddenly the money I had left didn't seem very much. I had promised myself that my last night in Egypt would be spent at the Cairo Hilton, which wouldn't be cheap, so I only paid for a 2nd class ticket on the night train back to Cairo.

A few minutes after I got on the 2nd class carriage, I realised I had made a serious and potentially fatal mistake. I boarded early, and got a window seat. People kept boarding until every seat was taken, at which point people sat on the floor, and others climbed into the overhead luggage racks. I was the only European in the entire carriage, sardined with about two hundred Egyptians. Call me skittish, but I felt a little vulnerable.

As the train headed north into the desert night, I decided that the alternative to staying awake all night was probably being filleted and thrown out for the vultures. As it turned out, staying awake was easy: the window next to me wouldn't close, so I spent all night being blasted by frigid desert air which contained lots of sand particles.

Nineteen hours later, I arrived in Cairo, filthy, smelly, sporting wind-tunnel hair and minus the first layer of skin on my face. I staggered towards the Hilton, moving like the tin man from the Wizard of Oz while my limbs thawed. I knew what the desk clerk was thinking as he looked at me:

"No, I'm sorry sir, you've arrived too late for the Derelicts' Convention – it was *last* week."

"Can I have a room please?"

"That will be $60US *in advance*."

I have never enjoyed a hotel room so much in my life, much to the detriment of the housekeeping staff, who were left with the task of chiseling two brown tide marks out of the bath. Resurrected, I got into my best clothes, drank the Hilton's expensive beer, and made a meal from the free nuts on the bar.

My seven weeks in the Middle East had served to confirm my grandmother's oft-repeated assertion that bankers were running the world. Russian funds built the Aswan dam, and American funds were now being used to repair it. The USA sold AWAC planes to Saudi Arabia to sponsor its own rapidly increasing defence budget, yet Saudi Arabia financed the

PLO who were sworn to destroy America's friend Israel. The USA favoured selling arms to any areas that gave it a strategic edge over Russia and therefore a strong position from which to argue for disarmament, while at the same time doing millions of dollars worth of trade (especially in wheat) with Russia. Money, obviously, crossed all borders and was multi-lingual.

The next day, I was back in the U.K. and spent a few days shuffling between London, Selsey and Yorkshire. On the Trans-Siberian, Derek and Den had met Murray and Wendy from New Zealand, who were now ensconced in a flat in Earl's Court with Megan. We camped on their floor, buying food and wine, and cooking as our contribution. We stayed up so late that mornings didn't exist, only afternoons. Megan was tall, olive-skinned and attractive, but there were dark circles under her eyes.

"Are you okay?" I asked her.

"Not really. I've been constipated for a month."

"You mean you haven't gone at all in that time?"

"That's right. It's a bit of a worry."

It was also the end of any potential romance; she was too much of an explosion risk.

Den flew out to Tel Aviv and Derek came up from Selsey to help celebrate my twenty-fifth birthday. I shouted Megan, Wendy, Murray and Derek to dinner at the Twin Brothers' restaurant, and Murray's natural reserve dissolved in shiraz. Back outside the flat, we had a snowball fight which predictably ended in wetness and laughter. Wendy began running down the street, and I pursued her. We ran down Eardley Crescent, and Wendy turned to face me, her back pressed hard against the brick and wrought iron wall of the Brompton Cemetery, resting place of Emmeline Pankhurst. We kissed with the abandon of farewell, the freedom of knowing nothing serious could come of it, for the next morning I would be gone.

Or at least, I tried to be gone. The plane that should have been ours was frozen in at Manchester, so Cathay Pacific bussed all 380 of us to the Metropole Hotel in Brighton. The following morning was more successful, and I found myself flying to Hong Kong between two precocious schoolboys.

After a few days shopping in Hong Kong, there remained one more flight, the flight taking me back to Western Australia on December 19, 1981. The future remained uncertain, but I knew whatever it held, the events in that Jerusalem garden would somehow remain central. If God valued me enough to pursue me, the least I could do was return the favour. I experienced an overwhelming sense of gratitude and linked it with my commitment in the garden. I had avoided commitment for years; now it felt like through this commitment, I had found a place to begin.

As we started our descent, the wind known as the Fremantle Doctor was buffeting the Cottesloe sand dunes and moaning above the long-gone Skinner Street cemetery. It seemed an appropriate time for poetry.

Now

Memories, like sepia prints
in someone else's album,
spindrift past, ownerless.

Yet what do I not owe,
and how to pay,
a debt a lifetime long
in a currency unknown?[5]

---

[5]   First published in the *Fremantle Arts Centre Broadsheet*, Vol. 3, No. 5, September-October 1984

On board the Turkmenia, leaving Fremantle in January 1978.
Left to right: me, Derek, Dennis.

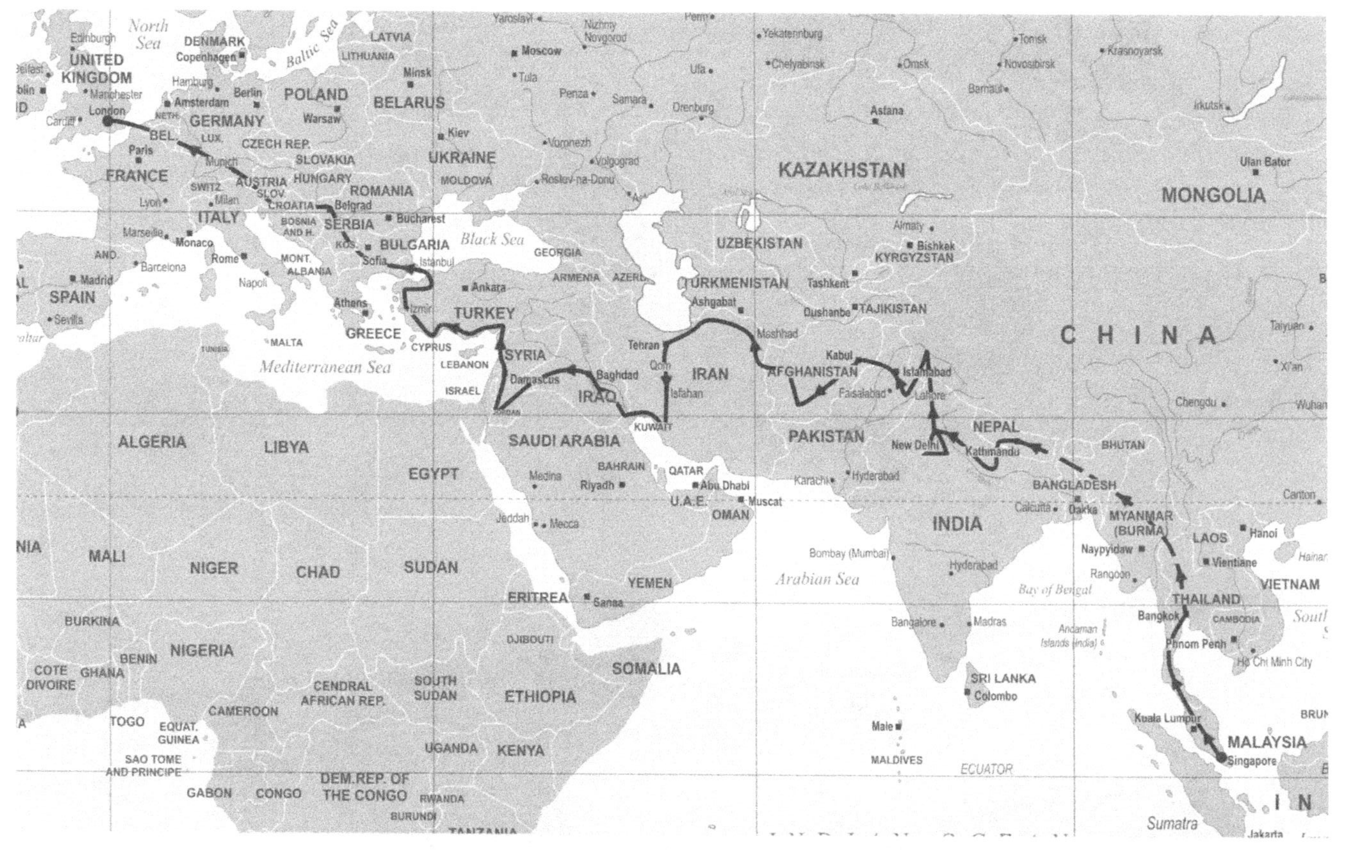

Singapore to London, including the world's longest bus trip: February to May 1978. (Route drawn by Joel Elliott)

Amber fort, India. Left to right: Alison, Derek, Dennis, me.

Dennis & Derek walking towards Fakhredin Al Maany,
Palmyra, Syria.

Diving in the Red Sea, south of Aqaba.

Dennis & me in Istanbul.

The cycling trip: May–September 1978.
(Route drawn by Joel Elliott)

In Selsey, after cycling.
Left to right: me, Derek (with Pip), Dennis

In Hyde Park, 1978.
Left to right: Dennis, Derek, me.

In our Malta apartment. Left to right: me, Derek, Dennis.

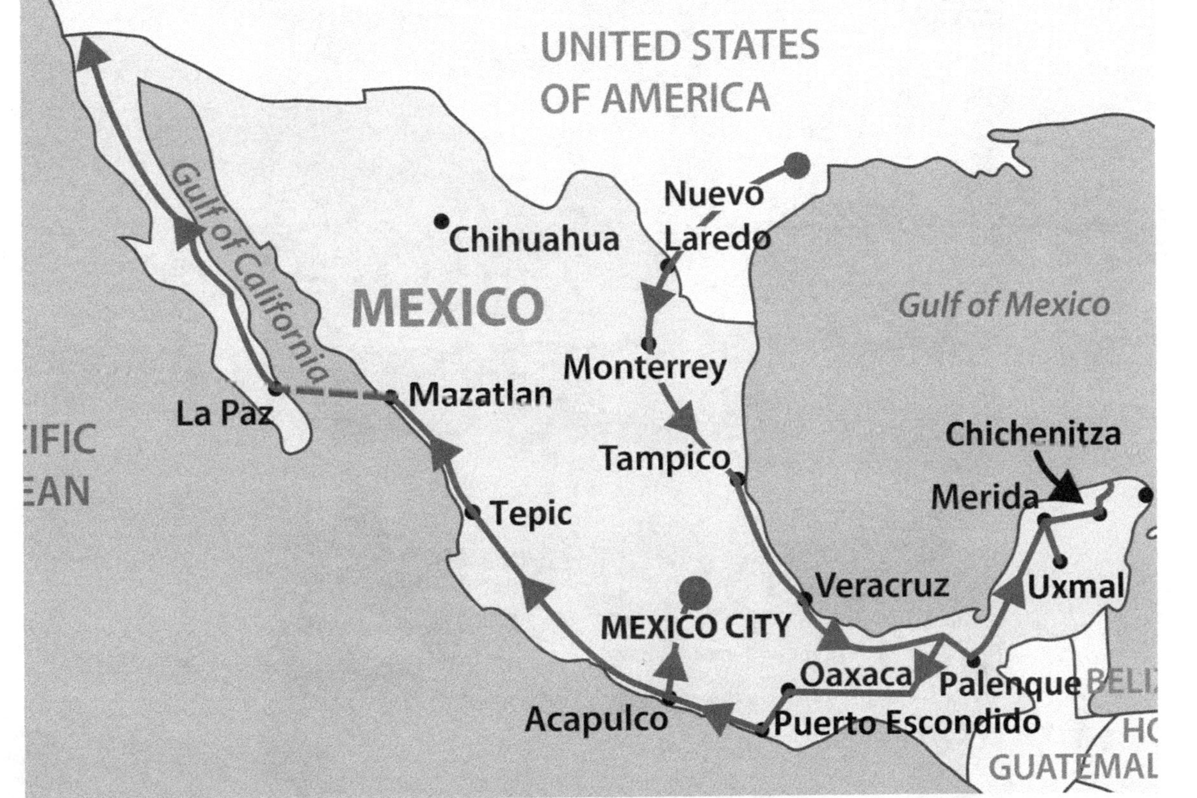

Mexico by local bus: December 1978–February 1979 (Route drawn by Joel Elliott)

Chichen Itza. Left to right: Dennis, me, Derek.

Me at Holford Green with Derek's parents, Pip, Grandad and Teresa.

Days of gold & madness near Leonora.
Left to right: Derek, me, Dennis.

Mum & me at Perth airport, June 1981. She's wearing black
because she's convinced I'm about to die.

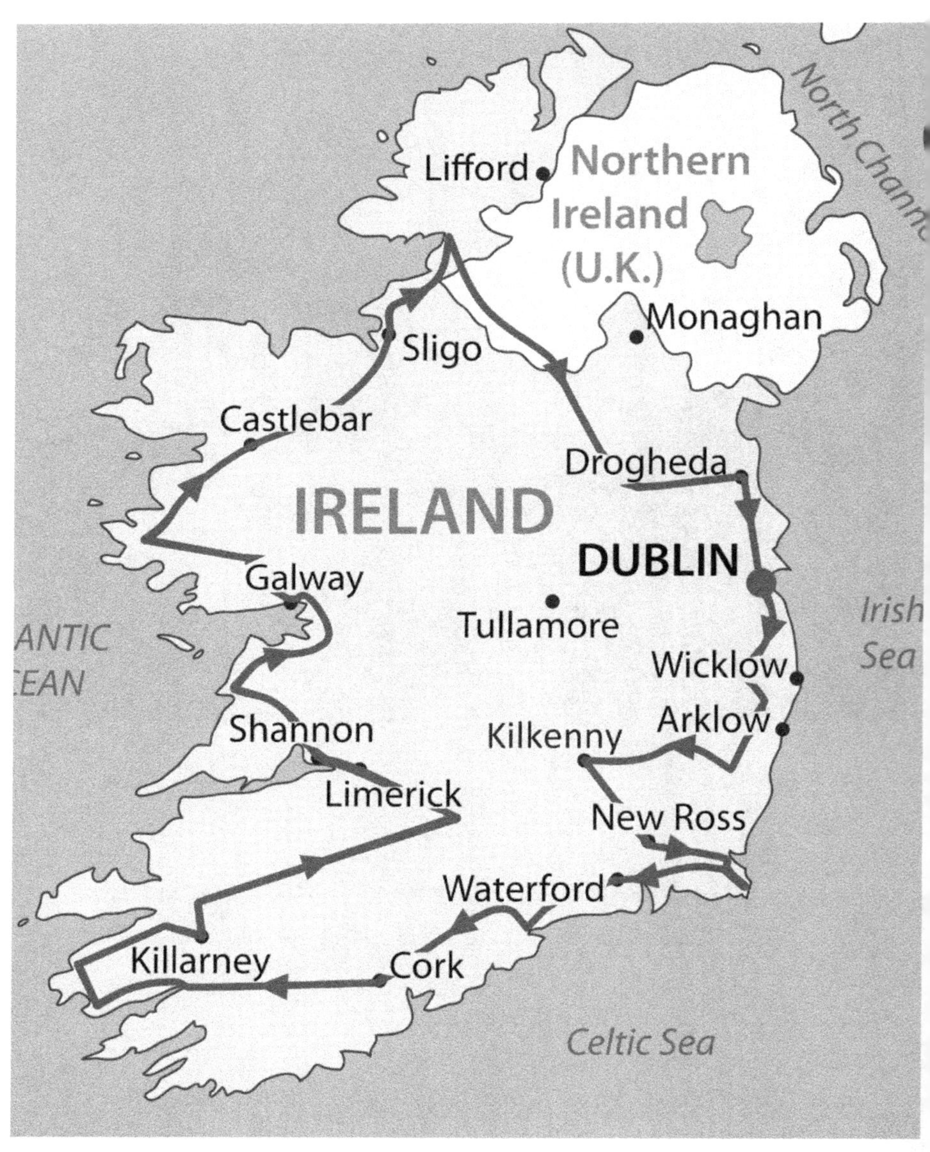

The Irish Ramble: June to September 1981.
(Route drawn by Joel Elliott)

CPSIA information can be obtained
at www.ICGtesting.com
Printed in the USA
LVHW011920180319
611006LV00008B/595/P

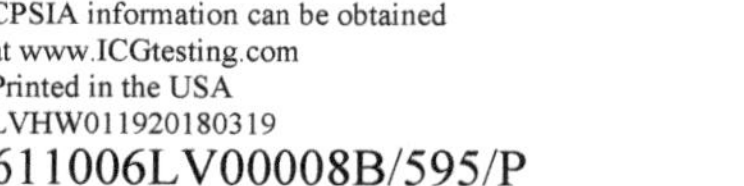

9 780648 441045